"*Made for This* accomplishes the vitally importa[...] life by bringing the Church's rich teachings on m[...] void left by the breakdown of family life and disr[...] intergenerational wisdom. Mary Haseltine's enga[...] la combine to make this a must-read book for exp[...] *Samuel J. Aquila of Denver, Colorado*

"Our Catholic faith helps to shed light upon the meaning and beauty of all our experiences. From her study of theology, the knowledge gained as a childbirth educator, and her own experience as a mother of five, Mary Haseltine, in *Made for This: The Catholic Mom's Guide to Birth*, unpacks the illumination faith brings to the miracle of the birth of a new life. This book is a valuable tool to help mothers experience pregnancy and birth as God intended — something beautiful, redemptive, and supernatural. It is a must-read for expectant mothers and fathers, for couples in childbearing years, and for everyone who cares about them." — *Archbishop Joseph F. Naumann of Kansas City, Kansas*

"My hope is that every woman will pick up this book and give it a read. Whether you are religious or not, have had children or not, this book gives a beautiful reflection on the female body and the amazing strength that is within all of us." — *Abby Johnson, pro-life advocate and founder of And Then There Were None*

"For mothers seeking a companion through pregnancy and birth, *Made for This* offers a wise and comprehensive resource as a Catholic alternative to popular how-to guides. Mary Haseltine celebrates the beauty and strength of women's bodies as part of God's loving plan. New and experienced mothers alike will appreciate the practical guidance and ways to pray through pregnancy and labor. A beautiful invitation to encounter God in the midst of bearing and birthing new life!" — *Laura Kelly Fanucci, author of* Everyday Sacrament: The Messy Grace of Parenting

"Birth is wild, raw, unpredictable — and absolutely beautiful when you allow God to meet you in this profound human experience. Mary Haseltine equips every mom — whether pregnant for the first time or expecting her tenth baby — to enter fully the mystery of childbirth. By educating her mind, preparing her body, and engaging her soul, this book provides every pregnant woman a crucial road map for the journey to motherhood." — *Edward and Beth Sri; Edward is author of* Men, Women, and the Mystery of Love, *and Beth is creator of borntodothis.org and mother of eight*

"Finally! This is a book that acknowledges not only the miraculous work that a woman's body is doing throughout pregnancy, but also the intrinsic value of the child. So many Catholic mothers (myself included) have had to lean on authors who understand only partially the miracle that is taking place when God chooses to co-create a human being with us. We've had to guard our minds, bodies, and spirits with our childbirth preparation courses and literature because the authors simply do not understand the richness of the reality that is taking place. I am so happy that Mary Haseltine has written such a comprehensive and authentic book for Catholic women to lean on as they come to understand fully the amazing title that God has given them as mothers." — *Leah A. Jacobson, MA, IBCLC, founder and CEO of The Guiding Star Project*

"Mary Haseltine has walked a delicate line with masterful precision, bridging the sometimes contentious gap between medicated and unmedicated birth with grace, mercy, and a profound dose of faith-filled wisdom. In a culture which tends to downplay the spiritual and struggles to acknowledge the beauty of fertility and childbirth, Mary has brought her formidable skills as a mother, a doula, and a careful theological thinker to bear on a profoundly important part of the human experience. As a woman and a mother who has experienced the gamut of hospital births, reading her book brought both joy and healing to memories I had relegated to the very dimmest places in my mind. Stock this title in every Catholic parish and medical practice and put it on your gift list for new moms." — *Jenny Uebbing, blogger at* Mama Needs Coffee *and mother of five*

"Mary Haseltine has given the Church a true gift by diving deep into the richness of countless aspects of motherhood. I only wish I had had this book years ago!" — *Sarah Swafford, speaker and author of* Emotional Virtue: A Guide to Drama-Free Relationships

"This is the all-in-one childbirth book I was looking for but couldn't find during my entire pregnancy: a balanced, evidence-based look at women's options for childbirth, beautiful theological reflections on the sacramentality of motherhood, and inspiring birth stories from Catholic women. I will be buying this book for every pregnant woman I know!" — *Christina Dehan Jaloway, Catholic wife, mother, speaker, and blogger at* The Evangelista

MADE
FOR THIS
THE CATHOLIC MOM'S
GUIDE TO BIRTH

MARY HASELTINE
WITH A FOREWORD BY WILLIAM SEARS, MD
AND MARTHA SEARS, RN

**Our
Sunday
Visitor**

www.osv.com
Our Sunday Visitor Publishing Division
Our Sunday Visitor, Inc.
Huntington, Indiana 46750

Our Sunday Visitor Publishing Division, Our Sunday Visitor, Inc., 200 Noll Plaza Huntington, IN 46750; 1-800-348-2440

ISBN: 978-1-68192-171-6 (Inventory No. T1884)
eISBN: 978-1-68192-175-4
LCCN: 2017961130

Cover and interior design: Lindsey Riesen
Cover art: Shutterstock

PRINTED IN THE UNITED STATES OF AMERICA

ABOUT THE AUTHOR

Mary Haseltine is a theology graduate and a certified birth doula and childbirth educator. With a passion for building a culture of life through the teachings of the Theology of the Body, she works to bring an awareness and practice of the teachings of the Church into the realm of childbirth, mothering, and pregnancy loss. She lives in Western New York with her husband and five sons. You can find more of her writing at www.maryhaseltine.com.

TABLE OF CONTENTS

ACKNOWLEDGMENTS

To the One who saw fit to make me a mother six times over,

To my heavenly mother, Our Lady of Childbirth,

To my earthly mother, who still bears the scar on her womb from the sacrifice she made for me,

To my husband, who has offered himself to me in every conception, pregnancy, and birth; who lays himself down every day, striving to be worthy of the call; and whom I often don't deserve,

To John Paul, Michael, David, Luke, and Benedict, for allowing me the undeserved privilege of motherhood,

To my Joseph Mary, whom I pray to meet in eternity and who showed me to the core of my being the worth of every single baby and every single moment,

To the ones who were with me and supported me during my own births,

To my sisters in heaven who have seen this project through,

Thank you.

....

Of course, my gratitude also to the many women who have given me the honor of sharing in their births as they welcome their babies into the world. My special thanks also to the women who were willing to share their stories in this book: Amanda D., Amanda P., Amelia, Angie, April, Bridget, Carolyn, Carrie, Cherie, Christina, Christy, Colleen, Dwija, Erin, Ginny, Haley, Janelle, Jennifer, Jill, Katie, Kendra, Lauren, Lindsay, Lisa, Lydia, Madeline, Mandi, Marchelle, Margaret, Mary, Megan, Melody, Micaela, Molly, Nancy, Nell, Nicole, Shannon, Teresa, and Theresa (and John and Greg, too!). May God bless you for blessing others with your stories.

FOREWORD

We are honored and excited to write this foreword to Mary Haseltine's most welcome and needed book, *Made for This: The Catholic Mom's Guide to Birth*. Since our reversion to the Catholic faith ten years ago, we have come to deeply appreciate the uniqueness of a Catholic approach to all aspects of parenting. The books we have written over the years were intended to pass on to other mothers and fathers what we had learned both as healthcare professionals and through our own pregnancies, births, and parenting, and to present God's design for the woman's body, which is made to grow a baby and give birth, and then feed and care for the child.

The main point we make about childbirth, one that all mothers need to know, is what we call the "hormonal symphony of birth." Mom is the conductor in this symphony, and when all the players are working in harmony, beautiful music — as she gives birth — occurs. The hormonal harmony during birth continues to cascade through both the mother's body and the newly born baby's body. God's design is in place to ensure a smooth transition from baby's life in utero to his or her new world of air-breathing and breastfeeding, and being held, warmed, and comforted skin-to-skin. This symphony can only unfold seamlessly when this design is given the time and conditions it needs. This is the science and the art of birthing you will be learning about in this book.

We experienced birth as naive young parents fifty years ago (fresh out of nursing and medical school), through seven more births, the last one in 1992, when we were present for our adopted daughter's birth. These ranged from our firstborn's birth with spinal anesthesia and forceps (1967), through two more hospital births (one of those unmedicated), then on to having the blessings of four home births. Each of these very different births taught us so much that we've been privileged to write about in several of the books in The Sears Parenting Library. We know firsthand the importance and the need for women to be fully informed and empowered on birth!

We have seen, in these past fifty years, both the art and the science of childbirth developing. Women have learned to trust their bodies in birthing, and at the same time they have learned to embrace the scientific advances that can help them benefit from truly evidence-based birth practices that are completely respectful of mom's and baby's natural biology. Partnering of the art of childbirth with the science of childbirth leads to making informed choices, and there are many choices to consider as you work toward the goal of a safe and satisfying birth. This goal fits perfectly with the culture of life we strive for, and it respects the dignity of women, understanding our feminine genius, as Pope Saint John Paul II taught in his *Letter to Women*.

As a Catholic mother, you want to follow God's plan for you and your baby, and it is good to know you truly are *Made for This*. You are made to be the mother of and to give birth to this child. There is a lot to learn about your pregnant body, and even more about your pregnant mind. And there is a lot to learn about what labor and birth will be like and what you need to know to meet the demands of giving birth. Recent research has correlated a happy, relaxed, informed pregnancy with having a healthy birth and baby. Still, there is no better stress-buster throughout your pregnancy, and especially as the time draws near for your baby to be born, than daily prayer.

Pregnancy is a precious nine months of physical growth and development for mom and baby, and emotional growth for mom and dad. Taking time for spiritual growth during pregnancy will bring husband and wife closer to God and to each other. We encourage you to use these nine months wisely. *Made for This* offers solid spiritual direction in addition to the excellent childbirth preparation you are looking for. Preparing spiritually for birth enhances every aspect of being ready, not only for birth, but also for the parenting of your child and the shaping of family life. This book is a unique resource: The author holds a degree in theology, and she is also a childbirth educator and a birth doula. Her book provides a clear road map for your journey of faith on your way to welcoming your baby into the world.

Dr. William and Martha Sears
Authors of *The Baby Book*, *The Birth Book*, and
The Healthy Pregnancy Book

INTRODUCTION
How to Use This Book

I am the mother of six children, five of whom I've been given the privilege to raise. I'm also a Catholic birth doula, birth instructor, and have been blessed to be with many women as they brought their babies into the world. I've studied, experienced, and seen firsthand the beauty of evidence-based birth and the complications that can result from the opposite. I'm not a doctor, a midwife, or a nurse. What I am is a disciple, a woman, a mother, a doula, a student of theology, a teacher, and a writer in whom God has placed a passion for the beautiful design and act of birth.

This book is meant to be a companion to your other preparation and prenatal care. I want to make very clear that this book is not meant to be a substitute for your own research or to provide any medical advice for your specific situation. My prayer is that it will help you approach your unique birth and motherhood with more information and draw deeply from the grace present during pregnancy and birth, entering more fully into your feminine genius. I highly recommend attending a quality birth class, conducting your own research, reading more books, and talking with your husband and medical provider when making plans for your birth.

It is outside the scope of this book to provide comprehensive information on every unique circumstance. However, I do believe there is something within these pages for every single woman as she approaches her birth. My prayer is that in these pages will be found encouragement, grace, hope, beauty, and truth. I hope that you come away knowing deeply that no matter what kind of birth you are called to have, you are indeed made for this.

May you and your baby be blessed with a healthy, happy, and, yes, *holy* birth.

1

WHY BIRTH MATTERS

"Whatever you do, do all to the glory of God."
— 1 Corinthians 10:31

"I did it. I can't *believe* I just did that!" Her words as she held on her chest the wriggling, slippery baby boy fresh from the womb were exhausted but euphoric. "I've never done anything so amazing."

It was the moment she had been waiting for, the moment so many women long for. And she, like so many other mothers before her, was transformed. Her hair was matted, her face sweaty, her body bleeding and aching, and yet she was radiant. Just moments before she had been absolutely certain she couldn't do one bit more, and then, like so many mothers before her, she did it.

And it changed her.

The shocking, raw, messy, agonizing reality of birth has an incredible power. In its very nature, birth — every birth — is designed by the Creator to be one of the most profound and intense moments of our lives, and women know that deeply. Millions of women have felt its power, and countless women long for it. It isn't just the intellectual and spiritual reality of becoming a mother, though most certainly that is part of it, but the actual process of childbirth itself has the potential to transform us. And it is meant to. The physical process of birth is intimately tied to a mental, emotional, and spiritual one. For the mother at the center, it's never "just" a birth. Birthing our babies isn't like a run to the store or a chore to check off a list. It isn't something we're meant to just grit our teeth and get through in order to have a baby. It is innately personal, involving our entire bodies and selves; it is emotionally charged and ingrains itself deeply. Birth is at once miraculous and earthly, wild and gentle, strong and vulnerable, normal and weird, natural and supernatural, bloody and beautiful. In the end, it is the way that God intentionally designed to transform us into mothers. Birth matters deeply to us as women.

The experience of birth stays with a woman forever — not necessarily every specific detail surrounding the birth, but on a deeper, much more intuitive level — how she felt, how she was made to feel, how she was treated, how well-prepared she was for the complicated emotions surrounding the arrival of this baby, how it changed her and gave her confidence in her motherhood — or perhaps the exact opposite. Each birth leaves an imprint on a woman's body, mind, heart, and soul. She is changed. We are complete persons, so what affects one aspect of our person affects everything else — physically, emotionally, spiritually, mentally. We have the opportunity to choose to invite the One who planned it all in the first place to saturate every part with grace before, during, and after birth.

In this book we will talk about why the act of birth is so powerful, why it is such a deep and important moment in a woman's (and man's!) life, and what God might have to do with it all. We'll learn why having a deeper understanding of our births is not "over-spiritualizing" but recognizing the truth of who we are, body and soul, and who God is. We'll share examples of how we as women can cooperate with the way that God designed birth to transform our bodies, minds, hearts, and souls. We'll hear from real women who have experienced profound grace through their births, and those who have allowed their faith to integrate their pregnancy, births, and motherhood deeply. We'll walk through some of the options you will likely have so that you can make the best decisions in your own unique circumstances. In opening ourselves to God's plan for each one of us, we open ourselves to the possibility of a beautiful, transformative, happy, healthy, and, yes, even *holy* birth for ourselves and our babies.

God's Plan for Your Birth

Whether a woman is Catholic, Christian, or of no religion at all, she is physically the same as any other woman, and the baby certainly seems to come out the same way regardless! The physical movements and techniques, physiological aids, medical choices, possibly *everything* on the outside may look similar.

So what might be different when we speak of birth from a perspective of faith?

Drawing from her faith, a woman can seek to honor the design and plan of the Creator, in whatever way that means in her unique circumstances. We have a God who desires to be intimately involved in each of our lives and who has a beautiful and unique plan for each of his daughters. He loves each one of us infinitely and eternally. That same God, so in love with each one of us, wants to be invited to play a part in the most important and transforming moments of our lives, including our experience of birth.

The mystery of love and the rich tradition of the faith can penetrate your unique birth and transform it into something holy. When our lives and souls are transformed through baptism, every aspect of our lives becomes a conduit for real and living grace. It seems entirely appropriate to expect that something so profound and intimate as the birthing process can be infused with that grace. These moments so intimately tied to our God-given vocations as wives and mothers can especially be part of God's plan to work in our lives and draw us closer to him. The same God who has concerned himself with the number of hairs on your head and who has searched your being and knows when you sit and stand is certainly concerned with you as you birth one of his sons or daughters.[1] He doesn't walk us through conception and pregnancy only to leave us at the door of the delivery room. Nothing is outside his reach and dominion and care. We can see his hand in all of it and ask him to be intimately involved in our pregnancies and births.

There is a temptation to compartmentalize the parts of our lives that don't feel or look holy (because sometimes our understanding of holy has been distorted) from our relationship with God. Some people may feel that God wants nothing to do with that "birthy stuff." Some may cling to the idea that birth is purely a physical or medical process — get in, get it over with, and get on with more important things. Perhaps some feel pressured by the erroneous belief that a holy or Christ-centered birth should look or feel a certain way, and that turns them off. But none of these are truly valid reasons to write off the reality that God can be — wants to be — a part of your unique birth.

We have a choice to make as women approaching our births. We can enter into it as something to get through, knuckles clenched and eyes squeezed shut, wanting it to be over as quickly as possible, seeing it as a flawed and dreadful design for meeting our babies. Or we can enter into it with hearts a bit more open, viewing it as the incredibly intelligent design of God himself, the way that he, our loving Father, mindfully and intentionally chose to build a family and transform his daughters into mothers.

I believe God wants to come with us into each pregnancy and birth and do something powerful. Whether it's your first baby or your twelfth, no matter what kind of pregnancy and birth he calls you to have, no matter your circumstances, his grace is present and available in extraordinary amounts. He wants to transform you and draw you deeper into his mystery of love right now, with *this* pregnancy and birth, in a way that speaks to your unique heart. God gives us the choice to work with his grace and answer the invitation to see our pregnancies and births from an eternal perspective. It is the vehicle through which the two becoming one is met face to face. It is here where woman participates in the creative power of God and where father and mother meet the new person that they, with God, have called into being.

Every birth looks different because *we* are all different. God calls each mother to have a unique pregnancy and birth. So, the idea of integrating our faith into birth is not meant to outline a specific formula for a holy birth. It is not meant to tell you the correct way to give birth or to pass off as doctrine what can be changeable — each woman's circumstance is unique. While we will talk about some, this book is not meant to go into every specific choice you will need to make when it comes to the birth of your baby, and it is outside the scope of this book to go into the risks and benefits of every single option in your pregnancy and birth. There are several great books that already do that, many noted in Appendix D. It is highly recommended that you pick up one of those books to complement this one, and consider taking a quality birth class, especially if this is your first baby. A good birth class will help you know the landscape of birth practices in your area and the providers that are better at giving compassionate, dignified, and evidence-based care, and will help you enter more fully and intentionally into your birth.

What this book is meant to do is talk about how we can allow God to transform our pregnancies and births into something beautiful, redemptive, and truly supernatural. It is meant to help women understand the design of their bodies and birth as well as some of the choices available so that they can best respect their own dignity, that of their babies, and the design of God's plan when it comes to birth. It is meant to help women access the tremendous redemptive and transformative power of birth. It is meant to give tools to the mother who wants to approach her birth in the light of her faith. We do nothing in a vacuum. The light of our faith has the power to transform everything we do — even, and in an especially profound way, birth.

Birth is an incredibly sensitive, personal, and emotionally charged topic, which only serves to highlight the point that it *is* important, it matters, and it affects us deeply. Because of this, there is no room for judging other women when it comes to birth choices. There is room only for listening, encouraging, offering valuable information when appropriate, and providing support, respect for others' situations, and genuine love. While we, of course, need to judge our own situations, be informed, and make the best choices we can in our own circumstances, it is not our responsibility to do that for others. My humble prayer is that as you read this book, defenses are laid down. I pray that you will be open to the idea that perhaps birth is such a sensitive topic precisely because birth is so central to who we are as women. Perhaps at the core of our being we know how much it truly does matter. And perhaps that is *exactly* how God designed it.

Six birth stories, each one different. I've been blessed by all of them, both by my babies and by my actual birth experiences. It's clear to me now that each birth was a lesson in virtues that I desperately needed. My first taught me acceptance. My second gave me courage. My third forced me to have faith and trust. My fourth required patience. My fifth was a lesson in humility. And my sixth was a refresher course on each virtue of my previous births. I would not be the same person without each of these births.

Yes, a healthy baby and mama are the most important things. But beyond basic survival, the ability to thrive and grow and change in a birth experience is important, too. For better or worse, a couple will carry the experience of their baby's entrance into this world forever. It only makes sense to hope, seek, and pray for a birth in which those first moments together as a family are ones that strengthen the family bond and promote love between the parents and child, and awe and gratitude to God as Creator. I've been blessed by six of those experiences, and I pray that every mother has the same.

Babies matter. Mamas matter. And birth matters, too.

— Micaela Darr, mom to seven on Earth
and two in eternity, birth educator

2

A CULTURE OF LIFE IS
A CULTURE OF BIRTH

*"Before I formed you in the womb I knew you, and before
you were born I consecrated you."*
— Jeremiah 1:5

When it comes to the overall culture of birth and specific practices and protocols, we might wonder if it is really a topic that concerns the Church. After all, "as long as the baby's healthy," right? However, the gift of a new baby is seen by the Church as the highest sign of blessing for the husband and wife and the visible reality of two people becoming fully one. Entering into the Sacrament of Matrimony, husband and wife oblige themselves to be open to life. Their "yes" to the question, "Will you accept children lovingly from God?" binds them to that promise. Babies are meant to be intimately tied with the sacrament of marriage, and every single one of those new babies enters the world by way of birth. By truly honoring birth and recognizing God's design for new life from conception through its fullness in birth, we also honor and recognize the dignity of marriage, the dignity of each human person, and the beauty of the One who planned it that way. When we honor birth, we honor marriage. When we honor birth, we honor God.

This doesn't mean that a good and beautiful birth is reserved for the "perfect" nuclear family, of course. Every mother and baby, regardless of their circumstances, deserves the best possible care and experience of birth because they are made in the image and likeness of God. Part of building a culture of life is advocating for the dignified treatment of every man, woman, and child at every moment, no matter the circumstances. This doesn't end in the birth room. As pro-life people, we are obliged to care about birth practices and healthy, dignified, evidence-based birth, fighting the stigma that the pro-life community only cares *that* babies are born but has no concern for the way mothers and babies are treated during the process and after.

We cannot be satisfied with a baby and mother who simply survive. We need to be concerned that babies are welcomed into the world healthy, with joy, and treated in a way that recognizes their God-given dignity. We need to be concerned that the dignity of every woman is respected, especially as she actively takes on the role of motherhood. We are bound as the body of Christ to help create a culture of birth where the totality of woman and baby — mind, heart, body, and soul — is respected and where the most vulnerable among us, the newborn baby and the mother giving birth, are treated with love and evidence-based care.

Catholics and Evidence-Based Birth

Catholics should be at the forefront of the movement in our country for respectful, evidence-based birth. The Catholic Church declares that the faithful should "distinguish carefully between the rights and the duties which they have as belonging to the Church and those which fall to them as members of the human society. *They will strive to unite the two harmoniously, remembering that in every temporal affair they are to be guided by a Christian conscience, since no human activity, even of the temporal order, can be withdrawn from God's dominion.*"[2]

This means that the Christian has an obligation both as a follower of Christ and as a plain old human to show concern for these types of life issues. Even issues that might not necessarily seem like "religious issues" are, in fact, still under the dominion of God, and his plan and law must be respected. We are called to use our well-formed consciences to discern how to live in this world, taking care to apply what we know to be true to every aspect of life. We don't leave our faith at the doorway of the labor-and-delivery room. However, because our approach to birth and the choices we make are not specifically an issue belonging to the Church, we are free to determine the answers and approaches that best suit our particular circumstances, always doing so with the basic laws of God and the teachings of our faith in mind.

Approaching life from a Catholic worldview, we know that every mother and baby has dignity and deserves to be treated as the image of God. If birth is not safe, or if a woman or baby is demeaned during birth, or if birth practices are not evidence-based and compromise the health and even lives of women and babies, then we are not promoting a true culture of life. Unfortunately, our modern medical system often places profit and efficiency ahead of human dignity, and this is especially true in pregnancy and birth. Our legal and medical model do not even consider unborn babies real persons. Impersonal healthcare too often forces us to sacrifice intimate care tailored to our unique situation. Many providers treat mothers and babies using "factory-model" protocols and treatment. Some even operate using outdated methods. Too often mothers are not listened to during their pregnancies or given the time, respect, and up-to-date information they need to make decisions in their best interests. Far too many women have experienced what they deem a traumatic birth resulting in serious health problems (or worse) for themselves or their babies.[3] Far too many women have walked away from pregnancy and birth feeling that they weren't listened to or were pressured into choices they didn't really want to make. Instead of receiving evidence-based, reverent care, they leave birth with wounds and scars on their bodies, yes, but also on their minds, hearts, and souls.

In the United States, many are surprised to learn that maternal morbidity rates of women are actually on the rise.[4] Compared with other countries, our infant survival rate ranks behind most of Europe and Asia at an unacceptable 57th.[5] The cesarean rate in the United States is more than double what is recommended as safe for mother and baby by the World Health Organization.[6] Women of color have a greater number of birth complications, and their infants die at higher rates — more than double the rates of other communities.[7]

Costs of birth have become inflated and pose a deep hardship for many families. Countless women relay birth stories filled with interventions that were not based on real evidence, frustration with a medical system that did not listen to them, and sometimes blatant abuse or disregard for their consent in treatment from the mother for herself and her baby. There is virtually no system of real care in place for a woman after she has had her baby, and often she needs to go back to work or her "normal" life before she has recovered at even the most minimal level from the birth.

Thankfully, small steps have been taken by many providers and hospitals to change birth practices to better reflect modern evidence and to provide more dignified care for mother and baby. But there is still a long way to go.

If we claim to support the dignity of every human person, then we as Catholics must be concerned with birth. If we are asking couples to be open to life, we have to do better when it comes to supporting them through the resulting pregnancies and births with real information and respectful care. We should be a part of the move toward a better system and an essential part of the discussion of creating a culture of birth that can fit seamlessly into a greater culture that recognizes and celebrates the beauty of family, womanhood, and the irreplaceable gift of every human life. How we approach birth as a culture and even as individuals will say a lot about what we value and what we truly believe. As Saint John Paul II stated, "Concern for the child, even before birth, from the first moment of conception and then throughout the years of infancy and youth, is the primary and fundamental test of the relationship of one human being to another."[8]

Both our intentions in our decisions and the way we do things matter greatly. We don't believe that the ends justify the means.[9] We have to be concerned with the "how" and take great care to ensure that every mother and baby is treated with dignity, that birth practices are based on solid science and evidence, and that God's original design of creation and natural law are respected throughout pregnancy and birth. We can reject the lies that birth is ugly, gross, shameful, or that it doesn't really matter how women and babies are treated as long as both are alive at the end. We as a Church can choose to claim birth again for God, recognizing that it is his design first, truly believing that he really planned it this way, and he is the great designer behind it all.

The Dignity of Every Baby at Every Moment

From the very moment of conception, Christianity recognizes that human person with a life just as valuable and important as that of any other person on Earth. No matter the circumstances surrounding conception, every baby is a unique and irreplaceable human person willed by God for his or her own sake. As Saint John Paul wrote in his 1994 *Letter to Families*: "God 'willed' man from the very beginning, and God 'wills' him in every act of conception and every human birth."[10] That reverence for every life needs to mark every single birth.

In the Christian understanding of the family, parents are not autocrats, and the worth of the individual members is not dictated by hierarchy or seniority. All members of the family are "equal in dignity," and parents are obliged to "regard their children as children of God and respect them as human persons."[11] The Gospel message transforms our understanding of each individual soul, helping us to recognize them as the image of God, regardless of age, ability, size, gender, race, or any other characteristic. "Inspired and sustained by the new commandment of love, the Christian family welcomes, respects and serves every human being, considering each one in his or her dignity as a person and as a child of God."[12]

This understanding of the dignity of every single baby must infiltrate how we approach our births as Christian women. The baby — unborn, being born, and newly born — has the same rights and dignity as the mother, father, doctor, midwife, nurse, or anyone else in the birth room and must be treated accordingly. In fact, Catholic teaching would take this one step further: the baby should receive in some sense *greater* deference as the weakest and "poorest" in the room. The message of Christ (and the teaching of the Church) contains a preferential option for the poor, which refers not just to the economically poor, but to the weak and vulnerable of the world. Inspired by the beatitudes and the command of Christ in Matthew 25, we believe we have a Christian duty to protect, honor, and defer to the weakest among us.[13] Whatever we do to the least of these, we do to him, too.

In pregnancy and birth, then, how can we best honor the baby, taking care to treat him or her as someone with complete dignity and worthy of compassion and respect? In their littleness and need, babies become another Christ among us. We as mothers can choose to recognize that reality with the choices we make in birth and in our attitudes surrounding their personhood. We can choose to honor that reality with how we approach our pregnancy, talk about the person within us, and defend his or her rights as equal to our own.

Before, during, and after birth, each child has an experience all his or her own. We understand very little about the unborn and newly born brain, but we do know that babies experience pain, fear, pleasure, happiness, comfort, and much more, possibly amplified since they do not have the context of experience or cognitive reasoning to temper their understanding of what may be happening to them. Their experience of the birth can and should be taken into account. It certainly helps us grow in compassion and love when we try to understand what the birth experience must be like for *them*. What a testimony it is to the inherent value not only of that unique individual life but of every life when we treat the tiniest among us with tremendous compassion and concern. As mothers, we can take our babies' experience into account when making birth choices, erring on the side of life, compassion, and honor for their dignity. After all, our babies' needs, emotions, and experience matter and are just as valid as our own.

....

Do we see the importance of the baby being treated with respect, love, and dignity as a complete and irreplaceable human being valued by God? Do we respect women and allow them to make informed choices about their bodies and their children? Do we use real science and a complete understanding of biology in our approach and methods? Do we recognize the profound moment in front of us as the mother welcomes the new child into the family and bow to that mystery before us? Do we do everything we can to respect the way God designed it to happen and respect the order of the family as God created it? Do we treat every mother and baby with the reverence and love they deserve? We cannot claim a culture of life until the answer to all of these is a confident yes.

Instinctively, we know that birth should be a joyous and happy event, and we can see its beauty — from a distant standpoint, at least. Can we dare to step a little closer and choose not to be scandalized by the sheer physicality and rawness of it all? Can we continue to see its beauty in God's plan? Just as womanhood is beautiful, marriage is beautiful, conception is beautiful, and motherhood is beautiful, so the end result of all those things — the act of birth — is also beautiful. Really. When we view birth as the natural result of the divine plan for marriage and family and a reflection of the value we place on human life, then we can see why it is entirely appropriate and fitting for Christians to care … and to do so deeply.

"The history of every human being passes through the threshold of a woman's motherhood," wrote John Paul II.[14] This means that the entire history of humanity, every person made in the image and likeness of God, passes through the rite of birth. There is not one human being on this Earth who is excluded from the issue. Physical birth is the avenue through which God himself chooses to continue his divine plan of love to multiply the human race. The more we acknowledge and reverence the beauty of birth, the more we will create a society where every life, every baby, every mother and father, and ultimately God himself, is revered and celebrated. Transforming how we view and approach birth affects the individual lives in front of us, and indeed, it can also transform the world.

Over and above such outstanding moments, there is an everyday heroism, made up of gestures of sharing, big or small, which build up an authentic culture of life.…

Part of this daily heroism is also the silent but effective and eloquent witness of all those "brave mothers who devote themselves to their own family without reserve, who suffer in giving birth to their children and who are ready to make any effort, to face any sacrifice, in order to pass on to them the best of themselves." In living out their mission "these heroic women do not always find support in the world around them. On the contrary, the cultural models frequently promoted and broadcast by the media do not encourage motherhood. In the name of progress and modernity the values of fidelity, chastity, sacrifice, to which a host of Christian wives and mothers have borne and continue to bear outstanding witness, are presented as obsolete.... We thank you, heroic mothers, for your invincible love! We thank you for your intrepid trust in God and in his love. We thank you for the sacrifice of your life."

— Pope John Paul II, *Evangelium Vitae*, 86

3

THE FEMININE GENIUS OF BIRTH

"So God created man in his own image, in the image of
God he created him; male and female he created them."
— *Genesis 1:27*

A woman can certainly have a great birth experience without choosing to delve into the deeper meaning behind it all. But understanding more about God's original design for us as women allows us to appreciate his plan more fully and integrate it more intentionally into our lives. As we make ourselves more available to the mystery of it all, we are better able to be who he made us to be, women created body and soul. It might be tempting to skip over talk about the spiritual significance of birth, but I encourage you to enter in. Understanding the deeper meaning of birth allows us to experience and integrate our unique births and motherhood in a powerful way. If we are hoping to approach our births as women of faith, it only makes sense to see what the Church and Scripture have to say about it. (And both have said a lot!) Perhaps God has something to share with you as you come to a better understanding of his design for birth and the amazing design that is you.

We have different gifts than men, and it is beautiful to acknowledge and celebrate that fact. The Catholic Church, especially through Pope Saint John Paul II, has spoken clearly and often about the "feminine genius." God imprinted on our souls something unique and beautiful, and our uniquely feminine souls glorify God and are a gift to the world. While it is becoming culturally unacceptable to say so, we know he created us differently, and he did so intentionally, out of his infinite love. That difference is both physical and spiritual.

The physical differences in our bodies teach us something about who we are, who we are meant to be, and what God's design is for us. Of course, the most significant difference is our ability to conceive and bear new life. Our wombs, our breasts, our organs, our hormones, our genitalia, our menstrual cycles are designed to bear and nurture new life.[15] Whether or not she ever becomes a physical mother, a woman is designed to bring new life into the world, and our bodies are a reflection of that soul-deep reality.

We also differ from men in our souls. Women are often more in tune with others. We bring tenderness to situations. We tend to be stronger multitaskers. On the whole, we are more intuitive than men. While there is much diversity in how we reveal these feminine gifts, women are created by God to love in a unique way, and we offer gifts to the world that our men cannot. Womanhood reflects unique characteristics of the love and care of God.[16] In her essays on women, Edith Stein (Saint Teresa Benedicta of the Cross) speaks of a woman's stronger tendency to sympathize; to serve another life; her more acute sense with children; her greater drive to cherish, guard, and preserve rather than fight and conquer; and her greater awareness of the needs of the creatures around her.[17] Women possess within themselves a unique and powerful strength that can change the world.

Physically and spiritually, every woman's femininity, by its very nature, points to motherhood. We know instinctively that there is no other relationship like that between a mother and her child. Motherhood calls for great sacrifices, and it holds a place of honor and distinction not only in the Christian tradition, but also in many other cultures. This respect for motherhood is written deep in the soul of mankind. As Saint John Paul wrote in his 1994 *Letter to Families*: "On the human level, can there be any other '*communion*' comparable to that *between a mother and a child* whom she has carried in her womb and then brought to birth?"[18]

As the tiniest seed of a person grows within her, the mystery of that union is soul deep, and she is forever changed into a mother, called to love, protect, guide, nourish, and give life. Not only do we acknowledge this transformation on a spiritual and emotional level, but researchers have recently discovered that the cells of an unborn baby, containing his or her DNA, can be found in the mother for the rest of the mother's life.[19] Even in the case of miscarriage, abortion, or the mother placing her baby for adoption, motherhood has transformed her down to a cellular level, and she is forever united to that child.

Our feminine souls and bodies are intrinsically united, and together they fully reflect our feminine genius as we become mothers: birth is a necessary part of that.

While he was on Earth, Jesus made clear in his actions that women are equal in dignity to men. In his apostolic letter *Mulieris Dignitatem*, Saint John Paul writes, "It is universally admitted — even by people with a critical attitude towards the Christian message — that *in the eyes of his contemporaries Christ became a promoter of women's true dignity* and of the *vocation* corresponding to this dignity."[20] Christ responded to the needs of women. He looked them in the eye and saw them for who they really were: beloved and precious daughters of his Father. Saint John Paul goes on, "Jesus of Nazareth confirms this dignity, recalls it, renews it, and makes it a part of the Gospel and of the Redemption for which he is sent into the world."[21]

We can and should demand that every single woman in the birth room be treated with the dignity that Christ himself has bestowed upon us. She should never be shamed, manipulated, coerced, lied to, laughed at, ignored, or disrespected. Quite the opposite, she should be reverenced, deferred to, cared for, and treated with the utmost respect.

The Lord wants our feminine hearts to be fully awakened and alive. In birth, our feminine genius can be brought to new heights. Our remarkable strength, determination, beauty, and self-sacrifice are all exemplified in the act of birth. For those of us called to physical motherhood, Christ certainly wants to be a part of the process. When women are treated with dignity and worth, especially in those profound moments that mark womanhood, they are "liberated" and "restored to themselves: they feel loved with 'eternal love,' with a love which finds direct expression in Christ himself."[22] It is a beautiful and transformative force for the woman's understanding of herself and her role as mother when this type of care and reverence marks her birth, and it should be considered a tragedy when it doesn't.

Every person is called to make a gift of himself or herself, and a woman partakes of that call in a unique way as she enters into the role of mother.[23] In pregnancy and birth, we experience at a raw, intrinsic level the reality that we only find ourselves through the gift of ourselves.[24] As she takes on the role of mother from the very moment of the conception of her baby, a woman becomes something new, and she experiences her womanhood in a deeper way. "Motherhood involves a special communion with the mystery of life, as it develops in the woman's womb. The mother is filled with wonder at this mystery of life, and 'understands' with unique intuition what is happening inside her. In the light of the 'beginning,' the mother accepts and loves as a person the child she is carrying in her womb."[25] Becoming a mother can awaken within us a new strength, a deeper love and self-gift, and a greater awareness of the mystery of God's plan.

We have a God who is deeply in love with each one of us, calling us to our own unique motherhood. He is a loving Father, and we can come to him in our pregnancies and births. After all, this is the vocation he has called us to. We don't have to be ashamed of or feel silly for asking him to be a part of it, and we can freely ask that our births be beautiful and holy and happy for us as mothers, for our babies, and for our whole family. We can also feel confident demanding that our dignity as his daughters be respected by our providers and others with us during birth. Our God is not a stingy God. He can and does want to be involved. He can and does want us to come to him in our need, especially in this most poignant time of our womanhood.

Your birth can be a beautiful moment of honoring and experiencing the feminine genius God has given you. He loves each of his daughters deeply and intimately. Not only does he want to meet you in your birth; he wants to work in and through you to bring both physical and spiritual life into the world.

> With all my births, I've experienced birth as a sort of "thin space," a place where time seems to stand still … a moment in which I can feel that participation in creation. I get to bring into the world a bit of heaven, pure innocence, which can only come from God. With all my sinful nature and ugliness, I get to help do that. I feel him. I feel God working through me to create another person, another soul, a unique individual. And I know I couldn't have done this on my own. When the head crowns and it hurts like nothing I've ever experienced and I push till the baby is out, and in the sensation of relief afterwards, I know, I just know, I was part of a miracle.
>
> — Megan Lyons, mom to four

4

THE THEOLOGY OF THE BODY: A THEOLOGY OF BIRTH

"This is my body, which is given for you.
Do this in remembrance of me."
— Luke 22:19

Is it crazy to talk about a "theology" behind birth? Some might think so. But God is not a haphazard designer. His intentional design of all of creation, peaking in his design and creation of the human being — specifically *woman* — is meant to bring glory to him and lead us back to him.

Christian tradition has confirmed time and again the goodness of the body as a creation of God. We see in our body the absolutely amazing, intricate design of a heavenly Father, and we believe God when he says his creation is "very good."[26] The human person is uniquely composed of both body and soul, not just one or the other. We are not pure spirits like angels. Pope Benedict XVI reminds us: "Man is truly himself when his body and soul are intimately united."[27] In fact, this truth is the foundation of the sacraments of the Church. It is only through our bodies that we have access to the sanctifying grace of every sacrament.

This means as Christians we should view and treat our bodies with dignity as a good and beautiful gift designed by God to be used as a gift to the world. As the *Catechism of the Catholic Church* says: "For this reason man may not despise his bodily life. Rather he is obliged to regard his body as good and to hold it in honor since God has created it and will raise it up on the last day."[28] We need to honor our body and the way God designed it to function.[29]

This gets confusing in our culture, which urges us on the one hand to worship the body, yet simultaneously digs deep at the hearts of women, convincing them that their bodies are never actually good enough. How many of us have been scarred by this view of the woman's body? From our earliest years, we hear that we must be sexy enough, pretty enough, thin enough, and readily available for sexual use. For many women, these wounds run deep. And these ideas seep into our images of and expectations of pregnancy and birth. How many of us can look in the mirror at nine months pregnant and feel truly good and beautiful? Precisely when we are at the epitome of our physical femininity, swollen with new life — our bodies doing exactly what they were designed by God to do — we battle feelings of being too fat, too ugly, too self-conscious, and too embarrassed to be seen in public. It can be a fierce battle to believe that our bodies are good and holy, designed by God for his glory.

Saint Gianna Beretta Molla, a brave Catholic mother and medical doctor who gave her life to save her baby, said, "Our body is a cenacle, a monstrance: through its crystal the world should see God." This remains true even at the end of our pregnancies and at the time of birth. If anything, it becomes even more clear as we prepare to bring new life into the world. Our bodies are made by God, and they are good. *You* are good.

Yes, with your growing belly, your swollen feet, your widening hips, and your exhausted eyes, you are very good. You are a visible witness to the world of life and hope. God designed birth precisely and intentionally. Birth may be a private act, but just like the conjugal act that brought this baby into existence, that does not make it any less good. In fact, just like that marital act of making love, we can say that our instinct to keep it private actually highlights just how good and holy it truly is.

Through the Incarnation, God redeemed the whole physical world, making our bodies holy. "Through redemption, every man has received from God again, as it were, himself and his own body. Christ has imprinted new dignity on the human body — on the body of every man and every woman … the human body has been admitted, together with the soul, to union with the Person of the Son-Word."[30] What we do with our body can give glory to God. Saint Paul reminds us: "The body is not meant for immorality, but for the Lord, and the Lord for the body.… Do you not know that your bodies are members of Christ?… Do you not know that your body is a temple of the Holy Spirit within you, which you have from God? You are not your own; you were bought with a price. So glorify God in your body."[31]

As a mother, you get to do exactly that in a very tangible way through your pregnancy and birth.

And the Two Shall Become (Really!) One

From 1979 through 1984, Pope John Paul II gave a series of talks during his weekly General Audiences. In the talks he formulated a brilliant worldview that tapped into the Catholic understanding of the human person being integrally united as body and soul. This series of talks over five years has come to be known as the Theology of the Body. The entire scope of the talks outlined the ways that our bodies can speak a theological language, especially through the Sacrament of Matrimony. The talks formulated the Church's traditional teaching in a new and more detailed and comprehensive way. In fact, many people were shocked by the pope's unembarrassed exegesis on the topic of sexuality and the ways in which it is designed to witness to God and even lead us to him.

Saint John Paul insisted that Christ gives us a model for understanding our bodies (and marriage and the family) when he speaks to the Pharisees about divorce.[32] We must go "back to the beginning" to understand God's original plan. The intentional design of our bodies as male and female speaks to us of who God is, and their very design proclaims the Gospel. Our femaleness and maleness, and the way they complement and quite literally fit together, tell us about God and his design for family, and they can be the instrument through which we become more like him. Sex is designed by God to be a way that married couples can experience and grow in holiness. In their very bodies, husband and wife replicate the relationship of Christ to his Church. Marriage is thus "a sacrament whereby sexuality is integrated into a path to holiness."[33]

Man and woman, through their bodies, provide a glimpse of the mystery of the Trinity.[34] They fit together, and neither the female nor the male body makes sense when seen in isolation. The husband gives of himself to his wife as the Father pours himself out to the Son, and the Son lovingly receives that outpouring. The love between Father and Son is so real that it begets the Person of the Holy Spirit. Mirroring this reality, the love between husband and wife is also designed to be so complete that it has the potential to create an entirely new person — a person who is then *born*.

Our bodies are good, holy, and beautiful, and sexual intimacy within marriage is also good, holy, and beautiful. "Since God created him man and woman, their mutual love becomes an image of the absolute and unfailing love with which God loves man. It is good, very good, in the Creator's eyes."[35] The physical love between a husband and wife has the capacity to bring forth a completely new and eternal human being. A decision to love with all our body has the potential to change eternity. What an awesome — and sobering — concept!

"Amongst the blessings of marriage, the child holds the first place," says the Church.[36] In the marriage rite, man and woman are asked if they will "accept children lovingly from God." It's not because having children somehow makes them "better" than childless couples, but because the child is to be seen as the highest blessing and natural result of the union of man and woman, God's plan for marriage and family made full. Their complete gift of self to the other in turn becomes a gift given right back to them. "In the newborn child is realized the common good of the family.... Its life becomes a gift for the very people who were givers of life."[37] Welcoming children should never be viewed as a threat to marriage. Children enrich, strengthen, and fulfill marriage. "The children born to them — and here is the challenge — should consolidate that covenant, enriching and deepening the conjugal communion of the father and mother."[38]

Being open to children naturally opens the husband and wife to birth. "Both in the conception *and in the birth* of a new child, parents find themselves face to face with a 'great mystery'."[39] Through the grace of their marriage, the couple has supernatural help as they walk through these "mysteries" of pregnancy and birth to enter into the new roles of mother and father.[40]

In some ways it would be easy to choose to stay a little bit selfish when it's "just the two of us." Yes, marriage is God's way of helping us learn to give of ourselves and grow in holiness, but parenthood? Becoming a parent takes it to a whole new level, and that is exactly how God designed it. Our time is no longer our own, our sleep is no longer our own, our hearts are expanded and made more vulnerable. The weaknesses and wounds and self-absorption that we've been able to hide thus far often become glaringly obvious under the light of motherhood or fatherhood. But in the new reality of parenthood there is a new and radical freedom — freedom to become who we were truly meant to be. We become real love. We are stretched to grow in living charity, which "is never satisfied with not giving more."[41]

You are a complex and intricate masterpiece beautifully designed to continue God's work of creation for the world. As your womb grows and you take on the work of pregnancy, you are able to see the love between you and your husband. As women, when we open ourselves up to motherhood, beginning with our very bodies, we are changed. It all begins with pregnancy and birth. Every part of the woman's body is at the service of creating and growing new life and then bringing that life into the world.[42] The profound mystery of the creation of new souls happens quite literally inside our bodies. And then our bodies are designed to bring that life into the world — to give birth.

But isn't this just over-spiritualizing it all? As Christians, we are an incarnational people. We believe that the material world is intimately united with the spiritual. Even more, we believe that God wants to work through the material world. He is revealed through his creation, through concrete, tangible things, from the beauty of nature to the soul-stirring power of music to the encounter with his very real flesh and blood in the Eucharist. Ours is a fleshy faith. God meets us and makes us holy through our bodies. If anything, it's over-spiritualizing to deny that God can and does want to work through our physical bodies as he intentionally created them. We'd also have to write off the entire Theology of the Body as over-spiritualizing. The work of birth testifies to deeper mysteries, allowing us to participate in the work of God, and this is a profoundly Christian idea.

We shouldn't be scandalized that our bodies and the powerful moments of birth reveal deep truths about God — the God of the universe, who became an unborn child, who gave water the ability to wash our souls, who designed sex to be a holy and spiritually profound act that reveals and leads us to the One who designed it all in the first place. We have a God who desires to be intimately involved in our lives and who reveals himself to us in and through our bodies — and that includes birth.

The births of my three children were all vastly different, but one thing was a constant — God was there, present with me, loving me. Always. Just because my first experience was traumatic doesn't lessen the fact that he was present. One doesn't negate the other; in fact, it can be the opposite. He stays with us in the hard places and can carry us through to the other side if we'll let him. And just because my last birth was peaceful and I was well cared for, that doesn't mean that his presence wasn't just as strongly felt. Birth can be an occasion for both joy and suffering, pain and ecstasy, love and fear. Our God is big enough for all of those things and more. By allowing him into the life-changing experience of birth, we are opening ourselves up to the true miracle of bringing life into the world.

— Christina Kolb, mom to three

5

BIRTH FALLEN, BIRTH REDEEMED

"When a woman is in labor, she has pain because her hour has come; but when she is delivered of the child, she no longer remembers the anguish, for joy that a child is born into the world."
— *John 16:21*

Ah, the chapter where it gets a bit more real ... or, more appropriately, where we feel it a bit more. All that nice theology talk sounds lovely and looks great on paper. But at some point we need to get to the reality of what that will actually mean for us in our bodies. Does God's plan affect what we as women physically experience during our births?

In his Theology of the Body, Pope John Paul II based his reflections and work on Christ's prompting to go "back to the beginning" to understand God's design and will for us, which helps us better understand what he wants from us, and what birth can become in light of the redemption.

Was Birth Supposed to Be Painful?

In the story of creation taken from Scripture, we are led to understand that God designed and desired childbirth. The very first command given to Adam and Eve after their creation was, "Be fruitful and multiply" (Gn 1:29). He wanted Adam and Eve to be intimate, to conceive, and to give birth! Sex, the physical, self-giving love between husband and wife, is good and desired by God, and it is meant to be fruitful both spiritually and physically. This means that the natural result — birth — is also good and desired by God.

As the fruit of the perfect love between a perfect man and a perfect woman, in the beginning birth did not include pain. Did it occur as naturally as other bodily functions, or was it even pleasurable or euphoric? We don't know. We do know, however, that things changed.

When Adam and Eve sinned, they upset God's original design for all of creation, which means God's original design for birth also got messed up. While the first command of God still stands, it now comes with caveats. Genesis tells us: "To the woman he said, 'I will greatly multiply your pain [*issabownek*] in childbearing; in pain [*be'eseb*] you shall bring forth children, yet your desire shall be for your husband, and he shall rule over you" (3:16).

This is not happenstance. The consequence hits at the very heart of who the woman is — bringer of life into the world. God doesn't negate that original command to be fruitful and multiply — sexuality, marriage, and childbearing are still good and desired by God — but now the original plan becomes more difficult. The effects of sin reach deep into who we are as man and woman, both as individuals and in relationship to each other.

In all of human history, the Church traditionally holds that only one woman ever underwent childbirth without suffering the consequences of original sin: there is a long-standing tradition that Mary gave birth to Jesus without pain, because she was conceived without sin through the future merits of her Son. The *Catechism of the Council of Trent* states: "To Eve it was said: In sorrow shalt thou bring forth children. Mary was exempt from this law, for preserving her virginal integrity inviolate she brought forth Jesus the Son of God without experiencing ... any sense of pain."[43] Many Church Fathers also wrote that Mary had no pain in childbirth.

Pain in childbirth is the lingering and deeply rooted effect of sin, and we regret that consequence. But this should not lead us to despair, or to curse Eve, or to distance ourselves from Mary. Rather, it is an invitation to allow our hearts to see the tragedy of sin, and then choose to find our own unique part to play in God's plan in light of the rest of the story.

The Importance of the Biblical Understanding of "Pain"

If we are seeking to understand God's design for birth, then let's try to understand what he himself says about it in Scripture. The first thing to note is the very words used in the original Hebrew texts. Translating from one language to another often loses some of the full meaning, and the connotation can change depending on the word used by the translator. The Hebrew masculine noun used for Adam's punishment — "toil" in his work (*be'issabown*[44]) — has the same root noun, *itstsabon*, as the feminine noun used for Eve's "pain" in childbirth (*issabownek*[45]): "To the woman he said, 'I will greatly multiply your pain [*issabownek*] in childbirth'" (Gn 3:16). *Itstsabon* is defined as "pain or toil."[46] A different word, *be'eseb*, is used in the next line from Genesis: "In pain [*be'eseb*] you will bring forth children." Both words come from the verb *'atsab*, which is simply defined as "to displease or grieve."[47]

Simply put, the "pain" in childbirth can have a larger connotation than our language offers. It might give us a truer perspective of pregnancy and birth to use a fuller definition. While there are women who are graced with nearly painless births (really!), the vast majority will experience some degree of pain. But it can be tremendously helpful to change your mindset toward what labor and birth will be. Prompted by a more complete understanding of the words of Genesis, let's take on the idea that labor is *work*. As Adam has his difficult work, so Eve has hers. Labor is called labor for a reason. Labor, birth, and recovery will be very, very hard work.

The preparation for and the act of birth is analogous to a marathon. There is much preparation involved, there is a lot of work to put in, and it's not at all easy or comfortable. It may, in fact, become very painful, and it will likely be a challenge beyond anything experienced previously. Yet the joy of making it to the finish line makes every drop of blood, sweat, and tears worth it. We may arrive there sweaty and aching in every muscle and ligament of our body, it may have been the hardest work we have ever done, but the joy overwhelms and deepens as we invest more and more of ourselves into the race. Like almost anything worth doing or in which we find the greatest pride and satisfaction, labor and birth will require commitment, an investment of self, and, yes, work. Some women may have to work harder, some may seem not to have to do much at all. But the Lord has picked out the perfect race just for you, and it's the one he knows is best.

Even the pains which, after original sin, a mother has to suffer to give birth to her child only make her draw tighter the bond which unites them: the more the pain has cost her, so much the more is her love for her child. He who formed mothers' hearts, expressed this thought with moving and profound simplicity: "A woman about to give birth has sorrow, because her hour has come. But when she has brought forth the child, she no longer remembers the anguish for her joy that a man is born into the world." Through the pen of the apostle, Saint Paul, the Holy Ghost also points out the greatness and joy of motherhood: God gives the child to the mother, but, together with the gift, he makes her cooperate effectively at the opening of the flower, of which he has deposited the germ in her womb, and this cooperation becomes a way which leads her to her eternal salvation: "Yet women will be saved by childbearing."
— Pope Pius XII, *Allocution to Midwives*

Entering the Story

Out of everything God could have chosen, he chose the act of childbearing to be where we as women would most directly feel the effects of original sin. There is something deeply significant in God choosing that specific way for women to bear the consequence of the fall. God could have decided that women also would have to work the land, or that we would have difficulty eating or some other activity, or have to be separated forever from man. God could have struck Eve dead on the spot and started over. But the God of the universe, who is wisdom and love itself, chose childbearing. And every single woman after Eve is now affected — which sometimes doesn't seem all that fair to our limited minds, does it? Yet those of us now faced with the prospect of physical birth have the opportunity to view it as a time to "enter into the story" of salvation history. Even if we don't fully understand it, we can view our experience of birth as a vehicle for our own sanctity and response to the problem of sin.

As Christians we believe that the incarnation of Christ and, ultimately, his passion, death, and resurrection — the Paschal Mystery — change the story. We believe that while the effects of original sin still remain, they can become vehicles of grace when we unite them with the Cross. Saint John Paul II writes, "The Redemption restores, in a sense, at its very root, the good that was essentially 'diminished' by sin and its heritage in human history."[48] Christ's death and resurrection didn't erase those consequences of sin we received. They redeemed them. And this changes everything. We now have the incredible chance to share in that eternal work of Christ. Before Christ, work was simply punishment for sin; now it is an avenue for redemption and grace.

In birth, we women have the opportunity to enter this mystery. Saint Paul refers to this reality: "Woman will be saved through bearing children, if she continues in faith and love and holiness, with modesty" (1 Tm 2:15). Our births are effective tools in sanctifying both ourselves and the world. During pregnancy, labor, birth, and after, we have the chance to allow our bodies to mimic Christ's as we lay down our lives for the sake of another. Through Christ, the pain of childbirth is redeemed and capable of eternal good, not just for ourselves or our babies, but for the whole world. Drawing upon his example and grace, we have the chance to embrace our own cross; offer our will, minds, and bodies; and bring new life into the world.

The *Catechism* reflects that invitation: "In his mercy God has not forsaken sinful man. The punishments consequent upon sin, 'pain in childbearing' and toil 'in the sweat of your brow,' also embody remedies that limit the damaging effects of sin" (1609).

Whoa. Read that again. We have the opportunity to view the labor and sufferings we endure during birth as a unique part of God's plan to redeem the world from sin! *Our births can be a "remedy" for the world for the effects of sin.* What a mind-blowing invitation!

Replicating the sacrificial love of Christ, we women offer our very bodies to the child within. We can do this in myriad ways, of course — through eating well and exercising, through the aches and pains of pregnancy, even through the unconscious continual nourishing of that tiny body through our own blood. Yet no act better replicates that type of complete and total sacrificial offering of self as the act of birth. A woman's body becomes the vehicle, the passageway, of new life entering the world. Just as Christ offered his body on the cross to give each one of us new life, so a mother offers her body on the bed, in the pool, on the table, to give that baby new life. What looks like pain and blood and even death becomes the very avenue through which the world will be changed.

Pope Saint John Paul said just this in his *Letter to Families*:

> The fact that a child is being born, that "a child is born into the world" (Jn 16:21) is a paschal sign.... The "hour" of Christ's death (cf. Jn 13:1) is compared here to the "hour" of the woman in birthpangs; the birth of a new child fully reflects the victory of life over death brought about by the Lord's Resurrection. This comparison can provide us with material for reflection. (11)

The mother's act of birth "fully reflects" the paschal mystery of Christ. The mother in her own little paschal mystery offers herself completely, despite the pain, the fear, and the sacrifice required to give her child life. In birth, the woman has the opportunity to use her body for the glory of God. Her body becomes a sign of Christ's love for each and every person, a sign for the world that redemption is real, and that Christ has won. Just as Christ first offered his body and blood in the Eucharist at the Last Supper, so a woman offers her body to the infant in her womb at conception and throughout pregnancy. And just as that first Eucharistic celebration culminated in the great sacrifice of the Cross, so a woman reaches that culmination of her bodily offering in the great sacrifice of birth.

Archbishop Fulton Sheen declared: "Not only a woman's days, but her nights — not only her mind, but her body must share in the Calvary of motherhood. That is why women have a surer understanding of the doctrine of redemption than men have: they have to associate the risk of death with life in childbirth, and to understand the sacrifice of self to another through the many months preceding it."[49]

It is important to note here that the language of a woman's body still exists whether she has a natural vaginal birth, whether it is medicated, or whether she has a surgical birth. Regardless of the method, her body is still a beautiful and profound sign of the Paschal Mystery as she lays it down at the service of new life. In any kind of birth, she gives of herself completely, vulnerably, to the point of her own blood being spilled so that her child may have life. The act of birth is by its very nature paschal. We as women have the opportunity to climb our own unique Calvary and ultimately give ourselves over as Christ did, offering our complete bodies — naked, vulnerable, messy, and beautiful — to usher new life into the world.

Our unique experience of birth is our chance to enter into the story — Christ's story. No matter how one's birth plays out, Christ continues to be present and available. No matter what kind of birth you have, there is opportunity for grace and growth, and an offering of self. There is an opening in the story of sin and salvation and redemption for you.

Will there be pain? Most likely, yes. But as Catholics we approach pain and suffering in a very different way from the rest of the world. Through Christ, pain has the power to become something beautiful and redeeming. God has endowed our bodies with a unique feminine strength to share in this work. We see it as an opportunity to grow in union with God, to become stronger, and even to participate in the work of saving souls. And, as almost any mother can attest as she looks her baby in the eyes, it is worth it.

In finding out that you are pregnant, you are able to be freed, liberated from the tyranny of yourself in this tiny world in which you were the most important. You are free to love and give and sacrifice. And that holy grace will make you something altogether different. You will be shaken, humbled, stretched, and broken. And it will make you a mother.

— Haley Stewart, mom to three

Mary, Our Lady of Childbirth

"Mary's maternity is the model of all motherhood."
— Saint Teresa Benedicta of the Cross

In the Incarnation, God was born of a woman. God chose to enter humanity through the rite of birth. If nothing written thus far has convinced you that birth is beautiful and has the capacity to be holy, this truth should.

The Son of God could have chosen any way to become human. But he chose, from all eternity, to be conceived and grown in a human woman and born from her very body. In Mary, childbirth is reclaimed again for God. In her "yes" (*fiat*) to the angel Gabriel at the Annunciation, Mary became the new woman of Genesis, the archetype for all women. Her "yes" is the reversal of Eve's "no." She is the new Eve. The consequences of Eve's disobedience can now be redeemed and made new through Mary's obedience. Willingly and freely Mary chose to offer her body as the vehicle for God to become man and bring eternal life to the world.

What an example we have in Mary's beautiful and bold openness to the will of God. What's more, we have the opportunity to do the same. United with her, we can give God the offering of our very body to bring new life into the world. Mary can be the model we need to open our hearts, bodies, and souls to new life. Even those experiencing a pregnancy unexpected or less than ideal can see themselves in her, for certainly Mary's situation was considered less than ideal on the surface! "In Mary, Eve discovers the nature of the true dignity of woman, of feminine humanity. This discovery must continually reach the heart of every woman and shape her vocation and her life."[50]

While Mary probably did not experience pain during the birth of Jesus, she certainly suffered as she stood at the foot of the cross, united with her Son in his work of bringing eternal life into the world. Calvary was her labor. As his mother, her "yes" opened her up in a unique way to the pain and suffering that was necessary for humanity to be redeemed. We can look to her as we share a piece of that in our pregnancies, births, and the rest of motherhood.

There is a beautiful sculpture of Mary in the Church of Saint Augustine in Rome called *Our Lady of Childbirth*. Beneath the statue are hundreds of pictures, testimonies, and offerings of thanksgiving from mothers who prayed there for healthy pregnancies and births. For centuries women have begged intercession from Mary under this title for healing of infertility, for help in pregnancy, and for healthy and even happy deliveries. This devotion is a tremendous witness to the importance and beauty of a woman's experience of birth — and heaven's concern for it. Not only should we pray for a healthy birth, but we are invited to ask that it be a "happy" one.

As a mother herself, Our Lady surely experienced profound joy, power, intimacy with the Trinity, and perhaps even ecstasy during her own childbearing, though her outside circumstances were far less than ideal. She offers us a share of her joy. Christ gave her to us, after all, and the Church declares that "she is a mother to us in the order of grace."[51] She is our heavenly mother, a good and devoted mother who wants the best for her daughters, and we can be assured that she desires and prays for us to have healthy, holy, and truly joyful births.

Our understanding of Mary as mother and the model for all women means that we can see in her an invitation to enter deeply into this time of pregnancy and birth. She can be our guide, model, intercessor, and comfort as we bring these newest sons and daughters of God into the world. Many women find that their relationship with the Blessed Mother grows deeper during their pregnancies and as they enter into their roles as mothers. In her, we have not only the inspiration but the powerful prayers needed to become the mothers that God created us to be. And she can mother us as we mother our babies.

I was due with two of my children around Christmastime. It helped to picture Mary pregnant with Jesus, especially toward the end. When pregnant with my son, I was getting very close to my due date on Christmas Eve and VERY ready for labor. I went to Christmas Eve Mass and sat toward the front. My priest saw me and at the end of Mass he mentioned to the congregation that I still hadn't had my baby. I responded, "I'm so glad I'm not riding on a donkey!" Mary trusted God so completely, not only to agree to give birth to God's Son, but also to trust when she had to travel to Bethlehem and then give birth in a stable! It helped me to be grateful for my clean birth, doctor, doula, etc., and also helped me to feel calmer as I meditated on her trust.

— Amanda D., mom to four

6

THE DESIGN OF BIRTH

"For you formed my inward parts, you knitted me together in my mother's womb. I praise you, for I am wondrously made. Wonderful are your works! You know me right well."
— Psalm 139:13–14

Knowing how our bodies work gives us a better understanding of the basic design of birth. Basic knowledge can play a tremendous role in dissolving the fear that creeps into our view of birth as a result of media portrayal, horror stories we've heard, or simply our own ignorance of the female body's design. Understanding also gives us more confidence in God's design for our bodies and helps us make decisions well so we can have the best birth possible.

It's amazing that many schools today cover the gamut when it comes to contraceptives and sexually transmitted diseases and all sorts of disordered sexual activities, but most high school students walk away from their biology and health classes with no idea how birth works, or even that sex and babies are designed to go together. Not only that, many have never studied the basic fertility cycles of the woman or the formation of the baby in the womb. They know about abortion but rarely know about normal birth.

In today's culture fertility is a liability. Even the government continues to seek to make contraception universally available as "preventative medicine,"[52] with the underlying assumption that the healthy female body somehow needs to be fixed and medicated. For the majority of parents today, their education in normal fertility, biology, pregnancy, and birth begins when they are actually going through it themselves.

This education vacuum is filled by the idea of pregnancy as punishment and birth as terrifying. The media's depictions of birth, filled with screaming, the mother's water breaking in some embarrassing place followed by immediate agonizing contractions and pushing, certainly don't help. Most new mothers and fathers need to be told that it's not usually like that.

When we understand how something truly works, we become empowered to utilize it. This is true with our fertility. In recent years, more and more women — Catholic and non-Catholic — have begun to realize the power and advantage they have when they better understand their fertility and monthly cycles. Our cycles are designed by God and we function best when we work with that design rather than against it.

There is a growing grassroots movement against the onslaught of contraception as women question whether it makes sense to tell their bodies not to function as they were designed. There are consequences to contraception that have become better known and studied as they've arisen. Intervening in the design of the woman's healthy body with chemicals and intrauterine devices can greatly jeopardize both a woman's short-term and long-term health, not only physically but mentally, emotionally, and spiritually.[53] When a woman understands her fertility, she can make better, informed decisions about healthcare, her prospects for a future pregnancy, when to be intimate with her spouse, and when she might not be fully healthy. There is a beauty and dignity to women's understanding the design of the Creator for their bodies and claiming and using that knowledge.

So, too, with birth. Having a greater understanding of how her body is designed for birth gives a woman greater ability to make decisions and foster better short- and long-term health outcomes for herself and her baby. Respecting a mother's intellect and her right to have good information recognizes her dignity as a woman and enhances her satisfaction with her birth.[54] Similar to fertility cycles and related decisions, there are also often unintended consequences to intervening without necessity in the natural design and process of birth. There is, of course, not a moral equivalency. There is no Church teaching on how a woman should give birth or make specific birth choices, as there is with contraception. Sometimes we can and should intervene in the natural process of birth. But learning how our body is designed to birth allows us to work better with that design and have a better, healthier, more informed experience for ourselves and our babies.

The Most Important Lesson

So what should a woman know about birth?

The female body was designed to give birth. Even if she never understands the precise logistics or anatomy of how it happens, a woman who has the confidence that her body was naturally designed to create and to bear life is at an incalculable advantage. As Pope Saint John Paul II expressed it: "The woman's motherhood in the period between the baby's conception and birth is a bio-physiological and psychological process which is better understood in our days than in the past, and is the subject of many detailed studies. Scientific analysis fully confirms that the very physical constitution of women is naturally disposed to motherhood — conception, pregnancy and giving birth — which is a consequence of the marriage union with the man."[55] The pope reaffirms this truth: Women's bodies are designed by God to birth. A woman's fertility, her ability to carry, birth, and nurse a child, are all representative of good and normal health. As Catholics we reject the contraceptive mentality that tells us fertility is a disease to be cured and the birth of a child a punishment to those who haven't been "responsible."

For good or for bad, a woman brings her past, her social environment, and her deepest beliefs and fears into her birth. When a woman comes from a line of women who have successfully and confidently given birth, when she maintains a healthy body image, when she views her marriage and motherhood as a calling from God, when her husband has confidence in her ability to give birth to their baby, and when she hears confident and beautiful words about her womanhood and motherhood from her provider and even leaders of the Church, she will then have deeper confidence that she was truly made for and capable of this work. On the opposite end, if a woman has only heard horror stories about birth, if she has never seen a woman undergoing normal labor, if her husband doubts her, or if she has come to believe that her body is broken, then she will often bring that into her approach to birth.

We know that the effects of original sin mean everything does not always go according to God's original plan. Infertility occurs. Miscarriage happens. Birth complications do happen. We know that the original design is the healthiest way for a baby to be born. When complications arise, intervening for the sake of the mother or baby also should be considered part of God's plan. Science and medicine are meant to be a gift to the world — at the service of life. We thank God for the obstetricians, doctors, and midwives who use their gifts to serve women and babies and intervene when appropriate.

Still, we trust that God planned birth, and *he knew what he was doing*. His design has been bringing new babies into the world for thousands of years. It makes sense, and it works.

The Everyday Miracle

Most of us know by now how conception works. The husband's sperm meets the wife's egg. At that very moment God infuses a new, never-before-existing soul into a new body. Within a week or two that blastocyst baby has traveled through one of the woman's fallopian tubes and becomes embedded in the uterus, an incredible miracle every time. There, he or she will hopefully stay tucked away in the mother's womb for another nine months or so, growing at phenomenal rates, developing organs, sustained by the mother's blood. The baby is attached via an umbilical cord from the abdomen to the placenta. That place where the umbilical cord is attached will eventually become a belly button. The placenta, truly an amazing thing and sometimes referred to in the birth world as "the tree of life," is an *entirely new* organ that the mother grows in order to feed and nourish her baby. It is firmly attached to the uterus on one side and to the baby via the umbilical cord on the other. It is the only organ that the human body routinely grows from scratch and then discards. For the baby in utero, it functions as almost every major organ at once.

All of this occurs with very little conscious "doing" on the mother's part. She may be eating well and supplementing with vitamins and doing her best to take care of herself for her baby's sake, which are all good and helpful, but she doesn't have to consciously *do* any of the growing or nourishing of her baby. Her body is giving, nourishing, and growing this baby, while she works and plays, sleeps and eats. We sometimes hear about women who don't even realize they are pregnant until halfway through or even further along in their pregnancies. Their body grew a baby without their awareness that it was happening. This, of course, does not mean that pregnancy is always successful. We know the heartbreak of miscarriage. Not every baby develops properly — sometimes this is avoidable and sometimes it isn't. But this doesn't discount the fact that the baby's development lies mostly outside of the mother's conscious will and work.

Where the miraculous meets the natural, a baby develops and grows against all odds and yet outside of any drastic intervention. The same holds true for birth itself. We can cooperate with our body's good design, work with it, understand what is happening, and have a good provider so that appropriate measures can be taken to help if needed. But it's truly transformative for a woman to realize that her body *already knows* how to give birth and the majority of the time would do it just fine without a whole lot of help.

When Are You *Actually* Due?

Before we discuss the biological interplay of how birth happens, let's talk about how long a pregnancy truly lasts.

When will that baby finally be ready, anyway? Babies are considered "at term" when they are anywhere from thirty-seven to forty-two weeks. This means, contrary to what your due date suggests, there is actually a full five weeks during which mom could naturally go into labor. Almost all women, when left on their own, will naturally go into labor sometime during those five weeks.

This is why it's helpful to consider your due date an estimate, and it's vitally important that it be accurately calculated. Women who practice natural family planning or who at least have an understanding of their cycles and fertility have an advantage in this area. They have a better idea of the signs of ovulation and can better estimate within a day or two when baby was likely conceived.

The standard for dating a pregnancy, even today, is still to go by the start date of your last period and count from there. This means that, according to the dating system most in use, pregnancy begins before the baby was even conceived! So, when a woman talks about being six weeks pregnant, her baby is actually only about four weeks old. And that's only if she ovulated right on day fourteen of her cycle — which is a big, and often incorrect, assumption. Using the date of your last period to determine your due date assumes that you experienced the "official" twenty-eight-day cycle and ovulated on day fourteen. But how many women have that textbook cycle every month? (It's worth noting that the same medical system that mocks the "rhythm method" actually uses it when dating pregnancies this way.)

This method of dating, based on gestation of ten lunar months, follows Naegele's Rule, attributed to a nineteenth-century German doctor. This method calculates the estimated due date by adding one year to the first day of the last menstrual period, subtracting three months, and adding seven days. The result is approximately 280 days (forty weeks) from the start of the last period, and this is how the paper-wheel calculators in your provider's office or online calculators usually work. It is actually unclear whether Naegele himself used the first day of the period or the last day to calculate the due date, which would change the calculation significantly.[56]

Clearly, there are many ways in which using the first day of the last menstrual cycle can give a flawed result. An accurate due date can make the difference between going into labor naturally with a simple, complication-free birth and being pressured into an induction (and the risks included) for being "late" because the doctor thinks the pregnancy is further along than it truly is. This can even mean the difference between a healthy baby and a baby sent to the NICU or who has other struggles simply because they were taken out before they were ready.

Many obstetricians nowadays use early ultrasounds to date pregnancy. Using the ultrasounds and measurements of the baby, they can make a fairly accurate estimate of gestational age and when the baby is due. While this method is more accurate in determining the gestational age of a baby than the last menstrual period is, there is still room for error. The most accurate ultrasounds are those done in the first trimester. Many moms, however, are concerned about ultrasounds since, despite widespread and frequent use, their effects have not been sufficiently studied in controlled trials.[57] The American College of Obstetricians and Gynecologists has also warned against non-medically indicated ultrasound use,[58] stating that it hasn't been adequately studied and additional side effects could be discovered. Dating a pregnancy can be considered a medical use, and it may be necessary for some women, but, if possible, the most accurate "official" due date comes from knowing within a day or two when the baby was conceived and calculating from there.

What we call the due date is simply the day of the pregnancy counted forward to forty weeks (based on the last menstrual cycle). This is the midpoint of when a healthy woman will typically go into labor. It's interesting to note that the number forty is used often in Scripture by God to represent the fullness of something. Certainly, this shouldn't be considered a coincidence! Recent studies have shown that (using the traditional dating) the *median* date for women going into natural labor with their first baby and an uncomplicated pregnancy is actually forty-one weeks plus one day. For multiparas (mothers who have already given birth), the median was forty weeks plus three days.[59]

It is important not only to know your true estimated due date, but also to know that the date is not an expiration or "eviction" date, as you may have heard some people say. Nothing dramatic happens on that date, and your baby does not have a calendar in the womb to know when his or her "due date" is. It is important for you to know how far along you actually are, as well as the current standards of care, which do not consider a baby "overdue" until past forty-two weeks.[60] New standards have been put into place and encouraged since 2013 based on research that showed when babies at term had the best outcomes. Those new standards broke the five-week span into three groups:

Early term — 37–39 weeks
Full term — 39–41 weeks
Late term — 41–42 weeks

Notice that it is only when a mother goes past that forty-two-week mark that she is considered "overdue" or "post date."[61]

Consider your estimated due date just that — an estimate. It might help to think of it and talk about it as a "due time" or "due month." The end of pregnancy can be challenging, and it can be discouraging to a mother when she and others have this magical date in mind. Some women don't even tell others the exact date because of the pressure then felt to have the baby, or to "perform" by that date. If you think others will be overly excited to have the baby born by that date, putting unrealistic or unhealthy pressure on you and the baby, consider telling people "sometime in May" rather than the exact forty-week mark. Remember, the due date is simply the date in the middle of the five-week window when you might have the baby. It is not an expiration date. Special circumstances aside, your baby will come when your baby is ready.

So-o-o, How Does It All Work?

Sometime during those five weeks at term, you will go into labor. When your body goes into labor, you are flooded (usually unbeknownst to you) with hormones that begin the work of opening the uterus wide enough to allow the baby to pass through. We break this down into three observable "stages" of birth:

Labor (First Stage): The womb contracts and gradually opens the cervix (simply the opening of the uterus).

Pushing (Second Stage): The baby is pushed out of the uterus by a different type of contraction.

Afterbirth (Third Stage): The woman's womb contracts again to release the placenta and begins to shrink back down to its pre-pregnant size.

What Starts Labor?

Interestingly, very little is known about how God designed labor to begin and what actually "triggers" it. We know that most babies do best when they are allowed to gestate until they are ready to come out, and theories have been growing that in a healthy mom it actually *is* the baby that decides when he or she is ready. Scientists have recently discovered that babies release a protein in their lungs that plays a part in triggering mom's body to go into labor.[62] We know the mother responds to that release with increasing amounts of oxytocin, and that is what stimulates the uterus to begin to contract and open up.

It is amazing that we don't actually know more about what "flips the switch," but we do know that God designed labor and birth, so it is wise to be very careful about intervening without sufficient reason. Babies that are brought out too early often have breathing difficulties, struggle with nursing, and are more vulnerable to infection and being sent to the NICU. If a mother's body isn't ready, the birth is more likely to have complications and end in a cesarean section. When it is possible and other situations don't arise, waiting until the baby's and mom's bodies are both ready gives the best possible chance for a simple, complication-free birth.

It can take a great amount of trust, especially at the end of a pregnancy, to know that your body will go into labor. Support and encouragement from your husband, like-minded friends, and provider are invaluable at this time. Have a project or two that you leave until those last few weeks, and keep making plans that you can look forward to. I even recommend making plans past the estimated due date, knowing that you can always cancel. Most women find it's more helpful to have things to do and stay active and positive, rather than clearing the schedule only to sit around waiting for labor to start. Those last few weeks of pregnancy are challenging enough without adding internal pressure and frustration with your body and your baby into the mix.

There are most certainly situations that can arise where it is best to intervene and artificially induce labor for mom or baby. A good provider will be diligent in care but prudent in intervening, doing so only when it is of pressing concern.

Opening the Womb

When labor begins, the body begins to release large amounts of oxytocin into both the bloodstream and the nervous system, and the uterus begins to contract. Oxytocin, known as the "bonding hormone," or "love hormone," is released in torrential amounts during three main times: orgasm, labor contractions, and while breastfeeding. It is also released in much smaller amounts through touch, kissing, low lighting, good smells, and good memories. Because it is a neurotransmitter (unlike the synthetic form Pitocin), it affects both our brain chemistry and the rest of our body.

One of the main purposes of this hormone release is to bond two people together, emotionally and chemically, as happens between husband and wife. This tells us something amazing about God's plan: husbands and wives are designed to be bonded for life, and mothers are designed and biologically created to have a real and lasting bond with their baby. *God's plan of family is written into our very bodies.* This is one reason why it hurts so much when a sexual relationship ends, why a mother who never knew her baby past birth can still feel eternally connected to him or her, and why we can feel bonded after birth to the people who were with us during it. Our bodies are meant to work with our souls and are designed to reinforce and work with spiritual reality.

Oxytocin release is encouraged when a mother feels safe, respected, and private. The opposite is also true. If she feels threatened, exposed, judged, or vulnerable, it can inhibit the release of this incredibly important hormone. This means that a woman's environment (both people and place) matters greatly to the birth process itself. The release of oxytocin begins contractions that are usually subtle at first but continue to grow and intensify. Most women who go into labor naturally have a difficult time pinpointing when exactly labor began. For most, early contractions begin gradually and gently, and are often not all that notable. There is usually not a concrete "this is it" contraction that begins labor, as we often see in the movies. The majority of women do not have their water break before labor begins, also contrary to most television and movie portrayals.

Usually, beginning contractions don't follow a specific pattern. Some women describe them as a "tightening," some as menstrual cramps that increase in intensity, and others like back pain that wraps around to their abdomen. Part of how they experience a contraction can be influenced by the baby's position (whether the baby is anterior or posterior) as well as whether this is their first birth or not. The contractions (or "surges," as some people prefer to call them) increase in intensity, working to pull the uterus muscle up and stretching the cervix open. The cervix, again, is simply the opening to the uterus. Before birth, it is thick, tightly closed, and sealed with mucous, protecting your baby until the time of birth. If you picture the uterus as a balloon with the opening pointed down, the contractions are first thinning out that opening, then pulling the opening wider, dilating it until it is about ten centimeters wide and big enough to allow the baby through. Contractions usually occur in a "wave." You can begin to feel it coming, it grows and reaches a peak, and then slowly releases. In a natural labor, there are breaks in between the contractions, allowing you to rest and reenergize for the next one. There are three stages of this opening: early labor, active labor, and transition.

The First Stage of Birth — Labor

Early Labor

In early labor, the cervix is thinning out and beginning to open. You may begin to see lots of mucous or what is called "bloody show," which is part of or possibly the whole mucous plug, sometimes tinged with a bit of blood, that was sealing up the cervix and protecting the baby. Contractions may be consistent or sporadic. You usually can go about your day in between these early contractions and should eat and drink and rest if you can so you have the energy you will need for later. It's important to know that for some women this stage can last for days. If you can talk between contractions, you're still in early labor. If you plan to birth at a hospital, it's not time to go in yet. If you can sleep, do so!

Early labor is usually defined as the cervix dilating from zero to about four centimeters, but it's helpful not to have numbers in mind. Just let your body do what it needs to do. Many women find the best coping strategy during this time is to go about their normal day as much as possible, "ignoring" the labor in a way. Keep a good attitude, knowing that the process could take a while and that the time frame between contractions can be all over the place.

Active Labor

As the surges pick up in intensity, you may find yourself gradually getting more and more serious. Your mood shifts, and your body begins to buckle down more in the work of labor. You are no longer excited and may find it more difficult to talk during or even between contractions. You are less likely to be joking around and aren't able to go about your normal tasks anymore, even when trying your best. You find the surges cannot be ignored. You need to breathe deeply through each one and focus. When a contraction comes, you will find yourself focusing inward, perhaps needing silence, your body swaying or leaning, or sometimes needing to be completely still, breathing deeply and intentionally.

Many women talk about the phenomenon of "labor land" during this part of labor, where reality seems to shift a bit. Time is strange and almost feels suspended. You are mentally, emotionally, physically, and spiritually in a different place. The time between contractions usually begins to lessen. The muscular walls of the uterus are pulling up and "collecting" at the top. The contractions grow in intensity, and many women begin to vocalize in moans or sighs.

Transition

Transition is usually defined as the cervix opening from seven to ten centimeters. It is the hardest work of labor, but, thankfully, for most women it is usually the fastest. This is the time many women begin to feel as if they cannot do it anymore, and they often say so. Surges can seem to come one on top of another, and they are most often very painful as the cervix opens that last bit to allow the baby through. At some point, as the contractions progress through transition, you will begin to feel slight pressure that continues to build. The pressure often comes at the peak of the contraction and feels like the urge to have a bowel movement. Most women unconsciously begin to grunt, and a skilled provider or attendant will know that you are getting close to pushing. The contractions build until you are fully dilated and the pressure is causing you to push.

The Second Stage of Birth — Pushing

When you are fully open, your body will begin to switch over into pushing mode. All of that uterine muscle that has stretched to open the cervix is now collected on top and ready to literally push the baby out. You can push along with your body, but even if you don't, your body would push anyway: this is called the "fetal ejection reflex." Your body is designed to do this. For many women, there is a period of rest between being fully dilated and being ready to push. For some, contractions may ease significantly as the body transitions to the pushing stage. Typically, there is no reason to hurry or to push before you feel that pressure and have the urge. This could be the body's way of building up some more energy for the big work ahead. When it comes time to push, if you have not had any anesthesia, you will most likely feel an uncontrollable urge to bear down as though you are having a bowel movement. In fact, that is exactly the way you will push. You will usually experience intermittent pushing contractions with breaks in between, just as before, but this time your body is bearing down with the contraction. As your body pushes, the baby moves down the birth canal, your vagina. The speed is determined by how hard your body is pushing, how the baby is positioned, and how you are positioned. For some women this can take hours, for others just a few minutes.

Often, especially if this is your first birth, the baby's head will take "two steps forward and one step back" as it opens up the birth canal for the first time, coming down a little bit lower with each push, but going back up in between. This is totally normal. The baby's head is beautifully designed to fit through the birth canal. In fact, the skull bones of a newborn are separate and able to overlap for the journey, allowing the baby's head to fit as needed. For some babies, a longer pushing stage will leave them with a little bit of a "conehead" after birth, but it will eventually round out in the hours or days after birth. For an ideally positioned baby, the crown of his or her head will move its way down the vagina first, gradually coming into view. The baby's head reaches the labia, called "crowning," and the woman will usually feel a burning and very intense stretching of the skin of her labia and perineum. Slow pushing is often encouraged at this point to allow the skin to stretch gradually and avoid a tear.

At this point she is so close to meeting her baby! As the head, the biggest part of the baby, crowns and is born, the relief is immense. Usually it takes just one or two more contraction pushes for the rest of the body to slide out.

What about That Water Breaking?

Every woman is different regarding her amniotic sac releasing. For some women, their water releases before they've felt any contractions, and it does prompt gentle contractions that gradually lead to birth. For others, their water breaks, but contractions don't start for hours or even days. For the majority of women, the membranes will rupture sometime during active labor or transition. There are even rare instances of a baby being born "in the caul," or still in the amniotic sac! Some cultures consider it good luck (and it certainly is neat to see). For some women, the release is a big "pop" and a gush of fluid; for others it is a slow trickle.

The amniotic sac serves an important purpose for the baby throughout pregnancy, holding the fluid and protecting him or her from germs and bacteria. During labor, it helps provide a cushion for the baby and for the mother during contractions. The water also makes it easier for baby to move around to get into a good position for birth. Many women notice a significant increase in intensity when their water releases, although some experience it as a huge release of pressure, especially if they are in transition. If a woman's water does break before active or any labor, she should be in communication with her provider. The release of her water means that baby will need to come out within the next few days to keep him or her safe from infection. Different providers have different recommendations about how soon after a woman's membranes have ruptured the baby should be born.

The Third Stage of Birth — The Afterbirth

While it may seem as if you should be done after pushing out that baby, you still have one important step of birth left. Your body will usually give a good rest as you meet and hold your baby for the first time, and then it will begin to contract again, this time a bit less intense than it was as the baby was coming out. The placenta after birth begins to close off the blood vessels that were securing it to the uterine wall and prepares to release. Once it is completely detached, it will slide to the uterine opening. You will be exhausted, but you will need to push a bit more to get the placenta out. This is not nearly as much work as the baby, thankfully, and the placenta usually comes out in one or two pushes once you feel the contractions again. It is important to wait until the placenta has completely detached from the wall of the uterus. Unless there is a serious concern, no one should be rushing the placenta along, but it is also important to make sure it comes out soon after birth and is intact. Many women want to see the placenta, and it truly is an amazing thing, this organ that has been the constant supply of oxygen and food and blood to your baby!

After the Birth

After birth, your body will immediately begin the process of recovering and healing. The uterus will continue to contract so that it can return to its pre-pregnancy size. These postpartum contractions are important for stopping the blood flow from the site where the placenta was attached. If the placenta is pulled out before the blood vessels have time to begin to close off, or if your uterus is not sufficiently contracting, it can cause a loss of blood that may be dangerous.

This is where that oxytocin knowledge helps again. Oxytocin is what causes the uterus to contract again. Remember the third time that oxytocin is released in huge amounts? When a baby is nursing! When the baby begins to suck at the breast, the released oxytocin not only helps stimulate your body to produce colostrum and then milk from your breasts, but it stimulates the uterus to keep contracting. This is one of many reasons why it's important to keep you with your baby and help the baby to nurse right away. If your baby cannot nurse (or if a doctor is concerned about blood loss), you may be given Pitocin, the synthetic form of oxytocin, via an IV in order to mimic that natural response.

Your body will still bleed heavily for the next few days, gradually lightening over the course of a few weeks. Thinking of it as the menstrual periods that were missed over the last nine or ten months is a helpful way to understand it. The lining of the uterus is still shedding as it used to, but this time it has had nine months to build up. Small clots are normal, and the overall flow should resemble that of a period — heavy red the first few days and getting lighter and browner as the days and weeks pass. If you begin to go back to bleeding more heavily, it is usually because you are not getting the rest you need and are being too active. One doctor explained it like this: the site where the placenta was attached needs to close up and heal. It's like a scab, and if you are doing too much before it is completely healed, you risk opening that scab back up and bleeding again, which means you need to heal again.

Immediately after birth, you will still look about five to seven months pregnant. The after cramping that comes with the uterus getting back down to size intensifies with each baby, since the uterus has more work to do to get back to that size. In the day or two following a birth, your provider or nurse will be checking your uterus to make sure it is firm and contracting well. The checking can be very uncomfortable! However, it is important to make sure that your uterus is contracting. Within a few weeks your uterus should be back to pre-pregnancy size. A good provider will make sure that this is happening well, that bleeding is controlled, and that your body is healing properly. You will be checked a day or two after birth, possibly a week later, and then there is usually a six-week checkup to ensure that your body has done the major recovering and there are no serious issues. Within two to four days your breasts switch from producing the extremely important thick yellow colostrum for baby to filling up with normal breast milk.

By natural design, baby will usually want to nurse frequently during these first few weeks. You often can't do much else but lie or sit and nurse the baby. The frequent nursing helps to heal your uterus and forces you to lie down and rest so your body can recover. This is the time when mothers need a good support system in place to take care of the home and other children, provide meals, and offer emotional support. This help is vital to a mother's physical, mental, and emotional well-being. The task of growing and birthing a baby is monumental, and it would be wise for us to recognize that a mere few weeks is not enough to heal and feel back to normal. This time is a tremendous opportunity for family, friends, the Church, and neighbors to pay their respects and play a part in building a culture that honors motherhood and birth.

The Fertility Cycle Design

Another interesting part of the design of the woman's body is that typically there is a period of natural infertility after birth (called amenorrhea). Each woman is different in how long it will last, but breastfeeding releases hormones that tell your body to suppress ovulation. It is nature's way of spacing births so that mom and each baby get the time they need before another pregnancy. The more often you nurse and the more that baby relies on your breast, the more often those hormones are released that potentially delay the return of fertility. For some women, the return of regular cycles can take eighteen months; for some it is only a few weeks. Factors that may increase the length of this time include nursing exclusively and not supplementing with formula or food, sleeping near the baby, nursing the baby during the night, not timing feedings but feeding on the baby's cues, and soothing the baby with the breast rather than with pacifiers or distraction. The more often your breasts are releasing milk (and prolactin and oxytocin), the more your body will know that it's not yet time to return to normal fertility. However, each woman is different, and God's timing may be different, too. It is definitely possible to get pregnant before the period returns if ovulation occurs before that first cycle. So, a woman who is hoping to avoid pregnancy should be observing her body and noting any signs of fertility, even if her period hasn't returned.

Familiarity with some form of natural family planning (NFP), or at least an awareness of your body's personal fertility cues, can be helpful to know what is going on and if fertility is returning soon. An NFP instructor, through an official method such as Billings, Creighton, Sympto-Thermal, or Marquette, can be invaluable to a woman who is experiencing confusing signs (which is normal postpartum), especially if there is a need to delay another pregnancy.

....

That, in a nutshell, is how the female body and birth are designed to work. It is absolutely amazing to realize that we are still learning the many interconnected ways that the systems of our body and our baby's body interact for the great act of birth.

The design is remarkably complex and intricate, and unless there is reason to intervene, mothers and babies have the best outcomes when the natural design is respected. We know that we have an all-knowing God who has planned us from all eternity, and that he is a God who desires only our good. His design for our bodies is not haphazard. We can honor and respect that design, which functions very well, while still acknowledging that sometimes we must intervene for good reason. We can thank God and praise him for the amazing design of our bodies, and we can use our bodies to give glory back to him. Our bodies are a gift to us, beautifully and intricately designed at the service of life. We truly are wonderfully made.

It's so strange to me now that the only thing we learned in school about our fertility was how NOT to get pregnant. I don't necessarily think it's the school's job to teach that stuff, but the irony is not lost on me that we didn't learn how the female body actually works, just how to keep it from working. It wasn't until I was an adult that I even fully understood my cycle. Learning NFP was really empowering for me. It taught me that my body made sense! I think that helped as I prepared for birth. I still had a lot to learn, but underneath [there] was a new confidence that my body worked, and when it was time, it would know how to birth.

— Teresa A., mom to five on Earth and one in eternity

7

THE BIRTH OF A FATHER

"Husbands, love your wives, as Christ loved
the Church and gave himself up for her."
— *Ephesians 5:25*

The role of the father is integral to the formation of a family. The conception of the baby within the mother's womb is the result of the God-designed intimacy between husband and wife — the most intimate act we can engage in with another human being. The spouses' physical act of love and self-gift results in the creation of a new, eternal, microscopic person.

The father, from the very beginning, is intrinsically involved in his child's life. It may not be a conscious, personal relationship as of yet, but his participation is designed by God to be necessary for the child's very existence. As the baby grows, men often find themselves becoming more and more aware of the true reality of this new son or daughter. They can develop a relationship with and a love for this baby even in utero, and the baby can learn to recognize the father's voice. The more a mother is taken care of by the father, the more she can offer a healthy and love-filled environment for her child.

A mother experiencing high amounts of stress during pregnancy creates high cortisol levels that can potentially affect the baby. Often it is by helping his wife to get the rest, nutrition, and exercise she needs to have a healthy pregnancy and birth that a father can best love his child even before he or she is born. Giving his wife a safe environment of love and support, helping alleviate stress for her, in turn provides a safe environment of love and support for his baby.

As the pregnancy progresses, and the baby grows, the father's relationship with his child is also designed to grow. It is entirely appropriate and beautiful then, as the role of the father increases, that he be an active and important part of the birth itself. In fact, Saint John Paul II stated that fathers should be attentive and involved in their wives' pregnancies and births: "Even though we are speaking about a process in which the mother primarily affects the child, we should not overlook the unique influence that the unborn child has on its mother. In this mutual influence which will be revealed to the outside world following the birth of the child, the father does not have a direct part to play. *But he should be responsibly committed to providing attention and support throughout the pregnancy and, if possible, at the moment of birth.*"[63]

There is a beauty, difficult to describe, when the father is an active part of the birthing process. Just as the spouses gave themselves to each other in the bedroom some nine months previously, they can complete that process in the birth room, offering themselves to each other for the sake of their family. As the mother literally holds the fruit of their love in her arms for the first time, it is a profound witness to the plan of God for the two to become one flesh. This flesh is now so real that they behold it with their eyes, hold it in their arms, and give it a name.

Birth is an unparalleled opportunity for a husband to witness the true feminine genius of his wife. There is a profound grace present in sacramental marriage, one that is ripe for the taking at the time of birth. As a woman labors she and her husband can draw upon God's grace. This may be through prayer, service, physical support, or simply interior knowledge. It is wise for you and your husband to talk honestly and plainly beforehand about expectations for the birth. This may relieve pressure and fend off disappointment and dangerous resentment. While you cannot know exactly how things will play out, or the role you will need him to play during the birth, it is important for your marriage that you at least be on the same page going in.

My accidental discovery of my wife's feminine genius during birth was a transformative experience for my marriage. It made me have a greater appreciation for my wife's uniqueness as a woman and gave me permission to appreciate my own uniqueness as a man. Differences do exist. We're equal but different, and there's a beauty in that difference. The uniqueness makes each one even more special. There's a liberation in understanding that … together, they bring what their children need to the family.

— Greg W., dad to five

Every man is unique, and each will have a different temperament and relationship with his wife. This doesn't disappear in the birth room! The men who are more emotionally involved in normal life will be the ones more emotionally involved and offering support during birth. A husband who has difficulty expressing emotion or who doesn't understand well how to best support his wife in other aspects of life will have that same struggle in the birth room. This is one reason why a good birth class can be so helpful. It can give him not only an understanding of what the heck is happening to his wife during birth, but also the tools to help support her.

A confident father is priceless to a laboring wife. Knowing that he is offering himself in whatever way she needs during birth gives her the freedom to labor with greater confidence. When he believes in her, it's much easier for her to believe in herself. One of the tremendous roles a doula, nurse, or care provider can play in the birth room is offering *the husband* relief tools and confidence so he can pass these along to his wife. A provider (or nurse or doula) should never get in the way of the relationship between husband and wife.

Some ways that a father can be truly invaluable in the birth room are through physical support, such as back pressure, massage, head rubs, holding up his wife so she can relax or sway into a contraction, and more. He can be emotionally valuable by giving constant encouragement, letting her know how well she is doing, and exuding confidence in her abilities, from which she can then draw. It is important that he doesn't make her feel embarrassed or silly at a time when she is especially sensitive and vulnerable, and that he recognize her beauty and power during birth and help her to know that. A husband should know his wife better than anyone else in the birth room, and from that he often best knows how to encourage her. Some women need active cheerleading and physical comfort; some may not want to be spoken to or touched at all. A husband's emotional strength and stability provide a safe atmosphere for his wife to confidently labor and trust her body. Spiritual support from the father is also priceless, especially as the father is the spiritual head of the family. Having a father pray with his wife during the pregnancy, pray over her during birth, bless her with holy water, or speak words of Scripture over her has the ability to tap into that sacramental grace that is abundant and present for the taking.

Another way that fathers are necessary is by acting as a protector to their wives. The husband has the ability to protect his wife's space, advocate for her birth plan, talk to the nurses and staff when she cannot, and let her know that she is safe. A woman in labor should not be worried about arguing for her rights or preferences, and if a provider, staff, or family member is not respecting her, their baby, or the space, the husband's voice is especially helpful and powerful in protecting all of them before, during, and after birth, allowing her to focus on the work at hand.

It can often be a jarring experience for husbands during birth to see their wives in pain and vulnerable, knowing there is nothing they can do to "fix" it. While they can, of course, offer comfort, encouragement, back pressure, and hand-squeezing, the realization that this is not something they can take from their wives or do for them can be hard, if not frightening. It is difficult to watch someone we love fight a battle that we cannot take from them. However, it is a beautiful and awesome thing for him to surrender that desire and simply *be* with her in the experience. During birth, he can best show love by giving her the confidence that she can do it. Rather than attempt to fix it, he can choose to see her incredible strength. Rather than pushing choices on her that she may not truly want, he can honor and encourage her hopes for the birth, regardless of his preference.

I think I had the sense that my wife's labor was something I could actively manage or "coach" and that was what was expected of the dad in the labor room. Our next birth was at home, and labor was very, very long. I found myself uncertain about my role during all of it, and this led to tremendous anxiety in me, which I am sure was reflected back to my wife. Over the next seven home births, I learned that the best role I could play was just to be present for my wife in labor — praying, a little comforting here and there when it seemed right, but being careful not to overdo it, keeping the house clean, and being the "tub guy." For me, watching my wife in labor was still very stressful, and it always sounded good to me to be in the hospital. But our family has been so blessed by the opportunity to birth at home; I am so grateful that my wife sought this out. I would tell any dad going into this experience to not underestimate the power of just being present and calm for your wife as she labors.

— John H., dad to nine on Earth and one in eternity

Fathers have the opportunity to be Christ to their wives in the birth room. Rather than simply wanting to take away the pain, a husband can do something more profound and Christlike — he can enter into it with her, support her through it, and allow her to live out this piece of her story, just as Christ had to allow his mother to endure the suffering of his cross.

Birth often leaves husbands with a newfound respect for their wives as they witness in a raw and unforgettable way the power of the feminine genius. Perhaps that is part of God's plan, too. Birth is an opportunity not only for the woman to become more fully who she is called to be, but also for the man to become more fully who *he* is called to be.

He was an integral part of the delivery. He believed in me, was present with me emotionally, and gave me the space to freak out while he calmly massaged my temples or wrists. This guy knew nothing about birth — but now we joke that he should lead doula dad conferences. Having a role — and an important one at that — bridged the gap between feeling like labor was foreign and mysterious and for women only to feeling like it was something we as a couple were facing together.

— Nell O'Leary, mom to four

Husbands can actively live out their love for their wives and babies during the precious postpartum time. During the weeks after birth, dad should ensure that mom is resting, eating well, drinking enough water. He should be as helpful as possible, keeping up with chores and other children, and guarding her time of recovery from outside stress and unhelpful visitors. *He should consider it his sacred duty to protect her during this time.* He should always remember to keep the needs of his wife and new baby at the forefront of his obligations, giving them precedence over the desires of grandparents, unnecessary work obligations, or his own wants. Dads are incredibly important to the postpartum time, and the more support a man gives his wife during this time, the healthier she, their baby, and, ultimately, their entire family will be.

Birth is transformative not only for the woman, but also for the husband. A healthy, good, beautiful birth, especially one in which he was able to support his wife well, can give him confidence as he enters into the responsibilities fatherhood brings. And while it is important for the father to be at the service of his wife, recognizing her primary role in the experience, it's also important for him to understand, especially afterward, how the birth may have changed him, too.

Whether it is before, during, or after birth, the man has a tremendous and beautiful opportunity to fulfill his sacred obligation to serve his bride and love her the way Christ loved his Church, laying his very life down for her sake.[64] It is in this that he becomes the fullest version of himself, rising to the challenge of true manhood, giving his life in ways big and small for the sake of his beloved.

My husband was Christ to me in a very special way during the birth journey of our firstborn. He was that Christlike presence to me in a way we had both never experienced before. He pursued my best interest with courage. He made prayerful decisions that were hard to make at different times. He remained by me during my most difficult suffering, smiled with me during the exciting times, cried with me during the challenging and joyful times, and so much more. All these gifts that he imparted to me, his wife, then and every day since then in both big and small ways, are what kept me positive and steadfast during the weeks of recovery.

— Amanda Perales, mom to three

When the Father Is Not Present

A couple undergoing difficulties in marriage will not leave that behind in the birth room. If there is underlying tension or trouble in a marriage, it is best to do what is possible to address that before the birth. It may be that the birth is a chance for the couple to renew their commitment and a reminder of their vows and love. But if their relationship is greatly stressed or in turmoil, it is important for the mother to discern whether the father's presence will be a help or a strain in the birth room. As we've mentioned and will discuss further, a woman during labor needs to focus on being completely relaxed, vulnerable, and open. If there is an emotional stressor in the room, even if it is from the husband, while it's certainly not ideal, it may be better for him to be more distant from the birth.

Unfortunately, there are many other instances, too, where the father cannot or should not be present during the pregnancy or birth. This might be due to death, marital issues, or military deployment. There is also the reality of single mothers who do not have a husband or partner to support them through birth. Rather than pretending it doesn't matter, we respect her dignity as well as the dignity of the baby and the plan of God by acknowledging that this is a very real loss and allowing her to process it as such.

While it is truly valuable and desirable to have an involved and active father present for his wife and baby, the mother without one can take heart knowing that this deep lack can be offered up and united to the sufferings of Christ. It is highly encouraged that a doula or other solid support people be present with her for the actual birth. When the father cannot be involved or present for any reason, this is a chance for the Body of Christ to step in and offer support to the mother and baby however they need.

Immediately after birth, be quick to place the child in the father's arms — as the ancient Romans were wont to do — but with a spirit incomparably more elevated. For the Romans, it was the affirmation of the paternity and the authority which derived from it; here it is grateful homage to the Creator, the invocation of divine blessings, the promise to fulfill with devout affection the office which God has committed him. If the Lord praises and rewards the faithful servant for having yielded him five talents, what praise, what reward will he reserve for the father, who has guarded and raised for him a human life entrusted to him, greater than all the gold and silver of the world?

— Pope Pius XII, *Allocution to Midwives*

8

CHOOSING YOUR CARE PROVIDER

*"But the wisdom from above is first pure, then peaceable,
gentle, open to reason, full of mercy and good fruits, without
uncertainty or insincerity."*
— James 3:17

The choice of a care provider is one of the most important decisions you will make during pregnancy. Your choice of provider will affect where you will birth, how you will birth, the tests and interventions you are likely to receive, and your overall experience of pregnancy. It will also affect your treatment during birth, your feelings about that birth, and your confidence and trust in future births.

Two Different Philosophies of Birth

Providers typically subscribe to one of two distinct philosophies of birth.

The first philosophy views birth as a normal process for the female body, a process that, except in unusual circumstances, a woman is able to do quite well on her own. In this view, the design of the female body is seen as complete, meaning that most often a woman's body does not need outside help to give birth. After all, women have been giving birth for millennia, and the human race has multiplied quite well thus far. Providers with this philosophy only seek to intervene appropriately when an anomaly or complication presents itself. These providers see their role more as a "lifeguard," ready to intervene if necessary but trusting that the birth process is designed to work well. A well-trained provider using this method has witnessed birth many times, knows what is normal and what is not, and is skilled in knowing how to recognize anomalies and complications before they become dangerous. This philosophy has come to be referred to in the last several decades as the midwifery model of care.

The second philosophy is what some call the medical model of care. This approach views birth as urgent. It requires that a birth prove itself to be normal before assuming it is. In this view, birth is seen as risky, and interventions are taken whether the mother and child need them or not —

just in case. Providers with this view believe that because complications do sometimes arise, it is safest to treat every woman accordingly. There is a standard "type" of birth considered normal and ideal, and women must not fall outside that norm. A provider in the medical model of care is trained to intervene and follow the same protocol for every woman. Many have never witnessed a birth without any intervention or some sort of management. If we consider our first provider the lifeguard, this provider is more like a swim instructor, hyper-vigilant and hands-on, requiring every swimmer in the pool to wear a life jacket regardless of circumstances.

These different philosophies can lead to quite different birth experiences. It's important to know where a doctor or midwife falls on this spectrum and whether that provider's beliefs about birth line up with yours. If you have had health problems in the past, you may find yourself less confident in your body's ability to birth without outside help, so you may prefer the medical model. If you feel confident in your body and have a positive image of birth, or if you have developed a distrust of the medical system, you may find yourself more aligned with the midwifery model. Of course, if you know you have extenuating circumstances with your health, your history, or this specific pregnancy, that should impact your choice of provider.

On the whole, midwives tend to fall under the midwifery model of care (hence the name), and obstetricians fall under the medical model of care. However, there are certainly many individual exceptions to this, so it's important to get to know an individual provider and his or her beliefs rather than assume. Midwives working as part of a group practice are often beholden to an obstetrician, or were themselves trained under the medical model, or have to follow hospital protocol regardless of their own personal preferences. And there are certainly obstetricians and family doctors that lean more toward a midwifery model of care in their work.

Which Model Is Right?

God designed our bodies beautifully. His design for opening the female body and birthing a baby works, and it works well. We know that, biologically and from research, when we follow that design as best as possible, things are ideal for mother and baby. However, because of original sin, we live in a world that is not always ideal. Complications arise, sickness exists, and pregnancy and birth are not easy. What was designed perfectly is now subject to the effects of sin, and outside interventions may indeed be needed.

We can trust that God designed our bodies well and expect our births to follow suit, but we can also recognize that sometimes complications arise. Expecting that birth will be complication-free, allowing it to happen according to its design, and making choices toward that end makes sense, but so does having an experienced, watchful provider with us, should intervention truly be needed. We can certainly see God's hand in any necessary interventions to help a mother and baby stay healthy. We can even allow these unexpected difficulties and interventions to become redemptive, joining us with Christ and his work on the cross.

Making the Choice

You will need to decide for yourself what model resonates with you and your specific situation. Where would you feel more peaceful? Which philosophy most aligns itself with your experience, temperament, and faith? Which philosophy has better outcomes from a physical, emotional, mental, and spiritual standpoint? Are there health complications or anomalies with the current pregnancy that you need to consider? How does your history play into the decision? Are there women you know who have had great birth experiences? Whom do they use? There is no cut-and-dried answer. Every woman is unique, with a unique set of circumstances.

What we can say, though, is that you should choose the provider who best fits your beliefs, circumstances, and family. This means you should never be afraid to interview different providers, ask questions, and switch when necessary. If a provider is hesitant, dismissive, too busy, or doesn't even know the answers to your questions, that can be an answer right there. You deserve to have a provider who takes the time to answer questions and concerns, and who sees the value in a mother being informed and "picky" about her provider.

Choosing a provider is not the time to be soft and passive. Many women find themselves afraid to ask questions or express their preferences for fear of annoying their provider. Others may know in their heart they want to switch, but don't want to make waves or risk offending anyone. Many women may begin to see red flags as their pregnancy progresses, but think it is "too late" to switch, or they have idealistic hopes that, somehow, they will be the exception. It is important for your health and the health of your baby, as well as your growth in confidence as a mother, that you view yourself as the authority. You are the one making decisions, and it is important for you to find strength and confidence in that. Your provider is offering a service for you, not the other way around.

I'm thankful we sought out all the information we could. We felt confident in our relationship with our midwife and trusted her completely. We interviewed a number of midwives. The one we chose was upfront [in saying] that she prays for all of her clients and even included an outline of sorts of what we could pray for each week as the baby developed. I loved the extra care I received from the midwife, compared with the medical doctor I had with my first [child]. We talked about stress, diet, exercise, and other aspects of pregnancy. I wasn't a number; I was a pregnant mom in her care whom she knew and was praying for.

— Cherie L., mom to four on Earth, one in eternity

A good provider will offer choices rather than telling you what will be done to you. A good provider will have an open conversation about options and will want you to have a birth that respects your role as the mother of your baby. While they may have recommendations and protocol, they will make sure that you are informed and have as much a say as possible in everything that happens. They will make sure you know the benefits and risks of each choice, encourage you to do your own research, and respect your intelligence and free will to make your own choice.

When choosing a provider, it's critically important to note whether the provider is part of a group practice. If a provider is part of a group practice, it's very important to know if every member of the group views birth and practices the same way. As part of a group practice, the provider you've chosen may not actually be the one who attends your birth! Even within the same practice, different doctors or midwives may have different protocols and opinions. You may agree with your primary provider, but the person who shows up on call at your birth may view things differently.

You, mom, have the right and obligation to pick a provider who is truly going to serve you and your baby well, with dignified and evidence-based care, and who will be there when it is time to birth. This person will be with you during one of the most important, emotional, and vulnerable moments of your life. Birth is messy, naked, and requires a tremendous amount of trust and vulnerability between you and the people in the room. Choosing a provider with whom you can be all of these things is not only important for your emotional satisfaction and care, but, as we've seen, can also play a huge role in the actual birth itself. A provider who offers you an atmosphere of safety and comfort, without shame or embarrassment, is profoundly important.

Picking the top name on your insurance company's provider list is not the best way to find a provider. Nor is doing a Google search for providers in your area. One of the best ways to begin your search is by word of mouth. Find other women who have been happy not just with the providers' demeanor but with their own actual births, and ask them for advice. If you have friends who haven't been happy with their care, take note of who *not* to use. Ask local doulas for recommendations. If you are on Facebook, find a local moms' or birth group and inquire there (but be sure to state what kind of provider and birth you hope to have). When you make appointments to meet with a doctor or midwife, do so with the understanding, even if only in your head, that this is an interview and you are *not* committed to using him or her. Your first commitment is to your baby and your care, not to a receptionist or to a provider. Find your voice with the nurses and doctors and let them know you are trying to find the provider who fits you best. Do not be afraid to ask questions. Consider bringing a notebook with you to jot down responses.

Below is a list of questions that may help you decide if a provider is right for you, offering you insight into a provider's practices:

- Where do you attend births (what hospitals, birthing center, home)?
- How long do my prenatal appointments last? How long will I see you?
- Do you work with other providers? Who will be at my birth?
- How many/what percentage of your clients end up with a natural/medicated birth?
- Do you provide care for the baby after birth, or is that transferred to someone else?
- What is your cesarean rate?
- What birth classes do you recommend or provide?
- How do you feel about a doula attending the birth?
- What tests do you typically require during pregnancy?
- Do you routinely use IVs or pharmaceuticals in a normal labor?

- Do you perform episiotomies?
- What is your policy on artificial induction of labor?
- What are your recommendations for a healthy pregnancy?
- Will you respect my beliefs and refusal of artificial contraception?
- Do you perform, prescribe, or refer for abortions?

Here are a few things to ask yourself or reflect upon after meeting with a provider:

- How did I feel during the appointment? Rushed? At peace? Cared for? Important?
- Did the provider look me in the eye?
- Is it important to me that my provider is a male or female?
- How much time did I have with him or her?
- Did answers to my questions satisfy me?
- Did I feel comfortable expressing my opinion or asking questions? Did the provider ask me my opinion?
- How did her or she talk about the baby? Was my baby referred to at all? Would I feel comfortable with this person holding my baby?
- Does this provider make me second-guess myself or my ability to give birth?
- If this was a first visit, did the provider just assume his or her role, and respect that I hadn't decided on a provider yet?
- If he was there, did the provider respect my husband and include him in the discussion and appointment?

Pope Pius XII actually addressed the topic, and his words are equally applicable to any kind of birth provider: "Undoubtedly nature's voice speaks in [the mother] and places in her heart the desire, joy, courage, love and will to care for the child; but to overcome the suggestions of fearfulness in all its forms, that voice must be strengthened and take on, so to say, a supernatural accent. It is your duty to cause the young mother to enjoy, less by your words than by your whole manner of acting, the greatness, beauty and nobility of that life which begins, is formed and lives in her womb, that child which she bears in her arms and suckles at her breast; to make shine in her eyes and heart the great gift of God's love for her and her child."[65]

What a beautiful thought! Does the provider you are considering have this deferential and reverent attitude toward your motherhood? Does this person recognize the sacred privilege of being with you during this physical, emotional, spiritual journey into mothering this new child?

Once you have selected a provider, remember that you are not beholden to him or her to continue care. If that provider is not right for you, don't let the fear of offending or going through the process of finding a new provider scare you. It's better to be a bit uncomfortable now than to live with the regret of knowing you ignored warning signs that then played out in your birth. Find peace in knowing that there is the right provider out there for you and that finding him or her is invaluable. If you are having trouble finding a provider or making peace with the options available, consider praying to Saint Brigid, patroness of midwives; Saint Raymond Nonnatus, patron of midwives; or Saint Gianna Molla, patroness of physicians, to help you find the right person. Pray with your husband and include his input in your decision.

Whatever your decision on a provider, know that, no matter what, you are the mother God gave to this particular child. You are the one entrusted with making the decisions for your baby, and God will give you the grace needed to do so in your particular circumstances.

With my first pregnancy, I saw a family practitioner who also attended births. I didn't have a very good experience with her, and I felt she wasn't very knowledgeable, so I knew for the next I wanted an OB-GYN. Between my first and second pregnancies, I experienced five years of infertility. I saw two different gynecologists, trying to get answers and help, both of whom offered me the pill. Around this time I was talking with a woman at my parish whose daughter saw a Catholic OB-GYN who specialized in NFP, infertility, and did not give out birth control. I was intrigued. I found out that his office was about forty minutes from my house, but the drive was worth it. I showed him my fertility charts, and he gave me some excellent advice. Why hadn't anyone else offered this advice instead of simply pushing the pill?! It turns out, miraculously, I was actually already pregnant on my first visit with him (naturally after five years!), even though it was too early to tell at the visit. I was so glad that God had led me to him even though I was already pregnant. He even prayed during my birth along with a recording of the Rosary I had playing. He and his partner were absolutely amazing, kind, and smart throughout both that pregnancy and my following pregnancy.

— Amanda D., mom to four

Should I Choose a Catholic Provider?

Some women don't have the option of choosing a faithful Catholic midwife or obstetrician, but in some areas there are practices or individual providers who practice from a Catholic mindset. They don't prescribe artificial birth control or perform sterilizations, don't participate in immoral or unethical fertility practices, and will never refer for or be complicit in an abortion. Often they are versed in or at least respect natural family planning methods and will not pressure patients into limiting their family size. These providers are a great asset to the Church and the community.

However, simply because a provider identifies as Catholic is not enough for a woman to choose that person for prenatal and birth care. The provider should still practice evidence-based care when it comes to birth and respect the rights of the woman to make informed choices for her birth. Part of living the Catholic faith is acknowledging the dignity of the mother and her rights over her body and her God-given authority over her baby.

A Catholic provider, especially, should never coerce or manipulate a woman into birth choices based on his or her ease and schedule. He or she should always ask before intervening in any way and respect the natural design of God for labor and birth. He or she should always speak respectfully to patients and recognize the mystery and beauty of the act of birth, and reverence and respect the mother in her God-given role.

There is no requirement by the Church to choose a Catholic provider, and every woman needs to choose the provider who gives her and her baby the best, most dignified, evidence-based care for her unique situation.

When I finally understood the sacredness of this vocation and knew without a doubt the inherent dignity of motherhood, I was able to find the confidence to seek out providers that upheld my dignity and my baby's. They weren't always Catholic or in a hospital setting, but they were out there.

— Angie W., mom to four

9

CHOOSING WHERE TO BIRTH

"Be strong and of good courage; be not frightened, neither be dismayed; for the LORD your God is with you wherever you go."
— *Joshua 1:9*

Another important decision you will need to make about your birth is where you will have your baby. This will be limited to what is available in your area and, of course, is closely connected to your choice of provider. You may love your provider and want to birth at home but find that your provider only attend births at a hospital. Or you may really want to be at the hospital, but your provider only attends births at home. You may want the in-between option of a birthing center, but there are none in your area or your provider doesn't attend there. Or perhaps your choice is affected by an at-risk situation, atypical circumstance, history, or finances. For many women in many areas, the choices are limited. However, it's important for you to know all the options you do have so you can make the best decision for you.

Ideally, your chosen place of birth and provider will match up well. When that doesn't happen, you may need to decide which is a higher priority for you — birthing in the place you are most comfortable and feel most at peace, or birthing with the person with whom you are most comfortable and about whom you feel most peace. Some women know as soon as they have a positive pregnancy test the place or provider they want to use, and they work their other decisions around that first decision. Others may yet have to decide on both and find a combination of the two that makes the most sense given their unique circumstances.

Let's go over options currently available for most women.

Birth at Home

Birth at home used to be the norm for all women. Before the early twentieth century, a woman went into labor, the local midwife or doctor was called, and the mother gave birth in her home. It wasn't until the advent of hospitals and the urbanization of the industrial age about 100 years ago that women began to be expected to leave their home and go to a hospital to birth. For several decades birth at home in the United States became almost nonexistent, as the hospital model became the expected norm and government regulations and lobbying made it almost impossible for doctors and midwives to practice at home.

The last few decades, however, have seen a resurgence in women choosing to birth at home for a variety of reasons, the rate nearly doubling in the last decade. In 2014, 1.36 percent of women in the United States had an out-of-hospital birth, and in some states the rate was as high as 6 percent.[66] As the cesarean rates have risen and maternal and infant mortality rates in the United States remain among the highest in the industrialized world, many researchers, doctors, and women are wondering if a woman experiencing a normal pregnancy and labor is actually helped or hindered by being at the hospital. While moving to the hospital made birth safer in some ways, the management of all births as emergencies holds its own set of risks for a woman and baby.

In the United States, a home birth is typically attended by a certified professional midwife (CPM) or certified nurse midwife (CNM), though there are some medical doctors still who attend births at home.

At home a woman is freer to labor as she wants, not as directed by hospital protocol or expectations. She can move as she wants, eat when she wants, shower if she wants, and have whomever she wants present. There is no rush to the hospital, and the provider comes to her. At home she may feel more relaxed and comfortable, which has a profound effect on the body's ability to open and birth. Home-birth providers will be less inclined to recommend artificial induction and are more comfortable with letting the woman's body work the way it needs to. They typically are used to a woman choosing her own labor and pushing positions and work around her rather than expecting her to labor as they decide. They often are much more experienced in helping a baby come in the most natural way possible, with the least intervention possible, and birthing in water can be an option.

A good home-birth provider will have a well-equipped bag, complete with emergency supplies, such as oxygen and pharmaceuticals, and will go over with a woman the different complications that may arise and how they will be handled. She will ensure that there is a plan for unexpected complications or anomalies. A drawback to home birth, obviously, is the small chance of a true emergency situation, for which there is no immediate access to cesarean surgery or a NICU. Many home-birth advocates claim, though, that a good home-birth provider is well trained to avoid the situations and interventions that make emergency situations more likely, and believe that many emergency complications in the hospital are actually the result of a cascade of unnecessary interventions. It is important when choosing a home-birth provider to interview and choose someone who is well trained, experienced, and respected in the field.

Home-birth laws and accessibility to providers vary from state to state. Some women who would love to have a home birth find they cannot locate a provider in their area because of these laws, while other women may have several excellent options to interview and choose from. Because home birth is growing in popularity, more and more insurance plans cover a birth at home and sometimes are legally required to do so. A simple home birth is actually less expensive than a hospital birth since you are now only paying for the services of the provider, not the costs of overhead, staff, rooms, and assorted fees. However, depending upon the provider's requirements and the insurance coverage, what a couple ends up having to cover from their own wallet can vary.

Another benefit of home birth is that typically the provider you've interviewed is the provider who will be with you throughout your whole birth. This midwife (or doctor) has already spent hours with you at appointments and knows your history, your family, your personality, your fears, and your desires. A mom in labor can focus on the work of birth rather than filling out paperwork or introducing herself and her plans to staff and nurses while in labor. On the whole, it is a much more personal, intimate, and private experience than a woman will typically have at a hospital.

In choosing home birth, a mother often finds that she begins to take a greater role and responsibility in her own care and the care of her baby. There is something about opting to work outside the common system that forces a woman to "own" her birth a bit more. Decisions made are hers and cannot be placed upon the shoulders of someone else. That can be a beautiful yet sobering reminder of the importance of the role of motherhood.

With a home birth, the provider is licensed to care for the newborn as well. In a hospital setting, babies are usually under the care of the nursery staff as soon as they are born, not the woman's doctor or midwife. A home-birth provider will stay after the birth for several hours to make sure the mother and baby are doing well and typically visits the home the next day, and a few days after that. The mother and baby don't leave the house for care until the last appointment at around six weeks postpartum.

I switched to a home-birth midwife when I was thirty-five weeks along. I had an eye-opening experience working with a doula client at the hospital where I had been planning on birthing the baby. I trusted my current midwives thoroughly, but saw that certain things were out of their hands and that I was faced with a big choice: either be prepared to do battle the first twenty-four hours of my baby's life to get only the procedures that I wanted, or switch to a local home-birth midwife and take on the responsibility of having a birth without a NICU right down the hall. I had NEVER thought that I would have a home birth — I was a very happy hospital birther. I had already had two great births in the hospital and just had no reason to switch to home. That being said, I have always thought home birth was a safe and very reasonable option, and approved when others made that choice. I think my husband was a little shocked when I told him that I was now seriously thinking about a home birth, and we spent the next few days talking it over and meeting with the midwife who would be attending us. After the meeting, my husband and I walked away feeling very comfortable and confident that this would be a good option for us. A few days later we officially made the switch, and suddenly we were planning a home birth.
— Lauren G., mom to five on Earth and one in eternity, birth doula, and educator

Birth at a Hospital

Most women in the United States — currently more than 98 percent — birth in a hospital (though most statistics don't differentiate between hospitals and specified birth centers). For about the last century this has been the norm. If you are using hospital-based providers, they will typically have one hospital where they have privileges and where they attend births, although some have privileges at more than one and a mother can choose which hospital she would prefer.

At the hospital, you will typically not know the nurses and staff who will be caring for you during your stay. The provider stays in contact with the hospital staff regarding your progress in labor and will come in once you are close to pushing. Once the baby and placenta are born and you are assessed for bleeding and tears, the provider leaves, and you are now under the care of the maternity ward. In a hospital, you are subject to the protocols of the hospital. Since the staff attending you don't know your history, you often have to fill them in and complete paperwork while you are admitted.

The benefit of the hospital for some women is access to pharmaceutical pain relief, such as epidurals or narcotics. Some women feel safer with access to surgery down the hall should an emergency arise. For mothers with other little children, sometimes they feel a hospital gives them the benefit of a bit of respite before having to return to the demands of older siblings.

Hospitals will have their own protocols for birth, regardless of the personal situation of the mother in labor. Some consider this a benefit; others say it is a drawback. A hospital may, for example, require that all laboring mothers have an IV even if the woman's provider disagrees that one is necessary. The provider is bound to the rules of the hospital. A mother, of course, always has the right to refuse, but often this requires her to sign a statement that she is going against medical advice. Women are often told what will happen rather than asked their choice, and because they are in a vulnerable state while in labor, they may agree to procedures and interventions they may not have truly wanted simply because the staff insists. Hospitals are often subject to stricter government regulation, especially concerning newborn procedures.

Choosing a hospital birth does not mean you cannot have a natural birth. With a supportive birth team and proper preparation many women have simple and natural births in the hospital.

It is important, if you are deciding on a hospital birth, that you understand the choices you do have. You may want to hear the experiences of other women who have birthed at that particular hospital and take a tour of the hospital labor-and-delivery unit before making your decision. Hospital protocol and amenities available vary greatly. Much of a woman's experience is determined by the staff present, amenities available, the overall philosophy and protocol of the hospital, your provider, and how busy it is when you give birth. Some hospitals are well equipped with birth balls, tubs, showers, birth stools, nicer rooms, and other amenities to help you feel more comfortable and to aid in labor, while others may be starker and less equipped.

Another factor to consider is the hospital's overall cesarean and intervention rate. Annual cesarean rates as well as rates of epidural use, spontaneous versus induced labor, forceps use, vacuum extraction, episiotomies, and mortality can all be found online, usually through your state's health department website. You should take this information into serious consideration when making your decision, choosing the hospital and provider that offers the best chance in your particular circumstances for the best birth possible.

Obviously, if you know that you will require a cesarean birth, your choice is limited and you will need to be in a hospital. (We'll discuss cesarean birth more specifically in a later chapter.) If you have a high-risk pregnancy or a known health issue for your baby, you will also need to be in a hospital to provide you and your baby with the extra care you will need.

> For me, a hospital birth has always been the right choice. It is where I feel most comfortable, and I know that during labor and delivery I need to be confident in my birth team and surroundings. I am very blessed with being friendly with the OBs and midwife in the practice at the hospital. They work hard to create an affirming birth atmosphere for women and babies, and I trust them. I have toyed with the idea of home birth, admiring the natural, calming aspects, but I always end up with lingering doubts, and it just doesn't feel "right" for me. So, while the hospital may not be the "perfect" choice in some aspects, I feel confident that it is the best choice for me, in my situation, and in my opinion that is what matters.
> — Shannon Lawson, mom to five on Earth and two in eternity

Birth at a Birth Center

Some women have access to a middle ground between home and hospital in the form of a birth center. A birth center is typically a more homelike environment that allows for more freedom of labor and more comfort measures than a typical hospital. Most birth centers provide tubs for water labor or birth, for example. They don't restrict food or beverages, have larger and more homelike rooms, and have staff better trained in natural management of labor and birth. Unlike a hospital, they specifically exist for and specialize in birth. They are usually attached or are close to a hospital should an emergency arise that needs more intervention. Often, birth centers are staffed by midwives, but some may have an obstetrician also present or on call.

A birth center is a good option if your pregnancy has not entailed complications and you desire a more naturally minded birth but are uncomfortable with the idea of birthing at home. If delivery goes well, you usually have the option to be discharged earlier than you might at a standard hospital. Similar to a hospital, you may tour the birth center beforehand to see if it is a place you feel comfortable and to ask questions about protocols and options for your birth.

Remembering my feelings upon entering the hospital the last time, along with some other unappreciated downsides of a hospital birth, we decided to have this baby in a birth center. I was glad that I wouldn't have to be in a hospital and ward off any unwanted interventions, but I didn't think my experience would be all that different.

However, the differences became clear even early in my pregnancy. While I had liked my midwives from my second pregnancy, the midwife I saw at the birth center was different. She would spend an hour talking to me about my questions. She asked me questions about my family. When I complained of one of those pesky pregnancy symptoms, she offered solutions that might help me be more comfortable instead of saying, "Yeah, that'll happen in pregnancy sometimes." And when I had false labor two weeks before my due date and panicked a little bit at 5:00 a.m. on a Saturday, she answered her cellphone and even had the grace to act as if it didn't bother her. She and the other midwives showed a level of care for me that was humbling. To put it simply, I felt God in them. I saw his care for me in how they cared for me. And in the moments before our second daughter was born, in between contractions, I remember looking up at the circle of women sitting quietly out of the way, but surrounding me, and thought once again that I could feel God's love through the presence of these women who truly cared for me. A few minutes later, our daughter was born, and despite the physical intensity of labor and delivering a baby, I've never felt so peaceful.

— Christina Kolb, mom to three

Making the Decision

All three of these options — home, hospital, or birth center — are valid choices, depending on your personal circumstances. There is, of course, no one right answer that applies to all women. When deciding where to birth, take into account the type of birth you hope to have, the normalcy and health of your pregnancy, where you feel safest and most comfortable, any personal birth history, the options and providers available, and whether the protocol and practices of the place and provider match well with your beliefs and circumstances. Over all of this, you and your husband can pray and make the decision that is best for you.

10

YOUR BIRTH TEAM

*"So if there is any encouragement in Christ, any incentive
of love, any participation in the Spirit, any affection and sympathy,
complete my joy by being of the same mind, having the same love,
being in full accord and of one mind."*
— *Philippians 2:1–2*

It's incredibly important to have people you trust and who understand and support your birth plan. Your "birth team" should include those who can support your vision for birth and who will provide a helpful environment in all aspects.

Your Care Provider

Hopefully, as we've discussed, you've selected a care provider you trust, one who will not challenge your decisions and will provide an atmosphere of support, respect, and confidence as you labor. It is important that you review your desires for birth with your provider before the time comes. Make sure you are on the same page and all decisions have been communicated to other members of your provider's practice and "approved."

If you are birthing vaginally in a hospital, your care provider will typically only be present toward the end of your labor, as you near the second stage (pushing). For a planned surgical birth, your obstetrician will be in the surgical room the entire surgery. A provider at home will typically be present for a longer time. No matter where or how you are birthing, choose a provider who creates a sense of confidence, calm, and peace, not one who will make you more anxious or undermine your decisions or determination. Choose someone who sees you, the mother, as the decision maker and will do everything he or she can to show respect for you and help you have an informed, happy, healthy, and grace-filled birth.

My midwife was centering and grounding. She helped
me regain control of my breathing and get into various

positions to provide relief. She was encouraging at the right times and urged me to try something different with confidence, but not in the false cheerleader way that makes me want to gouge out my eyeballs. She had been there, and she was in the pain with me. Only she spoke, while the other nurses whispered quietly but mostly remained silent, monitoring the baby's heartbeat in a way that I hardly noticed. There was a unanimous presence there of reverence toward the laboring mother and the process of birth that I now remember with absolute awe and appreciation. I've never experienced anything like it.

— Carolyn Svellinger, mom to five

Your Husband

Much of the husband's role was discussed in Chapter 7, but gone are the days when he would be forced outside the maternity ward to pace as he awaited news of the birth. Thankfully so! Husbands are now welcome as a part of the birth in most places. As the co-creator of this child and the one who shares the most intimate bond with the mother, his presence is important. While there are some husbands who don't want to be in the birth room, more and more fathers desire to be there with their wives. The time of labor and birth can be incredibly powerful and build an entirely new level of intimacy between a husband and wife.

A father should be involved in birth classes and, to the extent he is able, attend appointments and prenatal meetings with his wife. The more he is involved and active during the pregnancy, the more he will feel comfortable during the birth and care of the baby afterward. Ideally, he will be involved in learning about the different choices available and helping his wife discern a birth plan and make informed decisions. In the birth room itself, as discussed already, a father's strength is important. He will need to be confident and able to advocate for his wife and baby, to show strength and confidence that his wife can draw upon. He can remind her why they chose to do things a certain way and, since he knows her better than any other person in the room, can speak to her heart in a way no one else can. He can work side by side with the doula as they both learn what is most helpful for this particular birth.

It is helpful for a woman to talk with her husband about what she expects from him during labor and birth. While things may change, it is helpful for a man to have some guidance on how he can best support his wife during this work. Perhaps she knows that what she needs most from him is constant encouragement. Or she may know beforehand that she wants him taking care of everything "behind the scenes" so that she doesn't have to focus on anything but labor. Some women choose to make a list of ideas for their husband to have on hand during labor and birth that they would like him to be in charge of. However the role is manifested, his support and presence is an integral and powerful part of a woman's birth team.

Going through labor and delivery with your spouse is like going on a supercharged, intense marriage retreat. It is raw and emotional and unforgettable. Everything between you is tested: communication, endurance, vulnerability, compassion, trust. And, when your husband is as dedicated and present as mine is, the bond of marriage is strengthened and renewed. After all, you are working together toward the beautiful goal of welcoming your child into the world.

In truth, there is no way I could make it through labor without my husband. He prays through every contraction with me, helps me with back labor, and motivates me to keep going.

— Nancy Bandzuch, mom to four

Your Doula

A doula (from the Greek word meaning "female servant") is a trained woman who works independently of your provider and the hospital to provide informational, emotional, physical, and possibly spiritual support before and during your birth. Because she works only for you, you get to interview and hire her before the birth. In labor and birth, she is trained to support and serve you as you bring your baby into the world. It was common in ancient days to have female servants and attendants to help the mother during birth. In fact, many ancient icons depicting the Nativity of Jesus include a servant girl or midwife! We can also consider whether Mary herself served as a doula for her pregnant cousin Elizabeth. Certainly, it makes sense that this trip of service to help her cousin included her help when it came time for the actual birth.

More and more women are realizing the worth of reclaiming that feminine help and having a doula working specifically and only for them during their birth. The doula will help prepare you for your birth and develop your birth plan, be there during active labor and throughout the entire birth until an hour or two after, and then usually meet with you postpartum to process the birth and see how you and baby are doing.

Studies have consistently shown that the presence of a doula makes a real and important difference in birth. The presence of a professional doula lowers the rates of cesarean section, induction, pain medication, labor time, birth complications, vacuum or forceps delivery, and NICU use. Women who use a doula report a higher satisfaction with their birth experience than those who do not.[67] The American College of Obstetricians and Gynecologists even states, "Published data indicate that one of the most effective tools to improve labor and delivery outcomes is the continuous presence of support personnel, such as a doula."[68]

A doula can be a vital part of your birth team, providing the support and confidence you need to have a good and happy birth. Her role in the birth room is not to speak for you or make decisions on your behalf. She is not a medical professional and is not able to give medical advice or perform medical exams or procedures. Her presence in the birth room should be one of support and calm, helping you find your own voice and strength in the birth room to reach the goals for your birth that you discussed beforehand. The role of a doula may be so beneficial to mother and baby that some providers now require that their clients have one for their birth.

A professional doula should be trained in and knowledgeable about normal birth. She should have a variety of ways to help manage pain, provide emotional support, and strategies to help you through labor. Most doulas are familiar with non-pharmaceutical management of pain. A good doula will be able to make suggestions to help the labor progress and provide helpful information on interventions so you can make informed decisions.

Contrary to popular belief, doulas are not merely for women planning a natural vaginal birth. Even if you are planning on using an epidural or have a planned cesarean, you can still benefit from having a doula, who can help you talk decisions through before the birth and help you know when you are truly in active labor and should get to the hospital. She can provide help with non-pharmaceutical pain relief for as long as needed to postpone an epidural until labor is well established and the epidural is less likely to slow things down. After an epidural, a doula can help with turning you from side to side to help the baby descend and can attend to any needs that you may have — ice chips, music, prayer, cool washcloths, back rubs, head rubs, verbal encouragement, and more. For a cesarean birth, a doula can be a source of information and help relieve nerves, serving as a source of calm during the surgery. A doula can give you information about the baby if you are not able to hold him or her right away, and she can be a tremendous help in the hours after the surgery, holding the baby, helping you nurse, and making you as comfortable as possible. If you have a cesarean and would like a doula to be with you throughout the birth, make sure this is approved by the obstetrician and allowed by the hospital.

There is a beautiful, natural sisterhood that is being reclaimed with the rise of doulas in the birth room. Throughout history, the women of a community would come to the aid of the mother, surrounding her and supporting her during birth. In fact, for most of history and in most cultures men were never a part of the process. In that sisterhood was a collective wisdom that could guide the process and give the mother strength and encouragement during her trial. This surely can be considered part of what the Church has called the "genius of women." While having the father active and present in the birth room is important and strongly encouraged, there is something that women can provide that a man simply cannot, especially women who have gone through the work of birth themselves.

As Christian women, we shouldn't be afraid to embrace the unique presence and genius we bring to the birth room. Women can see deeper, connecting and relating in a way that allows us to see to the heart, and bringing a uniquely personal perspective to a birth, one that sees the individual mother and baby and advocates for their care. A woman is better able to see birth not just as a physical process but as a spiritual one. As Saint John Paul expressed it:

> Perhaps more than men, women *acknowledge the person,* because they see persons with their hearts. They see them independently of various ideological or political systems. They see others in their greatness and limitations; they try to go out to them and *help them.* In this way the basic plan of the Creator takes flesh in the history of humanity and there is constantly revealed, in the variety of vocations, that *beauty* — not merely

physical, but above all spiritual — which God bestowed from the very beginning on all, and in a particular way on women.[69]

Finding a good doula requires that you ask around for recommendations and then meet for interviews. Your provider or friends may be able to give you recommendations, and if you take a birth class, the instructor will likely know a few to call on. Internet searches and local social media groups can also help you gather some names and set up interviews. It is important to be aware that a "full spectrum" doula refers to a doula who will also support and assist a woman during an abortion. As a woman and as a Christian, you have the right to understand that and choose only a woman who fully supports not only your dignity, but the dignity and right to life of your baby. A doula should see her mission not only as helping mothers, but babies as well.

Most doulas expect an initial, obligation-free interview with a prospective client. There, you can ask any questions, find out the specifics of what she provides for her fee, and get a feel for her personality and style to see if she would make a good fit for your birth team.

What should you ask a potential doula? Here are a few suggestions:

- What made you become a doula?
- How much experience do you have?
- Are you certified through an organization?
- What is your fee, and what does that cover?
- How many births do you take on at one time?
- What are your beliefs on abortion?
- What are your experiences with water birth/VBAC/hospital birth/ etc.?
- Do you work or have you worked with my provider?
- What will you do during the labor and birth? What kind of support do you provide?
- Do you have experience with breastfeeding support?
- Have you given birth yourself?
- When will you come for the birth? How long will you stay after?
- Do you have a backup in an emergency?

The answers to all of these questions should be taken into account. However, probably the most important factor is simply how well you "clicked" with her. After you meet with a potential doula, ask yourself:

- Can you picture this woman at your birth?
- Did you feel at ease with her?
- Do you hold similar beliefs about birth and the dignity of life, and maybe even faith?

A doula can be one of the greatest assets in your birth team and overall birth experience. Don't be afraid to look for someone who fits you well and who can provide the support you need during whatever kind of birth you are planning.

I will never give birth without a doula again. I skipped it the first go-around and then came to my senses with the second. I had an extremely fast birth, so she was only with us forty-five minutes before my daughter came into the big world, but she was amazing. She was calm and focused but accomplished so much. She talked me down in the peak moments, she got a cold washcloth, got a birthing ball all set up, encouraged me, called the nurses, and helped me breathe when I was supposed to not push (yeah, right). Post birth she helped me set up a great nursing relationship, brought me an apple juice slushie and a warmed blanket, and took pictures for us. She did this all while letting me do my thing with my husband, never intrusive, only an extra bonus. I am so thankful to her. I can never thank her enough. My husband didn't really get why we needed one but opted for the "Whatever you say, dear" choice, and even he is so glad we hired a doula.

Madeline D., mom to two

Other Staff

If you are birthing in a hospital, there will be several other nurses, aides, and possibly resident doctors who will be present intermittently during your birth. In fact, the nurse assigned to you and on shift will most likely be there much longer than your doctor or midwife. The nurse has a great amount of control in the birthing room and has the ability to provide a supportive, positive atmosphere, respecting your birth plan and helping you have the birth you want. There are many wonderful nurses who have a heart of service for the mother in front of them, taking care of her and making sure she is respected and her wishes honored.

The nurse also, however, has the ability to do the opposite. Many women remember forever the nurse who was assigned to them and how she supported them (or didn't). If the nurse assigned to you is not helpful or is even disrespectful or dismissive of you and your birth plan, or is actively undermining your goals, you always have the right to request a different nurse or staff member to attend to you. (If this is necessary, this is a great job for husbands. Simply go up to the nursing station and request a new nurse.) A doula also often has insights into the hospital staff that may be helpful. She may be able to help you request a certain nurse who will be more suitable for your plan.

You also have the right to limit the amount of student doctors in the room. Hospitals that train doctors will often invite them to observe during births. If this is not something you want, you will have to tell them. You can note that in your birth plan or simply make your wishes known when you are there.

If you are birthing at home, often a midwife will have an assistant who may attend births with her. Usually, you will get the chance to meet this assistant beforehand, but not always. If it is important for you to know every person in the room, you can make that request known to your midwife to make sure you get the opportunity to meet before the birth.

Friend, Sister, or Mom

Many women invite a close friend, a sister, or their mother to be with them in the birth room. This can be a beautiful and powerful moment in a relationship and a wonderful witness of women helping and supporting one another in family and community. It is important, however, that you choose these people prayerfully and carefully. Do not ask someone to be there simply because she wants to, or out of guilt. In everyday life, a person's presence can bring a certain tone or "vibe." That power is even more intense in the birth room. You only want people who will be fully supportive of your birth plan and with whom you feel no pressure or embarrassment. Remember, you will need to be vulnerable and emotionally and physically naked around them. Choose only those with whom you feel completely comfortable and who do not bring an atmosphere of nervousness or self-absorption. The people you ask to be at your birth should bring a spirit of service and complete support.

The relationship between mothers and daughters can sometimes be tricky. Many women are blessed with a completely intimate and supportive relationship with their mothers that brings a beautiful addition to the birth room. The birth becomes a powerful moment in their relationship and draws them closer. However, many women do not have this type of relationship with their mothers, and the different dynamics and tensions of that important relationship can cause issues in the birth room. Many mothers have a difficult time seeing *their* baby in pain or struggling. They subtly or blatantly undermine her work of labor and confidence that she can do this. Some mothers are quick to encourage (subtly or not) submission to anything suggested by the hospital staff or provider, even if there are other valid and more evidence-based options. This could be a generational difference, or perhaps it is the vulnerability they feel as their daughter goes through labor. Either way, you should not feel pressured to abandon your previous decisions in favor of immediate relief of someone else's discomfort.

The decision to have other friends or family at your birth should be made carefully and with prayer. If you do decide to invite certain people, it is important to establish with them beforehand your expectations and needs during the birth. Share your plan and how they can help you achieve that, possibly giving them concrete tasks to help with or things to keep in mind. A few examples would be to refrain from talking during a contraction, leave the room if you need to make a phone call, be in charge of taking pictures, etc. Also, remember that you always have the right to switch things up if you need to, even during the birth.

Having (Other) Children at Your Birth

If you are birthing at a hospital, having older children present is often not the norm, though sometimes possible. At home and at some birth centers, however, older children may be welcome. This can be a beautiful witness of life and love, but it is obviously the decision of the mother in labor whether it will be helpful to have them present. It can be especially powerful for young girls to see birth and normalize it for their own possible vocation. Some parents worry that viewing the birth and their mother in pain may be traumatic to their children, but usually that worry is unfounded. The attitude you have about birth will most likely be the attitude your children pick up. But, of course, parents know their children best, and certain children may be better suited to attend than others. Toddlers, of course, are especially difficult since they have higher needs of their own and can't understand why Mom can't tend to them. If a mother will be distracted or annoyed by the presence of other kids, that should take precedence. Her main focus must be on giving birth. Ultimately, there is no "right" answer for this. Every family situation and dynamic is different.

If you do decide that your older children will be welcome, it is definitely recommended to prepare them for what it will be like and what you expect from them — for example, "I will be working very hard, and I may need you to be very quiet while I work." Especially for younger children, telling them you may be noisy and making sounds or seem very different can help assuage confusion or fears. It is important for kids to know that even if you look as if you are in a lot of pain, everything is okay. Some parents prepare their children with videos or books. It is a good idea to have extra help on hand for younger children, to occupy them in another room if needed.

My first birth experience was when I was thirteen years old. My mom gave birth to my brother at home, and I was able to attend. My mom also had my sister at home when I was fifteen. Those births affected me very deeply. Yes, I saw my mom in pain. But there my mom was, all normal and yet powerful, giving birth on a bed surrounded by her family. I was sold.

— Micaela Darr, mom to seven on Earth
and two in eternity, birth educator

Your Spiritual Support Team

Many women avail themselves of a spiritual support team in the form of a prayer chain or perhaps a few close friends who can pray them through labor and birth, even if they are not right in the room. This can include those we know in heaven, our patron saints, and our friends or relatives here on Earth. There is power in the Body of Christ and in people united in prayer. Some women don't want anyone to know they are in labor or having the baby until after the birth, while others aren't shy about the whole world knowing and asking for prayers.

The prayers of close friends can be a powerful source of strength and grace during the toughest moments of birth. Those friends can know the ways that you need prayer most and unite with you in this work of birth. They can know any specific concerns or intentions for the birth you might have and pray for them with you. However they choose to do it — perhaps a visit to the Adoration chapel, praying the Rosary, fasting, or lighting a vigil candle — their prayers can be a powerful support for a peaceful, happy, and healthy birth. Of course, they should be people who can be trusted to keep everything private until you are comfortable with them sharing any news with anyone else.

With my second birth, we got to the point of considering a transfer to the hospital, so we started a prayer chain. Things got moving again shortly after that, and he was born fifteen minutes into the hour of mercy, at 3:15 [p.m.]. Our friends were all praying the Divine Mercy chaplet. It helped me realize that I'm not in this alone. My friends' prayers helped me through the time when I thought I had nothing left in me, but leaning on Christ, my husband and I found a strength we didn't know we had. It was a truly grace-filled experience.

— Cherie L., mom to four on Earth, one in eternity

Whom Don't You Want

We have already touched on this a bit, but it is important to know the people you do not want at your birth. You do not want anyone in the room who will abuse you, disrespect you, or try to manipulate you. You do not want anyone who does not share the belief that your baby is a complete person with worth, dignity, and feelings. You do not want anyone who disagrees with your birth plan, undermines your confidence, or makes you feel nervous or agitated. Your work during birth is to have a baby, and that will take your entire mental, emotional, and physical focus. You should not have people around you during birth who will use up that energy on their own feelings or insecurities. You do not want anyone in the room who will pressure you with their schedule. The needs of you and your baby are the priority during birth. Birth is one of the most intimate acts of a woman's life, so choose people you will not be embarrassed to be naked in front of, and who will not be scandalized by seeing you naked.

Choose people who can support you and with whom you feel completely safe and vulnerable — physically, mentally, emotionally. Remember that oxytocin is released when we feel safe, loved, and taken care of. Therefore, the safer and more supported a woman feels during birth, the more she is able to allow her body to do the work it needs to do. Choose people who will help in that goal.

11

PREPARING ALL OF YOU FOR YOUR BIRTH

"Commit your work to the Lord, and your plans will be established."
— *Proverbs 16:3*

Motherhood will truly take all of who you are. When it comes to such a major work as birth, it is wise to prepare intentionally for that work of love in all aspects of who you are — your body, your soul, your heart and mind.

Our babies are directly affected by our choices before birth, and we are intimately united with them from the moment of conception. In fact, Saint John Paul II said: "The first months of the child's presence in the mother's womb bring about a particular bond which already possesses an educational significance of its own. The mother, even before giving birth, does not only give shape to the child's body, but also, in an indirect way, to the child's whole personality."[70]

No pressure, right?

We cannot, and should not, take responsibility for every single aspect of our child's healthy development, of course. There are many things beyond our control and outside of our responsibility. As we discussed before, our bodies are really good at creating these little people without our conscious help. But science continually shows ways that the baby's personality, physical health, and mental health develop within the womb, and much of that can be influenced by the mother. The time we have with the baby within us is precious (even if it doesn't always feel that way!). There is a deep and intimate bond that develops, and this time with them is important as we prepare to meet them face to face and to take on the work of mothering this specific and unique child.

Sometimes the months of pregnancy feel like an eternity. Pregnancy can be incredibly difficult. But it always ends, and the time of pregnancy, as long as the days and months sometimes feel, is finite. It can be a beautiful opportunity to grow in relationship with God, Mary, yourself, your child, and even the world around you.

Over and over we see that the couples who intentionally take the time and energy to prepare well go on to have a more confident, positive experience of their birth. They can make better decisions, understand what is going on, enter into the experience together, and walk away from birth not only with a healthier mom and baby but a closer relationship. There are no guarantees, of course, but it only makes sense to prepare together for such an amazing and important time in a family's life.

— Lauren G., mom to five on Earth and one in eternity, birth doula, and educator

The Power of a (Good) Birth Class

One of the best ways to prepare for birth in a holistic way is through a birth class. A good birth class is one that will give you the information you need to make the many choices before and during birth, and will provide solid, evidence-based practice and facts to help you integrate those into your birth plan. A good birth class will also help you understand the physiology of pregnancy and birth, will teach you methods of pain management, and will help you understand and navigate the local birth scene so you know which options may be best for you. A good in-person instructor can address specific questions, be a sounding board for your decisions, and help you practice good positions for labor and birth or show you firsthand how to determine your baby's position.

A *great* birth class will also go into nutrition and exercise during pregnancy, as well as breastfeeding and postpartum care, though some instructors split those topics up into different classes. Even if you know your situation will necessitate a cesarean birth, a class can be helpful in knowing what to expect, the choices you do have, and how to best manage the birth. While books and online classes are helpful (there are some great resources for you in Appendix D), there is nothing that can take the place of an experienced, positive, and engaging in-person instructor. A great birth class will also help you prepare emotionally and mentally for birth. Some women may have the option of a faith-based class that will include spiritual preparation.

Most birth classes are a series of classes, usually taking place during the late second trimester and third trimester of the pregnancy. There are several specific methodologies that offer classes, such as the Bradley Method, Hypnobirthing, or Lamaze. The teachers in these classes are often certified specifically to teach the that method of birth within a prescribed and exact curriculum. Other teachers draw up their own syllabus and offer independent classes outside of an established methodology. To find a good birth class, it is helpful to obtain recommendations through friends or midwives, social media, or by asking around the community. If you have hired a doula, she will likely be able to point you in the right direction. Some women, of course, may be limited by what is available and offered in their area.

On the whole, classes offered by hospitals are often not comprehensive and are not sufficient for a well-prepared and informed birth. Often (though there may be exceptions), hospital birth classes are merely one or two sessions that will take you through the hospital protocol and are more an informational talk on what will happen to you during your birth, perhaps including a tour of the rooms and explanations of procedures. They tend to be limited in scope and are not aimed at helping a woman truly understand birth and know the benefits and risks of certain decisions or offering specific methods and tools to handle the work of labor. These classes may be helpful if you are planning to birth in the hospital and would like a tour of the room, but for the most part they are limited in scope.

Simply taking a good birth class is not enough, of course. It's also important to integrate and apply it. It is good to take notes, have some detailed discussions about what was learned in class, and work together on practicing positions or physical or mental exercises that were recommended. I highly recommend that parents go through all the information together. If a suggestion or method doesn't click with you, that's okay. Be open to the wisdom, experience, and suggestions of the instructor, but know that your birth is *your* birth. You know best the type of support and encouragement you may need. Be willing to integrate the information you've received from books, classes, and friends into a plan and method that works for your particular personality and family.

For our first birth, we attended a birthing class and read lots, [which] helped us be as emotionally prepared as we could be. In the earlier subsequent births, I found it useful to get out the books or reread them, reminding myself of the steps of labor, mentally getting into the right head-space. I would encourage first-time moms to educate themselves! Knowledge is power, and it brings confidence. Believe in your bodies — they are created by an awesome God — and remember that giving birth, bringing a new child into the world, whether naturally or with assistance, is the most powerful action you will undertake. Giving birth, however it comes about, is the beginning of your child's story, and it's incredibly precious. It's worth preparing for.

— Erin H., mom to ten on Earth and one in eternity

I. Body — Physical Preparation for Your Birth

"Do you not know that your body is a temple of the Holy Spirit within you, which you have from God? You are not your own; you were bought with a price. So glorify God in your body."
— 1 Corinthians 6:19–20

We want to prepare our bodies well for birth. As Catholics, we recognize that our body is a gift and needs to be cared for and treated with dignity. Not only that, but the child within, as a person created in the image and likeness of the Creator, deserves to have his or her mother do the best she can in providing a healthy and safe living space. So, we need to take the reasonable steps — from the experience of others, research, and our faith — to care for ourselves and our baby. Pregnancy gives us a profound opportunity to practice a true gift of self.

Thankfully, God designed our bodies to be strong — strong enough to overcome sometimes less-than-healthy choices or decisions, which can be influenced by the situation we are in or the type of information we have — and even though it can be incredibly difficult, we need to do what we are reasonably able to take care of ourselves and our babies during pregnancy. Physiologically we know that the better a mother cares for her body during pregnancy, the better able she will be to have a healthy birth, healthy baby, and smooth recovery. The effort, time, and sacrifice needed to do this are also great training and preparation for the demands of motherhood, a gentle prodding to self-gift that will be needed even more when the newborn arrives.

There are many ways a woman can physically care for herself and her developing baby during pregnancy. Again, none of this is meant to be a substitute for direct care from an experienced provider. Nor should it be seen as a substitute for sound medical advice for your specific situation.

Diet

By far the most controllable factor in a healthy pregnancy is diet. While recommendations constantly change in small ways, it remains consistent that your diet should be filled with whole foods, high in protein and high in plants. It should be varied and rich in vitamins and minerals, especially iron, calcium, magnesium, B vitamins, and vitamins C and D. Eating food that is as close as possible to the way God created it provides your body and your baby with the nutrients and building blocks needed for proper growth and development. This means, as far as possible, cut out the junk. A diet high in empty carbohydrates, refined sugars, and unpronounceable preservatives increases your risk for gestational diabetes, obesity, and increases nausea and exhaustion. Filling your body consistently with these types of foods replaces healthier options, depletes the body of necessary nutrients, and leads to exhaustion, lightheadedness, anemia, swelling, and other symptoms. Of course, many of these things can happen even with the best of diets; we don't need to fall into dietary scrupulosity, but a poor diet exacerbates many of these ailments and can lead to interventions and complications that may have been preventable.

The following guidelines are the common general recommendations for pregnant women:

Protein: Aim to get 75 to 100 grams of protein a day. Protein is the building block of our bodies, so it makes sense that a woman growing an entirely new person needs lots of it! Great sources of protein are free-range eggs, meat, fish, nuts, dairy, Greek yogurt, and some whole grains.

Healthy fats: Healthy fats such as olive oil, coconut oil, avocados, and eggs are important. Fat is necessary to store nutrients and will help with milk production. Omega-3s are necessary for brain, nerve, and heart development and function. Stay away from hydrogenated (trans) fats.

Fiber: Healthy fiber is important for digestive health and the elimination of toxins from your body. The muscle-relaxing effect of progesterone and relaxin (the hormones of pregnancy), as well as the growing uterus can slow down intestinal movement, leading to uncomfortable constipation. Getting enough fiber can help prevent this. It also helps control blood pressure and to prevent preeclampsia. You should get 25 to 30 grams of fiber per day while pregnant. Beans, seeds, whole grains, vegetables, and fruits are all sources of good fiber.

Calcium: Calcium is essential for building the bones of your baby as well as keeping your bones strong and healthy. Pregnancy and breastfeeding can deplete the calcium in your bones, leading to osteoporosis, so be sure your diet includes at least 1,000 to 1,300 milligrams of calcium per day. Milk, cheese, yogurt, leafy greens, and beans are all great sources of calcium.

Iron: Iron is essential for blood volume and preventing anemia (one of the most frequent dietary problems for pregnant women). It is recommended that a pregnant woman get at least 27 milligrams a day. Too little iron leads to excessive fatigue, lightheadedness, and insufficient oxygen for you and your baby. Good sources of iron include red meat, dark leafy vegetables, beans, and whole grains. Cooking in a cast-iron skillet can also help. Even with a diet high in iron, some women may find their iron is low. If you need an iron supplement, consider one that is derived from real foods and will be less likely to cause nausea or constipation.

Magnesium: Many pregnant women in our culture are low in magnesium — an often-overlooked mineral. Magnesium is required for a whole host of reactions in the body, including but not limited to muscle and nerve function, immune health, heart and blood function, energy production, bone health, and regulating glucose. Being low in magnesium can cause leg cramps, headaches, preterm birth, and preeclampsia.[71] Dark leafy greens, dark chocolate, pumpkin seeds, and beans are foods higher in magnesium. Epsom-salt baths are also a great way to increase magnesium, as it is absorbed into your skin.

The B vitamins: B vitamins, which include thiamin, riboflavin, niacin, folate (sometimes synthetically produced as folic acid or folacin), vitamin B6, vitamin B12, biotin, and pantothenic acid, are essential for a myriad of functions in the body. B vitamins work together and individually in every cell and are responsible for a vast array of functions for health, including energy production and the creation of blood (which needs to increase by 50 percent when you're pregnant). They are also crucial for the development of your baby's brain and nerves. Vitamin B6 is often used to help combat pregnancy sickness and nausea. Low B12 levels can result in heart palpitations, feeling lightheaded and faint, and fatigue. It seems that current recommended daily values for pregnant women are lower than what many women truly need, so many pregnant women find they need to supplement these vitamins.

Folate: Folate is an essential nutrient and another B vitamin that is important in order to avoid neural tube defects and spina bifida in the developing baby. It is suggested that you get at least 600 to 800 micrograms per day. While the synthetic form of folate — called folic acid — is often found in supplements, it is best to receive folate as much as possible rather than folic acid, so check supplement labels. Researchers are finding that for many mothers with a specific MTHFR gene mutation, their body cannot use the folic acid found in prenatal vitamins, and it can actually cause an adverse reaction. This is not a problem for most women, but it is good to know about and, whenever possible, it is usually better to get vitamins and minerals via their natural design. Folate is found in sunflower seeds, green leafy vegetables, citrus fruits, and beans.

Vitamin C: You also need about 85 milligrams of vitamin C daily. Vitamin C strengthens the immune system, which is weaker when pregnant, and also helps build teeth and bones and metabolic function. Citrus fruits, dark leafy vegetables, and peppers are all good sources of vitamin C.

Vitamin D: The most efficient way to get enough vitamin D is through sunlight. Fortified milk and foods such as eggs and fish can help a little, but nothing can replace even a few minutes of sunshine. While the FDA currently recommends 200 IU of daily vitamin D, most health experts are now saying that is far too low and recommend at least 1,000 daily IU for optimal health. Vitamin D is necessary for bone health, mental health, immune support, and plays a role in helping your body absorb other nutrients. Importantly, women with low vitamin D levels have a higher risk of preterm labor.[72] Low vitamin D levels have even been shown to cause more painful labor![73] If you live in a colder climate or cannot get several minutes of sunshine a day, consider taking a quality supplement.

Supplements: It is preferable that you and baby get the vitamins and minerals you need through a healthy diet of real food, but a good prenatal vitamin or specific supplement can help to make up for anything missing. Our bodies are much better able to process and absorb supplements derived from real foods than those that are synthetically produced. These types are usually gentler on your system, with fewer side effects, such as constipation or nausea. So, if you do need to supplement iron or other nutrients with a general prenatal vitamin, try to find one that is derived from real foods. Check with your provider on whether there may be any concerns with supplements that you believe you need.

Water: One of the most important things you can do is drink lots of good, pure water. Not drinking enough can lead to dizziness, fatigue (beyond regular pregnancy exhaustion), heartburn, headaches, urinary infections, preterm labor, prodromal labor, low amniotic fluid, and an entire array of other pregnancy frustrations. A good rule of thumb with any ailment in pregnancy is to drink several glasses of water and see if it makes a difference. You should be drinking at least sixty-four ounces of water a day. While it may be frustrating to have to use the bathroom more, it's very important to stay hydrated. In fact, some have suggested that not getting enough water can actually increase trips to the bathroom, since the urine you are producing is more concentrated and irritating to the bladder. Do what you can to get a source of water that is well-filtered of contaminants (including hormones, chlorine, pharmaceuticals, lead, and more) that are often present in tap water. Keep a water bottle with you as much as you are able. If you need to, use little tricks to help you get the water you and baby need — lemon slices, fruit infusions, herbal tea, sparkling water, a small incentive for yourself after each glass, a gallon jug that you fill each day as your allotment — whatever helps you to make sure you're drinking enough and staying well hydrated.

A few special foods: There are several specific gifts in the natural world that God has provided for pregnant women. Two of these are red raspberry leaves and dates. Red raspberry leaf teas or infusions have been used by women for centuries to help tone the uterus and prepare for birth. Since it isn't a medicine, there isn't a recommended daily amount, but it is generally considered safe to drink as much as you want, provided that you listen to your body and stop if you notice any negative effects. It can also be a great way to get some of your water for the day.

Dates (the fruit, not a night out with the husband ... though those are helpful, too!) have recently been shown through a National Institute of Health study to have a significant effect on a woman's labor and birth. In the study, women who ate six dates a day for the last four weeks of pregnancy were much more likely to go into labor on their own by their estimated due date, be more dilated when they reached the hospital, *and* their labor times were almost half of those of the women who didn't eat dates.[74] The theory is that there is some enzyme or component in the dates (one that women in the Western world perhaps don't get enough of, since dates are not a common part of our diet) that helps prepare the body to respond more quickly to the physiological prompts for labor.

Of course, there are no guarantees with either of these foods, but it certainly is good and interesting information to consider.

A Special Note on Pregnancy Sickness and Hyperemesis Gravidarum

Let's just do away with this "morning" sickness idea once and for all. For most women, it hits at any or all hours of the day or night. Let's call it what it is: pregnancy sickness. While it is best to fill our diets with healthy, whole, real foods, pregnancy sickness — and especially the more serious *hyperemesis gravidarum* — can make that ideal nearly impossible. There are times in some pregnancies when anything (even water for some women) will make a mother sick. If faced with such extreme symptoms, it is best to eat and get calories and hydration any way you can stomach it. Seek help from your provider, friends, and the online community to help you with tools, solutions, and support in this huge struggle. Know that you are certainly not alone.

We do what we can, the best we are able to, and leave the rest to a Father who loves our little ones even more than we do. If you need to compromise the ideal, be at peace, surrender it to God, knowing that he can make up for it. We have a loving and merciful God who does not ask us to give more than we are able. Not only is this the only way to have peace in the midst of the trials of pregnancy sickness, but it is a great practice for the work of motherhood itself.

Exercise

Our bodies are meant for movement. Healthy movement and exercise are very important for a simpler, healthier birth and recovery. This doesn't necessarily mean you need to begin training for triathlons or join the local gym (though if you're inspired and have no extenuating circumstances, go for it!). It does mean that you should be trying to keep your body moving and flexible and have some sort of fitness regimen while you are pregnant. Maybe that means a home workout you stream online, or perhaps you join the local YMCA so you can swim twice a week. For some busy moms of many, it could mean taking the older kids to the park so you can walk the hills or do steps while they play. Maybe it means a daily early-morning or after-dinner brisk walk with your husband.

The type of exercise that works for you is going to vary based on your individual circumstances, health, and schedule. It is incredibly easy (and understandable) for most pregnant women to want to sit a lot and not exercise because, well, it can be *really hard*. Most of us will need to make a very deliberate decision to overcome that stasis and exhaustion to get in some good movement during the day. Not exercising or getting enough movement during pregnancy is almost always felt later, as the body isn't as toned or ready for the work of labor and has a more difficult time recovering. This is, of course, assuming a normal and healthy pregnancy. If you have a condition or complication that makes exercising unwise, your immediate health and that of your baby should take precedence.

There are several specific exercises you can do to prepare your muscles, ligaments, bones, and tissues for the work of labor and birth, and to improve your recovery. These exercises are especially important in the last trimester. Several of the resources in Appendix D include visuals if you need additional help in doing them properly.

Squatting: Spending time doing slow, deep squats is incredibly helpful in increasing the flexibility and strength of your pelvic floor. The stronger your pelvic-floor muscles, the less likely you will be to tear perineal tissue in labor, and the easier time you will have regaining strength after birth and avoiding organ prolapse or urinary incontinence. To do a proper squat, pretend there is a chair behind you and stick out your bottom as though you are going to sit. Instead of sitting in that imaginary chair, go all the way down to the floor and hold for as long as you can. Try to keep your heels on the floor. It may be difficult in the beginning if you're not used to it. Don't give up! Have something next to you to hold on to for guidance and balance, if necessary. Do this several times a day, increasing the length of time and amount as you can. Doing 10 to 15 good squats a day is a great way to prepare your body in the last weeks before birth. Regular squatting during pregnancy can also increase your muscle tone and make it easier for you during labor if you want to squat during birth.

Kegels: Combined with squatting, Kegel exercises are very helpful in strengthening your pelvic floor and helping you identify the muscles that we women are not used to giving attention. A good Kegel is done by contracting the muscles around your vagina and urethra, as though you are trying to hold in urine and then slowly and consciously releasing those muscles. Kegels should be done slowly and deeply. Aim to do 8 to 10 at a time several times a day, slowly tightening the muscles, holding each one for a few seconds at the "top," and then slowly releasing. Like squats, the more you do, the stronger you will get and the more you will be able to identify the different muscles needed, making a large difference. It's important to remember the conscious tightening and release. Pay attention to what that feels like as you do it. Consciously releasing and relaxing is helpful for labor and birth, while the tightening and muscle tone is important for long-term pelvic-floor health.

Pelvic rocks: Doing pelvic rocks, especially at the end of pregnancy, can be helpful for releasing back pain and encouraging the baby into a better birth position. While on your hands and knees, keep your back straight and slowly round your back slightly and tuck in your pelvis as though you are tipping your tailbone toward the floor. Allow your lower back to stretch and hold this position for 8 to 10 seconds. The rock can help baby's head to get into position while the hands-and-knees position gives the baby a bit more room in your hanging belly to turn into a good position for birth.

Avoid reclined sitting: It is helpful to avoid couch sitting, where all the weight of the baby and belly is resting on your back. While it may feel nice at the time, it promotes a posterior baby because the heaviest part of the baby (his or her back) will follow gravity. It's okay to recline and relax in moderation, of course, but do what you can to sit forward, perhaps using an exercise ball or sitting cross-legged, or simply sitting on the edge of the couch rather than sinking into the back. The more room you give the baby and the more you can help his or her back to position itself at the front of your uterus, the more likely the baby will stay in that optimal position, encouraging a simpler, shorter labor.

Chiropractic care: Regular chiropractic care can also be helpful in preparation for labor. Adjustments by a chiropractor who is familiar with pregnancy care (look for someone who is Webster certified) can relax ligaments and open up the pelvis so the baby can get into the best position possible for birth. Chiropractic adjustments can help a baby who isn't favorably positioned (breech or posterior) and can help a mother to have a simpler, more straightforward birth. They also can be extremely helpful for back pain and other aches and pains of pregnancy. Ask your provider, doula, or friends for a good recommendation.

Optimal Fetal Positioning

The baby's position can play a big role in the ease or difficulty of the birth. A baby that is optimally positioned at the time of birth is one who has his or her head down and engaged in the pelvis, with the back facing the mother's front or left side. While babies are often born posterior (with the back against the mom's back, also termed "sunny side up") or even breech (not head first), the labor can be longer and more difficult. Posterior babies often cause "back labor," where the mom feels labor strongly in her back as the back of baby's head presses against her spine and tailbone. The good news is that most babies, given the proper room, will position themselves well for birth, and in case they don't, there are things you can do to help them. You can learn how to identify how your baby is positioned by feeling where the head is, the curve of the spine, and where you feel kicks. An experienced provider should be able to tell pretty quickly how the baby is positioned and can show you if you have trouble.

If your baby seems to be positioned posteriorly, spend lots of time on your hands and knees to give baby the gravity and room to turn around. Avoid reclined sitting. Chiropractic care, pelvic rocks, exercise, swimming, walking, and acupuncture have all been shown to help a baby turn to a good position. A great resource for helping babies get into the optimal birth position is spinningbabies.com. Many midwives and doulas are also good resources on positions and techniques that can help a baby get into the best position before and during birth.

Babies who are not head down are said to be "breech." While a baby can turn up to the last moments before birth, if your baby is breech past thirty-four weeks or so, you may consider trying some techniques to encourage baby to move head down, since that is the simplest way for vaginal birth. Certainly, try all of the above positioning techniques. Also, spend time doing "inversions": lie inverted with your head lower than your abdomen to encourage baby to flip. You can use stairs, an ironing board, or place your knees on the couch while your head and arms are on the floor to do this. It sounds strange and is not comfortable, but it can be great way to help a baby turn, and it can avoid more invasive interventions. Another option is acupuncture or moxibustion, an Eastern treatment of applying heat to the feet. While it sounds odd, there is some evidence that it can help turn a breech baby. A Catholic wanting to try this route should make sure the provider will not be doing anything that would be antithetical to our faith.

If none of the above-mentioned interventions works, a provider can, as a last resort, offer an external cephalic version (sometimes just shortened to "a version"). This is where the provider manually tries to turn the baby from the outside through the woman's abdomen. It isn't comfortable, and some providers may require an epidural. This is so that if the water is broken in the process and baby is transverse breech, or if they go into distress, they are more easily able to do a cesarean. A footling breech (where baby's feet are at the cervix) or a frank breech (where baby's bottom is at the cervix) can certainly still be born vaginally, though many providers are not skilled or confident in managing that type of birth. Unfortunately, in the United States, most providers are no longer trained in the art of vaginal breech birth, so it is becoming harder to find providers who are willing to do one. Currently in Canada, there is a push to retrain doctors in the art of vaginal breech birth and offer it as a better alternative to cesarean, as has become the norm.[75] A transverse breech (where baby is completely sideways), however, always requires a cesarean for the best outcome for a healthy birth.

> Although both of them together are parents of their child, the woman's motherhood constitutes a special "part" in this shared parenthood, and the most demanding part. Parenthood — even though it belongs to both — is realized much more fully in the woman, especially in the prenatal period. It is the woman who "pays" directly for this shared generation, which literally absorbs the energies of her body and soul.
> — Saint John Paul II, *Mulieris Dignitatem*, 18

II. Mind — Learning the Truth, Unlearning the Lies

"Do not be conformed to this world but be
transformed by the renewal of your mind."
— Romans 12:2

The time of pregnancy is an opportunity to prepare our minds well, learning what we need to about birth and about ourselves, and unlearning the things that are not true. What we believe about our bodies and birth when we enter into it ourselves will have a major impact on our experience, the choices we make, and can even affect the outcome itself. If what we believe is not based on truth, then our experience and choices will be tainted. If we haven't taken the time even to *know* the options available to us and the reasons behind different choices, then, as they say, we don't truly have any.

A mother who takes ownership of her birth experience is more likely to bring confidence and ownership into her mothering. Conversely, a mother who is made to feel doubtful, who is condescended to, questions her capabilities, or surrenders all her choices to those she thinks may know better has the potential to carry some of that attitude into her mothering. We should use the time of pregnancy, then, to prepare our minds well.

The first step is to do exactly what you are doing now: spend time learning about your body, about birth, and about the truths God has revealed about who he is and who we are. Through reading, study, and a good birth class, you can sort through the information, unlearning what the media, the culture, or others may have told you about womanhood and birth.

Honestly confronting areas where we cling to untruths will reveal to us where we need to pray, learn, and find healing. We need to spend time with the truth of who we are as women and what God has revealed, allowing that to soak into our minds and hearts. Then we can approach birth and motherhood the way he wants us to — with freedom, confidence, faith, and peace.

Our Birth Inheritance

It is important to consider and reevaluate what women in the Western world today have inherited as our birth culture. In every age, the historical and cultural view of women, religion, science, and common birth practices of the time have profoundly impacted women's experience of birth.

We are made to live in community and are designed by God to pass on and share our experiences, knowledge, and culture to the generations after us. The attitudes, rites, procedures, and norms of birth are no exception to this. Handing down the collective memory and passing on tradition and knowledge is a very human, and Catholic, concept. This shapes our expectations, fears, and even specific choices made during birth. This reality can be a blessing or a curse, depending on the circumstances. If the culture around us views birth as beautiful, sacred, and worthy, we will absorb that experience into our births. But if our cultural view of birth is that it is gross, shameful, dangerous, or terrifying, that can greatly affect our own experience.

It makes sense, then, to examine a bit of what has been handed down to us and shaped our beliefs, attitude, and expectations about birth as women in the modern world.

A (Very) Brief History of Modern Birth

Unprecedented changes have occurred in the area of childbirth in the last century. For thousands of years, women in labor were tended to by local women, female relatives, and often a midwife or someone of a similar role in the community who was trusted for her birth expertise. Only in the last century, in response to the Industrial Revolution and the urbanization of communities, was there a movement in the United States for women to birth in a hospital setting.[76]

In 1900, less than 5 percent of births occurred in a hospital. By the 1960s, 97 percent took place there.[77] Entire books could be written on the consequences of that move, both good and bad, but for our purposes, it is important to know that birth has become more foreign to the collective memory of women as a result. No longer were female relatives and friends present at birth, and until the last several decades women usually went into the birth room alone. Fathers, who were never much involved in the actual process anyway, were not invited until around the 1970s. Birth moved away from the immediate community and became increasingly seen as a medical process to be managed by professionals, rather than a normal biological process done by the woman.

Related to the institutionalization of birth was the movement away from breastfeeding, which grew increasingly stigmatized as the choice for poor or uneducated women.[78] Overall, there was a growing sense within the post-industrialization community that the natural state of the woman's body was inferior to technology. Often, women were blatantly told so.[79] The advent of increasingly available contraceptive methods during that time, as well as the legalization and promotion of abortion as a "solution" to unplanned pregnancy, only fueled this growing trend of animosity toward the woman's body. The effects of such a generational movement of thought regarding fertility, birth, and breastfeeding have had a lasting effect on women.

This movement has meant that young girls no longer see labor and birth as a normal part of life, and mothers in labor don't have the support of other mothers and grandmothers who have gone through it themselves. The collective wisdom and memory of birth has in many ways been completely changed. While there have most definitely been some positive outcomes from these cultural changes, there have been unpredicted negative ones as well.

Much of modern provider and hospital protocol works primarily on an efficiency model, often determined by what makes more sense for the doctor rather than for the woman giving birth. An unfamiliarity with birth combined with a culture that views the natural female body as inferior has certainly affected the confidence and experience of a generation of new mothers. The rise in contraceptive use and the shrinking of family size has also played a part in the loss of this memory. With smaller families necessarily comes less exposure to birth. This is true not only in the community at large, but within families themselves, as children are often too young to remember the birth of their one or two younger siblings.

We can and should be grateful for the ways that modern medicine has helped many women and babies, yet still recognize that unforeseen consequences left a mark on our collective memory and even produced negative outcomes for many women and babies.

The Contraception Effect

The contraceptive culture has deeply influenced opinions and beliefs about our bodies and, consequently, birth. Women are told from girlhood that our bodies as they were made are flawed. Our natural fertility, so integral to who we are as women, has come to be seen as an enemy, something to be "fixed" or medicated, controlled, and feared. Pregnancy is often presented to young women as a threat. A baby (unless it is perfectly timed and planned for, and fits within the culturally acceptable number, age, and circumstances) will ruin a woman's chances of reaching goals and being successful and happy. No longer is a young woman's fertility seen as healthy and a blessing. In many ways, fertility — and, subsequently, birth and babies — are now viewed as a liability.

This distortion of God's plan for a woman's body is pervasive, whether we use contraception or not. It reaches into every part of our culture, and we see and experience it all around us and often deeply within us. For many of us, this entrenched belief that our natural bodies are broken and not to be trusted clings to us as we approach our births. After all, if the natural design for our fertility is flawed and needs to be managed and fixed, then certainly the end result of our fertility — birth — must be flawed and in need of fixing as well.

It can be incredibly challenging for women in the modern world to believe that we are beautiful. It's also a challenge to weed out the ways in which our culture has twisted our beliefs about who we are as women. Beliefs are passed on, actively or passively, intentionally or not, and affect us for good or for bad. It is certainly wise to consider this as we make decisions about and mentally prepare for our own births. For many of us, it takes time, education, healing, and prayer to recover from the messages we have been hearing about our bodies since our earliest years. For many, the belief that we are ugly, dysfunctional, not good enough, or inherently flawed is profoundly damaging.

As Catholics, we know we can reject these lies, but they can be deeply rooted. Drawing on the truths of our faith, we can begin to transform our beliefs, aligning them with the truth of who we are, so that we can bring these beliefs with us into our experience of birth.

Recovering the Truth

To experience an informed, positive, and even holy birth, it is important to assess honestly what you believe deep down about your body and about birth. I encourage you to spend some time with these questions:

- Do you truly believe that your body is good and beautiful?
- Do you believe that God designed women's bodies (and that means your body) to give birth and do it well? Do you think those are just words?
- Do you believe that birth is something inherently dangerous? What is behind that? While complications during pregnancy and birth are real, do you see that these circumstances are deviances from the original plan?

- What have you been taught about fertility and birth either actively or passively by your family, friends, medical professionals, or the culture?
- If you have valid health issues that complicate your situation, do you believe that God is still a part of your birth, that he has a plan in it, and that he still wants you to have a good birth?

Reclaiming Language

Words are powerful. Whether spoken out loud, in our own heads, or in the cultural messages surrounding us, words shape what we believe and what we are capable of doing. People who don't believe they can do something will have a much harder time actually doing it. If we tell ourselves over and over (or hear from someone else) that we can't do something, those thoughts and words shape our reality. And the opposite is true: When we tell ourselves that we can do something, that also shapes our reality. This is especially true for birth. Many of us may need to work on convincing ourselves that we are up to this task and mentally prepare to handle roadblocks. This mental preparation will be of tantamount importance when it comes to the most difficult parts of labor and birth.

This is why it is important to surround yourself with people who believe in you, who have wisdom and experience to share (if you want them to), who have had great birth experiences themselves, and who truly want the best for you. Some women who perhaps had less than ideal and informed births themselves seem to enjoy sharing horror stories with new expectant mothers, subtly or blatantly undermining their confidence. Perhaps these women were never able to fully understand or process their own births and now carry resentment, anger, regret, or sadness. But it is rarely helpful for a new mother to have other women dog her with terrifying narratives or unwanted advice. However, it can be helpful to have other women share in a respectful and positive way things they wish they would have done differently and why. The words and support around you are important as you approach your birth.

For this reason, it's also important to choose your own words carefully, filling your mind with words that are true and encouraging. The Church has long taught that "we pray what we believe and we believe what we pray."[80] This means that the words we pray matter and have a direct impact on what and how well we believe. And what we truly believe has an impact on what we pray. A similar concept can be applied to our thoughts: what we say out loud shapes what we believe, in this case what we believe about birth. And what we believe about birth will shape how we approach labor and birth.

Speaking affirmations before and during birth can be powerful. These are words you can speak to yourself or out loud, words you can pray, especially when thinking about your birth or confronted with fear or doubt. As the living Word of God, Scripture verses are especially powerful. An affirmation could also be a quote from a saint, or a simple statement such as, "I am made for this," or "I am fearfully and wonderfully made." It could also be a reminder you know you will need in labor: "My body is relaxed and will let my baby out."

This practice may feel silly, since so many of us are not used to being in touch with this side of ourselves, and perhaps you feel self-conscious about anything that feels too "psychobabbly." But the truth is, it works. Our words form our thoughts, and just as we need to pray in order to believe, we sometimes need to speak what we know to be true in order to better believe it in times of doubt.

You may choose to print or write out your affirmations, prayers, or Scriptures and hang them in your home before birth as a reminder. (There is a large list for inspiration in the Appendices.) Many women do the same for labor and birth. Having a supportive husband and a doula who can remind you in moments of doubt that you have what it takes, that you are capable and strong, and that God knew what he was doing when he designed you is priceless before and during birth. Perhaps one of them can speak those affirmations out loud during difficult moments, reminding you of the truth and giving you confidence when things get hard.

Mind Training

Mental preparation for birth not only consists in knowing what is true, but actually living it.

I can know what it means to run a marathon, and I can tell myself over and over that I can do it, but in order to actually do it I have to develop my strength and willpower, pushing myself beyond what is easy or comfortable. I have to prepare my body, yes, but just as importantly I have to transform my mind and challenge myself beyond anything previously done.

A woman giving birth will have to overcome negative thoughts, words, and beliefs, especially when it begins to become really, really difficult. Almost every woman in labor comes to a point where she feels as if she can't go on. Runners call it "hitting the wall." This is the moment when you realize no one else but you can complete this great work. It is then that you will need to will yourself to go on and live out what you have been telling yourself for months: You were made by God to do this, and he will give you the strength in each single moment to keep going.

In the really difficult moments, everything you have been telling yourself and learning may be tested, bringing you face to face with what you believe about yourself. If you have chosen a natural birth, this is the time when you will need to decide to own that choice and climb that wall. You will need to access that reserve of mental strength, digging deep within yourself and relying on the grace of God to find the will to keep going. Just as Scripture tells us we are strong when we are weak, you will find the ultimate strength in surrendering to the pain, to the struggle, and to the grace of God and the work happening within, allowing yourself to be broken and weak. So often in that surrender women find they are stronger than they ever imagined. It is especially important to be surrounded by a good birth team, whose strength and belief you can draw from during those most difficult moments. When we can't believe in ourselves any longer, sometimes it is only the presence of someone we truly trust believing in us that keeps us going.

You were made to be the mother of this child. You were made to give birth to this child. The Creator of the universe planned this for both of you. Preparing mentally for birth, entering into it with trust that God created you to perform this great work, will give you the confidence you need to complete the task. You can approach your own unique birth confidently, knowing that God has called you specifically to this birth.

Growing up, my mother never felt she had much strength as a woman, and that passed on to me. In the end, I was an only child because she decided not to have any more. So, when I got pregnant with my own child, I didn't have a lot of confidence in my ability to give birth or breastfeed. I had a very medicalized birth with my first, BUT it showed me that I was able to do it! My body worked! It sounds silly, but I was actually surprised I was able to do it.

After my first birth I had the confidence to try an unmedicated birth with my second. It was the hardest thing I had ever done, but it was also life changing. I felt that if I could do that, I could do anything. I went on to have an even harder birth again with no pain medication. It isn't easy. It was excruciating. But I was able to do it and make it to the other side, and I feel that I could do it again if God gives us more children. It was a huge step in separating myself from the idea of being weak. My mom always focused on her weakness, and growing up with that as my model was tough. I still struggle with confidence and liking myself, but one thing I can always know is that I was strong enough to give birth three times and twice without pain meds (which greatly improved the overall experience). I want to have a different way of speaking about birth and breastfeeding with my own daughter. I want her to know that she can do it. That she is strong. That it takes great courage, but that God will be there for her.

Amanda D., mom to four

III. Heart — Addressing Emotions and Wounds before Birth

"Peace I leave with you; my peace I give to you; not as the world gives do I give to you. Let not your hearts be troubled, neither let them be afraid."
— *John 14:27*

The emotional component of birth is profoundly important, but often overlooked. Just like our minds and bodies, our hearts also need to be prepared for birth. Your emotions have the potential to color the way you view and live out motherhood. If you are humble and confident in your pregnancy and birth, recognizing it as part of God's unique call and plan for you, you will take that into the mothering of this child.

On the other hand, doubt, insecurities, anger, bitterness, fear, or other unresolved emotional issues can follow you into your experience of birth and motherhood. Personal fears and negative emotions can wreak havoc in our minds and hearts before and during birth, consciously or unconsciously disturbing our peace and ability to enter into this stage of our life freely. An anxious, fearful spirit can have a powerful effect on your body and its ability to open up fully and smoothly during birth.

To enter into a positive and beautiful birth experience and into this calling of motherhood with greater confidence and peace, it's important to honestly assess your emotional health, especially regarding your body and birth. If we believe that our vocations as wives and mothers are our path to holiness, a true calling from God, then it makes sense to address any emotional issues that may be interfering with our ability to live them out well. It is important that you be free to approach your birth emotionally healthy, with joyful expectation, experiencing fully the beautiful truth happening within your body. You want to approach it free from irrational fears, pain, anger, or baggage from your past.

Birth is innately personal and incredibly powerful, and having a baby and becoming a mother is obviously a big deal! Underlying emotions, personal and family wounds, and fears may be exposed and experienced more intensely during pregnancy. Ignoring them doesn't help anyone. Trust that God is still in control. Perhaps he wants to use this pregnancy and birth to draw those things out in order to heal them.

When you were little, did you dream about becoming a mother one day? Chances are you thought you would be thrilled with the announcement of the pregnancy, joyfully expectant, and able to enter into birth readily. Instinctively, we want this to be one of the most beautiful and happy times of our lives. If this is true for you, thank God for that. If you are entering into this pregnancy and birth full of joy at the gift of this child and believing that your body is capable and beautifully made to do this work, that is a wonderful gift. Embrace, celebrate, and use that during your birth.

But perhaps your reality is not quite that ideal. Many women encounter fear, specifically, in a unique and painful way before birth. Maybe this is you. Your fear may stem from something clear and tangible concerning pregnancy and birth — fear of the pain, the previous loss of a baby, an adverse diagnosis, a past traumatic birth, or knowing someone else who experienced a traumatic birth.

Or perhaps you are dealing with a fear that's a little less defined but nonetheless ingrained. Perhaps you struggle to trust the medical profession, or maybe you are in a crisis pregnancy with little or no support. If you were not expecting or hoping to be pregnant, you may also find yourself fearful at the prospect of being able to care for this new baby. Maybe you are going into birth and motherhood without a husband present or available. Perhaps it is simply because you've never done this before, and all you know of birth are those horror stories from television. Whatever the cause, it's helpful to know that fear is a common struggle during pregnancy.

Fear of labor really hit me strongly when I was pregnant with my sixth baby. There were three things that really helped me overcome those fears and have a peaceful labor. First of all, I talked about it. Acknowledging the fear and owning my feelings were hugely important. My poor husband heard the most, but also other experienced moms and even the midwife herself. Some offered me empathetic ears, some eased my fears, and everyone was optimistic for me when I couldn't find it in myself.

Second, I really prayed that God would allow for a "normal" and "easy" labor. Labor is hard work, no doubt about it, and I prayed that I would not be given more than I could handle. I attended Mass frequently, and made sure to receive the Sacrament of Penance regularly to get any extra graces I could. I also asked friends for their prayer intentions that I could offer up during labor to make my suffering more meaningful.

Third, I looked at each specific fear I had and came up with a plan. Because I was anxious about the pain of childbirth, I made sure my midwife knew I wanted the option of anti-anxiety medication. Since I thought I would hyperventilate (again) during labor, I made sure an oxygen mask would be available. My biggest fear of having the baby in the car because of my history of fast labors was erased because we moved in with my parents around my due date so I could be super-close to the hospital. Having a specific plan, unique to me, was so helpful. Any time fears would creep in, I would just remind myself it was all taken care of.

I ended up with one of my most peaceful and uneventful labors and births of all.

— Colleen Martin, mom to seven

Fear isn't the only wound you may be facing. For too many women, deep and painful wounds are present that need profound healing, often related to a dysfunctional family, abuse, body image, or past sins. If we see our body as too ugly, too fat, too skinny, too sick, too weak, too shameful, or anything else, then that can have an effect on how open we feel in birth and how well we feel our body will birth.

A disordered sense of modesty can also hinder a birth. A woman who is embarrassed or ashamed in the birth room will have a significantly harder time feeling safe, and we know that relaxation and safety is imperative for oxytocin release and for allowing dilation to happen. Some women cannot pinpoint exactly why they are hounded by a spirit of fear, anxiety, shame, denial, or guilt, but it is there nonetheless.

As you approach your birth, is there fear, anger, or shame that needs to be addressed? Is there something that makes you feel ugly, broken, ashamed, jealous, or unworthy? We can know in our heads that we are made for this task and that our bodies are good, and that our motherhood and this baby are gifts from God, but sometimes that truth needs to make it to our hearts as well.

If any of this rings true for you, it is important to confront those feelings directly and work to heal and deal with them. In today's culture, chances are we all have a bit of work to do in encountering the negative emotions and lies that can surround what we believe about ourselves and our womanhood. Some wounds are common; some hide deeply and we may not recognize them immediately. Thankfully, the Divine Physician specializes in them all.

I wasn't emotionally ready for another child. But in my experience, nine months is the perfect amount of time to reflect and prepare and come to terms with a change in plans. The pregnancy was my hardest in a lot of ways, and it caused me to spend a lot of time in deep reflection of the connection between love and suffering.

I had a wise priest during this time remind me that it is okay after three births, including some scary ones, to be apprehensive about another child. It was okay and normal to have a bit of fear and question God's plan. But I needed to work on that separate from the child in my womb and never let those emotions be directed at her. It was beautiful advice as I worked through another layer of growing in motherhood.

— Angie W., mom to four

Finding and Healing the Wounds

There are many emotional wounds that can affect how we are able to enter into something so intimate and intrinsic to women as birth. Maybe you are struggling with depression, anxiety, or marital issues. Perhaps you have issues with body image or an eating disorder, whether from your past or currently. Maybe there is sexual abuse in your past that has shattered your view of your body's goodness or scarred the way you view and live out your womanhood. Perhaps this pregnancy has come after a long trial of infertility, making you question whether or not your body really does work the way it should. Maybe you have an abortion in your past that haunts you, and you feel you don't deserve to have a healthy and beautiful birth and baby. Perhaps this pregnancy wasn't planned and you have little support. Maybe your pregnancy is even the result of rape. Maybe there is a traumatic birth experience in your past that you haven't healed from. Perhaps your understanding of family has been wounded by a broken one.

If you are struggling with any wound, I would like to speak right to your heart for a moment. No matter what has happened in your past, no matter what you've been told or how you feel, no matter who or what has hurt you, God made you beautiful. Period. Do you believe that? Truly, deep down? When you look at your pregnant (or non-pregnant) body in the mirror, do you see goodness? Do you believe it is capable?

God made you, out of all the billions of women in the world and from all eternity, to be the mother of this particular baby. He made your body good, holy, and capable of bringing this baby to life in your womb. No one can take that away from you — not your past choices, not an abusive relationship, not your broken image of how your body works, not even the devil himself. God made your body to bring this baby into the world. Whatever cross you are carrying, whatever lies have a hold on you, they can be redeemed through his love, his healing, his power, and his truth. Perhaps he wants to use this pregnancy and birth to do just that.

Dear sister in Christ, know that those voices, whether they are of the culture, in your head, from your past, or from another person, are blatant and evil lies. They are the voices that say you are ugly, not strong, not good enough, that your sins are too great. They are beliefs you may not even realize you hold: that birth is gross, that it doesn't matter, that motherhood is weak, that this baby was a mistake, that your body is broken. These voices are not from God. As women we are called to bring life into the world, and the devil — who desires death and our destruction — wants to tear us apart at the heart of who we are. From the very beginning he attacked humanity through the woman. Today he attacks us through contraception, abuse, abortion, the lies in magazine ads and commercials, and, yes, even through birth. The devil is not a gentleman and will cross into every avenue of womanhood to drag us away from God and our life-giving mission. That's why it is so important to recognize these lies for what they are and bring them into the light of Christ.

The grace of God can heal and redeem anything. Take time to soak in the truth about birth and about who you are as a woman. Surround yourself with people who see your beauty, and with words and stories of people who believe in you and honor your dignity. Embrace the words of God in Scripture and take time in prayer to allow him to speak truth to your heart, to change and heal you. Take any sins to confession and receive the holy Eucharist, allowing Jesus, the Divine Physician, to scrape out the infection and replace it with the truth. In the surgical room of the confessional and in the medicine of the Eucharist we experience in a very real way the healing of the Divine Physician. Spend time in his healing presence in Adoration. Even if you don't know exactly how, or if you need to prepare for birth emotionally, the time given over to God is never in vain. He will work in you even if you don't understand what needs to be fixed. Just give him time and access to your mind and heart.

Depending on the issues you are dealing with, it may also be wise to find a professional counselor, preferably one who understands our faith, or talk with a trusted and faithful priest.

Remember that God is the one who created and planned this new little person. Remember that he makes all things new and he delights — yes, delights — in doing so. He is there in your wounds, in this pregnancy, and he will be there in the birth. He longs to heal what has been broken and pour out his grace upon you. He longs to see you fully restored and fully alive. He longs to see you living freely and fully as the woman he created you to be. This birth is a part of that. It does not need to be something you just get through. It can, in fact, be a profound opportunity for healing and grace in many areas of your life.

For many women, the experience of birth is God's way of bringing a sense of empowerment, freedom, deep healing, and even joy. His plan is not haphazard, and his desire is only for your good. This birth may be exactly what you need to experience his healing and love.

When I reflect on my own experience of pregnancy, childbirth, and breastfeeding, I cannot help but feel deep and heartfelt gratitude to God for the gift of motherhood and the empowerment that I have experienced through this gift. It's truly amazing how the simple reordering in my mind of the purpose of my body wasn't simple at all. It changed how I thought of myself and how I defined my place in the world.

Having been sexually abused for seven years in my childhood, it was so profound to me that the very parts of my body that were associated with so much shame and pain had brought forth and then sustained this precious child. These parts of my body were no longer designed for men's sexual pleasure. I began to finally and truly know that I wasn't a thing. In fact, I was created to give life! Not just physical life, but metaphorical life as well. I'm called to bring life to others, to bring hope, and to nurture the goodness already present in other people. I finally knew that I had dignity. Having been so utterly convinced of my pervading "badness" throughout my life, the discovery of my goodness profoundly moved me. I knew I couldn't be bad if I had brought forth something so good.

Reflecting on pregnancy, childbirth, and breastfeeding, it seemed as though God was saying to me: "This society may act like you are an object. But that is not how I see you, and that is not how I created you." I had doubted my ability to carry to term, to give birth, and to breastfeed, but I had done them all. I stopped feeling resentful about how my body worked and began feeling grateful for how awesome a gift it is to be female. I wondered what other amazing things I was capable of doing that I had never considered before. I wondered what other gifts and talents lay inside of me still unknown even to me. Today, I don't know who or where I would be without God giving me the gift of motherhood.

— April Jaure, mom to four on Earth and four in eternity

●

IV. Soul — Supernatural Preparation for Birth

"But from there you will seek the LORD your God, and you will find him, if you search after him with all your heart and with all your soul."
— *Deuteronomy 4:29*

As the work of pregnancy stretches and demands more and more from your body, your feminine soul is also preparing for the work of birth. You are a mother now, but you are also still God's daughter, and he cares infinitely for your unique soul. Through your openness to life, God has the chance to work deeply in your soul. As you offer yourself willingly for your baby, you become more like him. As you allow your heart to be transformed, you open yourself more fully to the love of your Father and give him room to change you into the woman he designed you to be — a woman who gives herself in love.

Preparing your soul during pregnancy is not only about transforming your own heart. Your work of pregnancy and birth can potentially affect your child, family, and the outside world, too. As Christians, we know our private actions and prayers can make a significant impact on the people around us. What we do affects the entire Body of Christ, most especially those God has placed directly within our care. This reality is a beautiful opportunity to bless our children, as a mother's prayers and offerings for her children are especially powerful. Your spiritual life during pregnancy can have a profound and beautiful effect on this new little person and far beyond.

So how can you prepare spiritually during pregnancy for the birth and the work of motherhood? Each woman's spiritual journey and relationship with God is unique, but there are universal and time-tested ways that can be considered and used in spiritual preparation.

Personal Prayer

Setting time aside every day to pray is always important, and during a pregnancy is no exception. Whether you read Scripture, pray the Liturgy of the Hours, have personal devotions, engage in spontaneous conversation with God, or a combination of them all, Our Lord desires your heart as much as ever. Some women are able to set aside a certain time of day for deeper prayer, while others find it best suits them to pray throughout the day. However you do it, without a doubt the Lord will bless any time you give him. Having a strong, real relationship with God will only help as you meet the challenges of pregnancy, the work of birth, and the complicated fears and emotions that often arise. Your personal faith can be the anchor that keeps you grounded when you are tempted to doubt or fear, and it can be the root of an even deeper experience of joy.

An active life of prayer in relationship with Christ is what can guide your decisions and be the root of all your preparation. It allows you the most openness to the birth that is God's holy and loving will. Finding the time to quiet your heart and soul and listen to the voice of the Spirit is profoundly helpful in discerning and finding guidance for the choices you will need to make. As mentioned earlier, God desires us to come to him in our pregnancies and births, and you don't have to be shy about asking him to bless yours. Pray directly for a happy, healthy, and holy birth.

Your Husband's Prayers

Prayer with your husband can also be a powerful spiritual preparation as the birth approaches. The graces of the Sacrament of Matrimony are available and can be powerful during this time. As often as possible, ask your husband to pray with and for you as you both prepare to meet your baby. This might be through spontaneous prayer, a novena, the Rosary, fasting, or something else. He can also lay his hands on your belly and ask for God's blessing upon both of you as a way of inviting God's grace into the pregnancy and birth. With your husband, you as the mother can pray for a beautiful and healthy birth and the providers and staff that will be with you at the birth.

The father's decision to be truly invested in the spiritual well-being of his wife and child has a powerful impact. A mother gains comfort and strength from his involvement, while a father gains confidence by doing something so important for his wife and child. Praying together for the health and birth of this child they created together is a beautiful way to acknowledge and live out marriage.

My husband and I have together consecrated each one of our babies to Jesus through Mary. The thirty-three-day consecration starts before the birth, involves daily prayers together for the baby, and ends on or around the baby's baptism. It's been such a powerful way for us to remember that this pregnancy, this birth, this baby all come from him. I know the graces from that are with me during birth and stay with that child forever.
— Teresa A., mom to five on Earth, one in eternity

Praying the Scriptures

The Word of God has power and can pierce our hearts and souls like nothing else. As you prepare for birth and for mothering this unique soul, you can turn to Scripture for guidance, confidence, peace, trust, healing, and grace. You may find yourself drawn to a particular verse or story of Scripture as you await the birth. Ask the Lord if he has a verse or word for you in this specific pregnancy. Meditating on that verse (or verses) and pondering it within your heart as Our Lady did is a profound way to allow God's Word and Spirit to work within you, transforming your pregnancy and birth and saturating them with grace. Staying connected to the liturgical readings — either the daily Mass readings or even the Liturgy of the Hours — is also a powerful way to open your heart to what God has to say to you.

During our most recent baby's pregnancy and birth, I relied heavily on the Scripture "Trust in the LORD with all your heart, and do not rely on your own insight" (Prv 3:5). Whenever I would feel anxious, doubt, or lack clarity about labor decisions, I would call this Scripture to mind. Immediately, I would have an inner peace and a strength that came from relying on my heavenly Father's protection.

— Janelle Horn, mom to six on Earth and four in eternity

Offering It Up

There is a Catholic practice of "offering up" our difficulties, pains, and trials to God as a sacrifice of love. Pregnancy certainly provides many opportunities for that! These little offerings can be united with Christ's suffering and death, allowing us, like Saint Paul, to "complete what is lacking in Christ's afflictions for the sake of his body" (Col 1:24). Not only do these offerings purify our hearts and souls, but they can be used as a prayer to help someone else. So the 2:00 a.m. heartburn, the sometimes excruciating pelvic pain, the "morning" sickness that hits at all hours of the day, or the back aching with the weight of this new life — all of these can be used to strengthen your soul, for your intentions, and as a prayer in themselves. "Jesus, I offer this [kneeling at the toilet bowl/third trip to the bathroom/insomnia/muscle cramp/insert difficulty here] for ___" can be an extremely powerful and effective prayer.

My fourth pregnancy was tough — probably my hardest one yet. I was overall very healthy, but there were just so many more difficult spots than with the others that made a lot of days really a challenge to get through. Throughout the pregnancy we prayed and trusted, knowing that somehow God had a plan bigger than we could see at the moment. That prayer didn't make it feel any easier, but it gave purpose to the suffering as we united everything to the cross and the good of our family.

— Angie W., mom to four

The Holy Eucharist

Receiving the Eucharist frequently at Mass in a state of grace is another powerful spiritual practice that is intensified during pregnancy. How beautiful it is to meditate on the Lord giving his very body to nourish us, while you are replicating that within your womb! And it is such a gift to your unborn child to be sharing that physical proximity to Jesus in the Blessed Sacrament. There truly must be an extraordinary amount of grace for both mother and baby when a pregnant woman receives the Eucharist often.

I have always particularly loved receiving holy Communion while pregnant. I taste the precious Body and Blood and imagine it entering my bloodstream, traveling through the placenta, and circulating blessing through my baby's body as well as my own. I feel the deepest surge of true thanksgiving.
— Katie W., mom to six on Earth and four in eternity

On a similar note, time spent in adoration is a great way to silence our hearts and place our hopes, dreams, fears, struggles, and decisions before God. As you offer your body as a gift to your unborn baby, you gain strength and peace before Jesus, who did the same for you. Spending time in silence with the Eucharistic Lord has the power to draw each of us deeper into the mystery and reality of motherhood.

God played an intimate part in our pregnancy journey from the moment the doctors told us we had a 9 percent chance of conceiving, to the miracle of our daughter's natural conception, to the way he worked through my doula, family, and doctors, and finally in our daughter's birth. I knelt before Our Lord in gratitude every week at Adoration during her pregnancy. I know that gave me a full heart throughout the pregnancy and eased my fears and self-doubts. It is only through him that our beautiful miracle baby was born.
— Bridget A., mom to one

Frequent Confession

Ask any mother who has been at it awhile and she will tell you that motherhood challenges her in ways she never thought possible. As mothers, we know and feel deeply when we fail, and often it is motherhood itself that shows us how weak we are. Approaching the Sacrament of Reconciliation often before birth provides extra grace and strength for our role as mothers, as well as a deep understanding of our own weaknesses and ways we need to be healed. Many women find a great deal of peace especially when they go to confession in the last weeks before birth.

Something I always try to do is go to God in confession as my due date draws near. Sometimes more than once. It brings me a lot of peace and comfort and grace during those final weeks, when the anxiety and fatigue of waiting has me stretched thin.

— Nicole Wright, mom to eight on Earth and one in eternity

The Rosary and Devotion to Mary

Pregnancy makes it easier to understand and identify with Mary as a woman and mother. As a mother, she can empathize with and intercede for you in a unique and beautiful way. Mary is an especially powerful mother to those women whose relationships with earthly mothers are strained or broken. She is the perfection of motherhood, and while she cannot replace an earthly mother, she can provide a unique grace to those who long for that motherhood, especially as they become more keenly aware of that lack during pregnancy and birth.

The Rosary is one of the most time-tested prayers to Our Lady. Meditating on the mysteries in the life of Mary is a powerful way to prepare for motherhood, and it is at once joyful, enlightening, sorrowful, and redeeming. Mary's example during these moments of motherhood gives the rest of us inspiration, example, and strength to follow in her footsteps.

During my fifth full-term pregnancy, more so than during my other four, I felt, for some reason, quite unsettled and nervous about labor and birth, and I wasn't sure why. I kept feeling as if I should be doing something more to prepare for the birth, that I had to practice so that I could "do" birth perfectly. As I prayed about it one day, I felt a sense of peace and could almost hear Jesus whisper, "Just trust me." I knew then that God was asking me to give this to him: the worry, the fear, and the suffering. Yes, I can do all things through him, but only THROUGH him. I looked around the church and my gaze rested on a statue of the Blessed Virgin. That is when I decided to begin a fifty-four-day Rosary novena during the last two months of my pregnancy. That is what was missing from my birth preparations. I had been stuck thinking about how I could physically and mentally prepare so that I could power through the labor and birth well. What I needed to do was prepare spiritually by admitting that I couldn't just power through it; I needed to surrender it all to God. I needed to daily hand it over to our Blessed Mother and her Son and ask for the grace to trust in Jesus and his will for this birth.

— Shannon L., mom to five

Devotion to the Saints and Angels

Pregnancy is a great time to seek out prayers and encouragement from the saints and angels. We have a beautiful gift in the Communion of Saints, and there are many saints to choose from. Many mothers choose particular saints whose stories speak to their situation. Sometimes a particular saint may "choose" you.

Saint Gianna Molla experienced cancer while pregnant and chose to protect the life of her baby rather than receive treatment. Saint Gerard Majella is considered the patron saint of expectant mothers because he interceded for a miracle for a woman in childbirth. Saint Brigid is the patroness of midwives and newborns. Saint Anne, mother of the Virgin Mary, is the patroness of those struggling with infertility, and her intercession is often credited for babies conceived after infertility and brought to a healthy birth. Saint Raymond Nonnatus was born via cesarean section. Saint Margaret of Antioch is traditionally called upon to intercede for pregnancy, birth, and a good milk supply. Saint Zélie Martin (mother of Saint Thérèse, the Little Flower) is another beautiful witness of motherhood. She lost three of her eight children in infancy, and the five who lived became religious sisters. Saint John Paul II, with his encouragement to women and mothers, is certainly a powerful patron during pregnancy and birth.

If you know the gender and name of your baby already, consider praying to the child's patron saint before birth. Your personal patron saints will be interceding for you before and during birth, and there are hundreds of other canonized saints who were parents or who have a particular care for pregnancy and childbirth.

The saints, though, are not limited to those who have been canonized. Those you know who have died in relationship with God can intercede for you, too. While we don't have the same assurance of their place in heaven, you can still pray for them and ask them to pray for you. You can ask mothers, grandmothers, friends, and even miscarried children (perhaps most especially) who we hope and pray are in heaven to intercede for a healthy pregnancy and birth.

The guardian angels are also powerful friends, both your own and the guardian angel given to this unborn child. From the moment of conception, how amazing that you have two angels with you! Certainly, they will pray for both you and baby as you approach the important moments of birth.

Saint Gerard has been so important for me in my pregnancies. With every pregnancy, we say a novena for his intercession. I received a medal while I was pregnant with one of my children. Since then, as soon as I find out I'm pregnant, I put on that medal. I've also felt especially close to Our Lady of Guadalupe during pregnancy.
— Cherie L., mom to four on Earth, one in eternity

Birth Blessings and Other Sacramentals

Sacramentals are sacred signs that can be powerful channels of grace through the intercession of the Church. The *Catechism* says that "they prepare us to receive grace and dispose us to cooperate with it."[81]

The primary sacramental at our disposal is blessings given by people, most especially (but not limited to) those given by a deacon, priest, or bishop. The Catholic Church so values motherhood and the sanctity of birth that there are several official blessings available during pregnancy. There is a Blessing of a Mother Before Childbirth, a Blessing of Parents Before Childbirth, and a Rite of Blessing for a Child in the Womb, all three of which are referenced in Appendix A. Consider asking your priest or deacon to give you and your baby one of these special blessings sometime before the birth. Perhaps it could be done after Mass, or consider inviting your priest over for dinner before the baby is due and asking him to do the blessing then. Some dioceses or parishes offer periodic Masses for pregnant women that include this rite of blessing. If you cannot arrange it with your priest or deacon, have your husband or friends provide the words of blessing while praying over you and your baby.

Other ways that blessings can be incorporated into pregnancy are with simple words of prayer over you or baby, or with the Sign of the Cross traced over your forehead and over your womb. I found it a beautiful practice during my last few pregnancies to physically trace a small cross over my growing womb at the beginning and ending of Mass. It helped remind me that the Mass blessings are for everyone present, including my baby.

There is a newer trend in the birth world of hosting a birth blessing (sometimes called a "blessingway") for a mother before her birth. These gatherings are not exclusively Christian, but the idea behind them is certainly in line with what we believe. As with a baby shower, a mother's friends and relatives gather before the birth in honor of the new mother. They can pray with and over the mother and baby, offer their love, and celebrate this new life. At a Catholic blessingway, prayers such as the Rosary can be prayed and perhaps blessed candles distributed that can be lit for you when you are in labor. The event could also incorporate gifts or frozen meals for the birth family. What a beautiful way that sisters in Christ can honor the work of the mother in bringing this new life into the world, and can offer her the spiritual, emotional, and practical support she needs before the birth.

Many women find themselves especially drawn to the power of other sacramentals during pregnancy. Frequent use of holy water or wearing a blessed medal or a scapular are simple ways you can draw on your faith during pregnancy. One of the traditional uses of the Saint Benedict medal is specifically for a timely and happy birth. There is even a little-known, ancient sacramental called an *Agnus Dei* (Lamb of God), which is a special channel of graces during difficult pregnancies and birth. The *Agnus Dei* is a tiny piece of wax taken from the Paschal candle in Rome, impressed with the seal of a lamb, and consecrated by the pope. They are then usually encased in a pouch to protect the wax, and you wear it or keep it with you. These sacramentals are difficult to come by since no popes have consecrated any since Pope Paul VI, but they are another powerful testament to the importance of pregnancy and birth. If you'd like to find one, consider calling different traditional religious orders nearby that might have them available, or asking your diocese if they know where you can find one. (It is not recommended to look for them online, as it's difficult to ensure their authenticity that way.)

....

God in his goodness gives us an abundance of ways to prepare our souls to enter into birth. You may find yourself drawn to specific ways, depending on your spirituality and personality, and you may even find it different with each pregnancy and birth. The most important thing is to open your heart and soul to where and how God may be calling you to deepen your relationship with him during this pregnancy and as you prepare for birth.

12

ENCOUNTERING THE
WORK OF LABOR

*"Therefore, my beloved brethren, be steadfast, immovable,
always abounding in the work of the LORD, knowing that in
the LORD your labor is not in vain."*
— *1 Corinthians 15:58*

It is incredibly helpful to have some sort of plan for how you will handle the pain and work of labor. This is where birth classes can be a great asset to both you and your husband. A birth class will give you hands-on tools and practice for ways to approach, work with, and manage the pain. Books covering specific childbirth methods are a great help. There are also a variety of physiological aids that can be helpful.

The Mind Game of Labor

A large part of the work of labor and birth is completely mental. The most important aid you will have is your own mind. How you view the work of labor and birth profoundly affects how well you will respond, both physically and mentally.

Viewing the contractions as good and helpful and actually trying to welcome them, rather than fighting them, will free your body to put all the work into opening the cervix and delivering the baby. Fighting contractions, fearing them, or tensing up against them makes it much harder for the body to do what it needs to do. This mental shift can be very difficult, especially in the active and transition stages of labor. We are naturally inclined to fight pain and avoid it at all costs, after all. Therefore, it is helpful to practice beforehand and to keep your mental game strong. This is also probably why women who experience chronic pain, who have dealt with injuries, or who are avid athletes often do well with labor. They have conditioned not just their bodies but their minds to deal with discomfort and pain. They probably have developed specific coping strategies, and they will bring those strategies into labor. So, too, women who have experience in fasting or who have trained themselves in self-denial have a better understanding of welcoming physical discomfort for the sake of something greater.

Transforming how we think about birth and the work involved will help us enter it and allow it to happen more efficiently. Can we train ourselves to view birth as very hard work rather than something painful to fight? It may be difficult to retrain our minds to welcome and accept something physically painful, but it is definitely possible. The more we do it, the more we will enter into the story of our birth and see it as the beautiful opportunity and gift that it is. Women who are able to accept the toil and work of labor and birth, rather than resent or fight it, often walk away with a much more positive experience.

Another point to consider: tension equals greater pain. Fighting a contraction actually makes it more painful. We can see how this reflects a deep spiritual reality! Christ tells us that we are to take up our cross, but that his yoke is easy and his burden light. The more we transform our view of pain and suffering as a way to refine ourselves and unite with Christ, the more our pain and suffering become bearable. We may even dare to find joy in the midst of it. In labor and birth, relaxing your muscles into a contraction helps manage the pain, makes the contraction more effective, and contributes to the cervix opening. Women who can relax the rest of their bodies allow the work to happen right in the uterus, where it needs to, and will usually dilate more quickly.

It is helpful to think about how most mammals handle birth. The very first thing most animal mothers in the wild do when nearing the time for birth is to hide somewhere safe. I remember clearly as a girl, having several cats that gave birth, we would often notice that the cat disappeared for a day or two, and we would have to go in search of the new kittens, hidden somewhere difficult to reach. There is a protective instinct within the mother to ensure she is not under threat and is completely safe. If she feels compromised, oxytocin levels drop and labor may stall and even threaten the life of the baby. Professional breeders and zoologists often remain hands-off during an animal's birth, knowing that intrusion on the process could stall labor. Like human mothers, an animal mother will most often begin labor at night. Most animal mothers are not frantic. They often lie completely still, the rest of their body looking nearly asleep as their abdomen contracts periodically. In some larger mammals, you will see them pace or walk through it. Any sounds made are low, long, and open, not high-pitched and tight. Their body pushes instinctively. They will lick their newborns clean, which cleans the nose and mouth, but also is critical for mother and baby learning each other's smells, bonding them and ensuring the baby's survival. The placenta is pushed out shortly after without help and then consumed. The baby often crawls (or walks, depending on the animal) to its mother's nipple completely on its own. Of course, human mothers are much more emotionally and spiritually complex than animal mothers, and we also have the consequences of original sin that animals do not, but nature can still provide valuable insight on how birth naturally and instinctively occurs for other mammals.

Relaxing in the face of direct pain is difficult to learn. It goes against everything we've been taught and how most of us have trained ourselves to think of pain. Think for a moment of what you do when you stub your toe. The first reaction is often anger and to "fight" the painful feeling and make it go away as quickly as possible. Now consider doing something different. The next time you stub your toe or step into a cold shower or have an injury, plan *not* to fight that feeling. Just allow it to happen. Instead, breathe into it and keep your body relaxed as much as possible, rather than tensing up against the pain. Relax your face, the rest of your muscles, and actually feel what is happening. Feel the way the pain is experienced, feel the blood rushing to the site, feel the response of your nerves. It might sound silly, but practicing how we approach pain and discomfort is critical not only to birth but to how we experience the Christian life. The better we can take that response to pain into labor, the better we will be able to handle it.

The more you can retrain your mind not to be shocked by pain, the more capable you will be of "ignoring" early labor. The best thing to do as things are starting but birth is not imminent is to go about your day, sleep when you can, and ignore it as long as possible. The biggest mistake many women make when it comes to labor and birth is dropping everything at the first contraction, or realizing that today might be the day and getting too excited. It's helpful to know in the back of your mind that labor is starting, but also to continue to go about your daily plans and not be too invested in what is happening yet.

As your body progresses, it will let you know when you should no longer ignore it. The more you can consider it not a big deal just yet, the better you will be able to enter into and handle it when things really do become more intense and difficult to manage. This attitude will keep you relaxed and reserve your mental and physical energy for when you really need them. If you are sure labor is beginning but are still able to sleep or rest, do so, unless there is some pressing reason why you may want to speed things along. When things no longer become ignorable, or contractions are coming closer and closer together, then you can begin to avail yourself of your support team and other tools to handle labor.

With each pregnancy, I always have the desire to have a natural birth, but the fears take over most times. Two of my children were born without medication. For the rest I had an epidural, with some of them being great, and some of them not working so well, having complications, or wearing off. I thought a lot during the pregnancy of my eighth about natural delivery. I checked into a doula a couple of times. A couple of my friends tried hypnobirthing and recommended I read a couple different books, which I did. My cousin loves the Bradley Method, so I did as much research as I could. My other cousin loves having home births, so some of her thoughts regarding childbirth affected how I handled contractions. I remembered a few tips from my friend that were so helpful in the early parts like rocking back and forth to take off the pressure and let the contractions happen … don't fight them. I remembered her words, and when I felt the urge to tense up I would try to relax. My sister's husband is one of sixteen children. His mother offered several tips to her regarding early labor that I remembered, and they proved to be helpful.

With all those small tidbits put together and the grace of God, I truly had the most wonderful and memorable birth with him. As my husband said, "Whatever you did this time, please do it next time." I felt so good after he was born. I didn't ever feel as if I had a baby. I hope to remember how I mentally handled each contraction and worked with them instead of against them.

— Lindsay Boever, mom to ten

Tools for Handling the Work

Any physiological aids that help you enter a more relaxed state of mind and body will contribute well to your labor work, as will aids that specifically alleviate pain. Will every option work the same for every woman? No. Nor are any of them going to be magic cure-alls for the work of labor. No secret trick is going to get around the fact that labor is difficult work that takes everything we have. But God provides methods and tools that we can use to help in that task. Every woman's labor is different, and every woman will respond differently, which is why it is helpful to have your own unique "toolbox" for this specific birth. These tools can then be used as needed to manage the pain and help your body do the work it needs to do.

Movement

When in active labor, it is almost always good to move. You should be able to move freely and work with the contractions in any way that helps. Some women need to walk, some squat down during a contraction (you can definitely feel them intensify and work harder when you do that), some rock back and forth on a ball or on hands and knees. A whole lot of women will find themselves swaying or "dancing" during a contraction. Usually, the first trick to try to get a slowing labor moving again is to go for a walk. All of these are the body's way of working the hips, helping the cervix open, and getting the baby into the best position to move down. Follow those leads and intuitions of your body and allow gravity and movement to help your baby down and out.

Freedom of movement makes labor smoother and easier. For me, walking is the best pain control there is … better than breathing exercises, better than massage, better than soothing music. This has been my experience at least. I walk through labor and walk through contractions. I walk all the way to pushing, if at all possible. I really believe our bodies are meant for walking, for movement, and for activity, especially during labor and birth. If at all possible, I stay active and on my feet.

— Amelia B., mom to five

Deep Breathing

When it comes to breathing during labor, panting (as seen on many outdated television shows) is not helpful. Take deep breaths through the nose that go all the way down into the lungs. Controlled and steady deep breathing keeps you and baby oxygenated well and is conducive to deep relaxation. Think of how you breathe when you are most relaxed or even on the verge of sleep. Think of your breath needing to reach the baby. Or maybe think of each breath as going right down into your uterus and giving it the energy it needs to pull open. Try to keep any vocalization low and deep, not high and tight. When in pain or when things get very difficult, we often unconsciously tend to speed up our breathing and take shorter breaths. It's very helpful to have a spouse or doula reminding you to breathe deeply, to relax all your muscles, and focus the energy.

During labor, my midwives would often call attention to my being very tense — eyes shut, jaw clenched, neck tight, shoulders hunched, etc. I would try to remedy this with breathing. Breathing in deeply and then breathing out. As the breath was going out, I would imagine it traveling through my body. I would inhale deeply, and I would imagine each exhale traveling down my head and out my eyes and mouth. On the next, traveling down my neck and into my shoulders and arms and hands. On the next, the exhale traveling down my chest and into my abdomen and uterine muscles … then through my hips and pelvis and down my legs … then the final exhale out my feet. If a contraction came during this breathing, I would try to breathe through it. Wherever I was in this breathing cycle of my body, I would try to focus on the breath relaxing in that area rather than on the intensity of the contraction.

— Lisa H., mom to nine on Earth and one in eternity

Positions

If labor is well established, you can get into whatever position is comfortable for you. Positioning can help labor intensify or ease it. Some women love sitting on an exercise ball during labor. Most hospitals now have them in the room, but if you are planning on laboring or birthing at home, it might be nice to have one on hand. Some women prefer to lie completely still in bed in a runner's position so they can relax their body.

Some women love to stand, and some find it works best for them to be on their hands and knees. In most circumstances, you can be in whatever position feels right for you. If there is a reason or desire to speed things up, you can use positions that intensify your labor. For many women this is squatting, walking, or even sitting on the toilet. If you need to take a rest, use positions that best let you do that, such as lying down or kneeling with your upper body supported by a bed, tub, or another person.

Counter Pressure

Often direct pressure to the lower back or on the hips is extremely helpful in labor. If you are having back labor, that pressure on the back can be a gigantic relief. Sometimes the husband or doula needs to be there nearly the whole time, pressing on the lower back near the sacrum. Another often-used technique is putting pressure on both sides of the hips and doing a "double hip squeeze." Not only can this relieve pain, but it also works to open up the pelvis a little bit more to help the baby drop down. I'll never forget one mother's reaction when I arrived at her labor and began to do this pressure during a contraction. Her face changed, and afterward she breathed, "I'll be honest, I wasn't sure what difference you would make, but *that* ... that right there was worth everything I paid you."

I really liked having hip compressions, and I was very clear, directing my husband on just the right way to do it. I was leaning on the ottoman with him sitting behind me on the birth ball and squeezing my hip with his knees. I kept thinking that I wished he would use his hands, too, since it did not feel strong enough. Later, I saw a picture of him squeezing so hard you could see all the muscles in his arms! I remembered that was the same with my second labor — I could not get hip compressions strong enough, but they did help, so we kept doing them.

— Lauren G., mom to five, birth doula, and educator

Massage

Massage can be relaxing for tense muscles and can release endorphins, and it may also greatly help in labor. Massage of the shoulders, temples, back, calves, thighs, or neck are all worth trying in labor. If you are having trouble releasing tension in labor, sometimes your face and mouth and neck can become very tight. Consciously relaxing the face and jaw is helpful in allowing the whole body to follow suit. It may help to have someone massage those places during the contraction while you consciously relax the places that are tense. That, in turn, helps the rest of your body release tension and labor more effectively. That physical touch (for some mothers) also is helpful in strengthening oxytocin levels and progressing labor.

Hot Water

A hot shower, or, even better, a hot tub, can feel amazing during active labor. Many midwives and doulas agree that it is best to wait to use this method until later in active labor, when the labor is more difficult and you may need extra help. Sometimes, if you get in too early, you can slow down the labor or the relief isn't as noticeable. But in strong, active labor, nearing and through transition, if you can avail yourself of a hot shower or birth tub, the effects can be incredible. Not only does pain and pressure become alleviated, but being submerged in the water helps you to enter into different positions and relieves the weight of your body, helping you to better relax. Many hospitals are now supplying birth tubs for this purpose, and most already have showers available to use during labor. If you have a movable showerhead, you can even place it directly on your back or where you are feeling the greatest discomfort. Women who are birthing at home can use their own tub, though often, if they are planning to birth the baby in the water, they will need to rent or buy a deeper birth pool.

Whenever I'm in labor, I can't get into the tub fast enough. It changes my labor totally as it allows me to relax more (the water takes some weight off my body), feel better (I position the jets to hit my achy back), and gets me ready to deliver quickly! My first natural birth went so fast in the tub that my baby was born in the water (against hospital policy), but I would do them all that way if it was allowed!

— Colleen Martin, mom to seven

Heat

Hot packs or compresses can be helpful, especially for back pain, and they can also be used on your belly, shoulders, feet, or anywhere they feel good. Many doulas carry a rice bag or heating pad with them for this purpose, or you can have one of your own ready at home or packed in the hospital bag. Most hospitals will have a microwave available somewhere on the floor that you should be able to use. As long as fever or infection is not a concern, using heat is a safe and noninvasive method that can bring a lot of relief during laboring.

Visualization

Many women, either before birth or in the midst of labor, practice visualization. To do this, close your eyes and envision something that connects with you that symbolizes opening and helps your mind and emotions to work with what your body is doing. This can be extremely helpful in transforming how you experience a contraction or surge. A popular image that many women seem to gravitate to is that of a rose or another flower blooming. That may feel a bit foreign and "out there" to some, but it can be incredibly powerful. Even Pope Pius XII referred to a woman in birth as "the opening of the flower."[82]

Scripture often uses similar symbolic language to talk about a woman's body. Throughout the Song of Songs (also known as the Song of Solomon) the woman's body is described with deeply symbolic language, including a garden and a gate. In our modern world, we've lost some of that poetic understanding of ourselves and creation, and we would do well to tap into that imagery again.

Another image may resonate more with you: Some women picture riding each contraction as if they are riding a wave in the water. Some are helped tremendously by simply picturing their own cervix stretching and opening with each contraction. Visualize your baby's head placing pressure on the cervix, and with each contraction it is getting wider and wider. Focus on the baby moving down and out. Simply having these words and "attitudes" in mind can be powerful — words such as "open," "down," and "out" can help your brain accept and work toward the end goal. Your husband or doula can help keep this frame of reference for you.

I visualize each contraction opening me up, bringing me closer. In the later stages of labor, when they're strong and more intense, I visualize them as waves on the beach, [and] I go in and out with them. Don't fight them, but work with them.

— Erin H., mom to ten on Earth and one in eternity

Essential Oils

More and more women are becoming familiar with and using essential oils during birth. These are potent, highly fragrant oils derived from various plants through distillation and are said to have therapeutic properties. Clary sage is supposed to be helpful specifically in labor. Peppermint can be helpful if you need a burst of energy or are feeling nauseated. Orange can help with providing energy. Lavender and other blends promote relaxation. If anything, simply smelling something pleasant can release endorphins that alleviate pain and can help you feel more at ease and better able to relax. Oils can be used directly on the skin with a carrier oil, diffused in a room, or put on a cloth that you can smell as needed. In the hospital, these oils can counteract that "hospital smell" that might affect labor and relaxation. If you are using essential oils, it's important to know how to use them safely, and to make sure you have no allergies or negative response to any of the smells.

Lighting

Our bodies respond physically to the lighting and atmosphere of the room we are in. Dark, dim lighting is relaxing. Bright, fluorescent lights, on the other hand, feel invasive and harsh. Low light can help you relax and feel safe and secure, while bright, institutional lighting can make you feel overexposed and vulnerable. Science has also shown that there is a reason most women who go into labor naturally do so at night. Melatonin, the hormone released for sleep and which is affected by light, works with oxytocin to stimulate contractions.[83] This means that keeping the room dark while you are laboring can help your body make contractions more effective, not only because you are more relaxed, but also because your oxytocin response will be stronger. Dim lighting can help you feel safer, more private, and freer to labor as you need, and it is also more conducive to rest between surges.

With almost all of my births, I've gone into labor in the middle of the night. I really like that. It feels safer somehow, quieter. I love the idea of beginning labor in secret, and keeping the room dark feels more natural to me. In a lot of ways, it's actually like sex! It's beautiful and good, but it's private. Feeling safer helps me to relax and enter into the labor better.

— Teresa A., mom to five on Earth, one in eternity

Music

If you are a person who responds strongly to music, it can be helpful to use that during labor. Music has a profound ability to change our mood and speak to us in ways that other languages cannot. If you are hoping to use music in labor, it is usually best to choose songs that you can breathe into and that enable your body and mind to relax. Songs that have a particular meaning and are associated with good memories can be powerful and helpful, contributing to the release of oxytocin.

Acupressure

There are certain acupressure points on the body to know: in the hand, on the lower back, between the eyes, and more. Pressing firmly on those points can provide some relief during labor, and different points will be helpful to different women. It may be helpful for your husband to learn these pressure points beforehand through classes or simple online searches or videos, or to have a doula who is familiar with trying these points.

A Doula

A skilled doula will be knowledgeable about and practiced in the above aids, and she can help you discern which may be the most helpful for you. She is often the one providing the counter pressure, dimming the lights, massaging the back, preparing the shower or bath, and talking mom through each contraction. She should be helping your husband to support you as much as you are both comfortable with, giving him tools to use with you. She should know different positioning techniques to help you best handle the work of labor and get the baby in the best position for birth. All of these physiological aids are extremely helpful, but perhaps most important of all is the constant encouragement and emotional support she offers. Your doula can help you believe you can do it when you no longer do. She will remind you that you have what it takes when things get hard. The physical and emotional support of a doula can make a tremendous difference in the outcome of a birth.

Will, Surrender, and the Grace of God

During most labors, there will come a point where you believe you cannot do it anymore. And most women will say exactly that (sometimes along with other choice words, also totally normal). For many women, this is when no tool, technique, or method is going to fix it. It is here that you can make the choice to face the pain and enter a place that is all at once weak yet strong, vulnerable yet impenetrable. This is when you actively choose to give every ounce of yourself over. It is a place of raw beauty as you decide to journey straight through the pain, giving everything you have to the service of life. If having a natural birth is important to you, this is the point at which your commitment to that goal and your strength of will in achieving it will be tested. You will need to access that faith in your body and the process, truly believing that you have the ability and strength, and the help of God, to make it happen. The people and support surrounding you will be incredibly important. They can remind you how close you are, helping you to trust that you are doing well and that your work is for a beautiful purpose.

In each [of my births], which have all been vastly different experiences and run up and down the scale in terms of difficulty, there has always come a point where I could do no more. I have always reached a limit where I could not go on, or at least by myself, in all of my own littleness and me-ness. A place where I would hit the wall of pain, difficulty, exhaustion. I could not control or think or reason my way out of that place. Be it in a contraction, during transition, after endless hours of laboring, or pushing, these are the painful events that forced me to let go and trust with everything I could muster.

It's then that I simply trust in God. Not out of my own holiness, or intellectual efforts, or nice feelings, but out of desperation. A desperation to be seen through to the other side of pain, unknowing, fear; to the beauty that is my child. And because of the gravity of those moments, even when those moments take forever, an awareness of the importance of trusting in God's will at that instant and in that very vulnerable circumstance overcomes me to the point where I feel the trust in a palpable way. In trusting in God, I felt a more intimate closeness with him and the peace of knowing he was in control like no other I had previously known. Trusting during childbirth consumed every part of me, not just my body, but all my emotions and the entirety of the love I felt for my child.

— Christy Isinger, mom to five

From somewhere deep inside, mom must find the strength and will to keep going through the pain to the other side, coming to the sobering realization that no one else can do the work but her. It is here that her will is tested and she realizes keenly that the only way out is through. She has the choice then to give her will over to that reality and the process, mentally allowing herself to be broken and for God to be her strength, holding her through each moment.

This is the roughest stage of labor. Transition is the biggest test of a natural childbirth, the moment when you simply must give up the idea that you are in control of this life and especially this process. God challenges you to realize that he is stronger than you can ever be, and that you must give over your pain to him. Trying to own it alone can only lead to feelings of uncertainty and despair. Allowing the Lord to manage it for you is the only way to keep yourself present for the new person who is about to enter your life.

— Dwija Borobia, mom to seven on Earth
and four in eternity

Here you will come to a place of complete surrender, a profound place of trust that there is life and resurrection waiting at the other side of the cross, and that "he who began a good work in you will bring it to completion" (Phil 1:6). As raw and difficult as these moments may be, they are also some of the most spiritually transcendent moments of birth. Simply opening yourself up to the reality of the grace present and allowing yourself to be used for this great work is intensely powerful. Giving your entire body over to the process, you will find a surrender and trust that perhaps you have never experienced before. It is here, when you believe that you can't do one bit more, that you are so very close to meeting your baby.

While these moments may be incredibly difficult, the grace present can sometimes be almost tangible. As you get nearer and nearer the moment when you will push that new life into the world, God is there, offering himself to you, giving you the grace and strength to go on, even if only moment to moment. For many women, these last stages of birth become a new and transforming experience of God and their own feminine genius and strength. They experience, firsthand, in their bodies, the paschal mystery of birth.

You can trust that God has brought you to this point, and he will see you through, working in and through you to create something beautiful. In this moment of surrender, he will do the last work he needs to do to prepare you for this birth and the welcoming of your baby.

That right there is the moment for me, in every birth, when I can feel God, I'm on my knees (literally and figuratively), begging for mercy, begging for God to take all the pain away. In that moment, I'm laid bare. I'm finally ready for a miracle, because I've gotten out of my own way. That is the gift of grace. I must decrease so he can increase.

— Micaela D., mom to seven and childbirth educator

The Decision: Medicated or Natural

The decision on how you will approach your birth is incredibly personal. What is most important from a Catholic point of view is that you are treated with respect and that you receive all the information you need to make a truly educated decision. You should not be pressured or lied to. You should feel completely free and knowledgeable enough to make the decision that is best for you and your baby. From an ethical point of view, it is required that any intervention be given with full consent, which means you understand the risks and benefits and freely choose to make decisions without fear, coercion, or abuse.

Some women know from the beginning that they would like a natural birth. The term "natural" in the birth world usually refers to a vaginal birth with no medication or pharmacological pain relief. Often women choose natural births for a combination of reasons. Some women are uncomfortable with the risks associated with the various options for medication. Others feel well prepared with birth classes and have an inner confidence that their body was made to give birth. Some women feel strongly that, since they were designed to do this, they only want intervention if there are strong medical indications for it. Still others are persuaded by spiritual reasons and the opportunity to enter into the story of salvation and the sufferings of Christ. Other women dislike the effects or process of medication, be it the needle required for an epidural or the feeling of helplessness if their body is numb and they cannot move around on their own. Some women have had a negative experience with an epidural or another drug with a previous birth and decide to forgo it for the next.

The option to use medicated pain relief or anesthesia during birth is also valid. For some women, the idea of at least having it available brings peace and relieves fear. Other women who struggle with anxiety or fear may find that they are better able to relax with help from medication. (Be aware, however, that the effects of certain drugs may actually increase anxiety symptoms.) Often, women choose an epidural when they reach a point of exhaustion during a long labor, as it allows for some necessary rest. For some women, an underlying condition, induction, or planned cesarean may require the use of medication or anesthesia, and their choices may become limited.

Again, what is most important is that you understand well the decision you are making and the possible risks of that decision, and that you make the decision with full consent and are given respect.

I was 30-something hours into my labor with my first child; I had labored with my doula and my husband by my side for over a day. When it was time to go in, I knew that I was going to be almost fully dilated and getting ready to push. However, as I arrived and was checked, I wasn't even close. Although I had been eating and drinking and "resting" for over a day as I labored this baby down into the birth canal, I was fully exhausted. I could barely stand up and couldn't keep my eyes open. I had taken a natural childbirth class for several weeks with my husband, and I wanted to have that experience for my baby and me. I had dreamed about it, visualized it, prayed for it. When it came down to that 30-something hour, something snapped in me. I KNEW I would not have the energy to push this baby out if I did not rest. The only way I could rest was to give my body a break and get the epidural. I knew I didn't want the other drugs. I knew I didn't want my water broken. I knew all the things I wanted and didn't want. Nobody was pushing me to induce this labor or move it faster … but I couldn't do it without help. I was so proud of myself for making it as far as I had. Forty-one hours after my first set of contractions I was able to meet my first child, a son, and it was quite the story I was able to tell. It was one that I wouldn't change for anything, and it was the most beautiful experience.

— Carrie D., mom to two

If you are unsure what you would like to do, reading quality birth books and attending birth classes can be invaluable in helping you make a decision. Most privately taught birth classes will discuss the risks and benefits of different choices during birth and will be able to tailor the discussion to your individual needs. They will give you all the options for your birth, depending on the location you have chosen, and help you make an informed choice on how you will handle labor. A good birth class will also give specific tools and non-pharmaceutical ways to handle labor during each stage. It's also incredibly valuable to talk with other trusted women (not those who will tell you horror stories) and get their input and experience. Special consideration should be given to women who have actually recounted birth as a positive and healthy experience. Talking with your husband and taking the decision to prayer is invaluable. These decisions are important and have consequences, sometimes huge. They are certainly choices to be made with a great deal of discernment, information, prayer, and support.

Some questions to consider before your birth when discerning how you will approach medicated pain relief:

- What are my reasons for not wanting/wanting to receive medication?
- Will this medication affect my emotions, my ability to be fully present during my birth?
- What are the possible risks and benefits to my baby with this approach?
- What are the possible risks and benefits to me with this approach? (This will be discussed further in a later chapter.)
- Are there other options I can consider?
- Has this drug or anesthesia been studied for safety? (Be aware that some hospitals and providers use medications outside of their approved FDA use.)
- Have I ever responded poorly to drugs or anesthesia? Do I have other allergies?
- Have I learned the possible short-term and long-term side effects? Do I understand that this decision could lead to other interventions?
- Am I being pressured into making one decision or another?
- What does my gut say? What option leaves me with the most peace?
- Have I taken it to prayer?

Once you have decided how you want to approach your birth, whether natural or medicated, it is important that you share that decision with your provider, husband, doula, and any other support people you will have with you. Some women choose to write out a birth plan to share and have on hand during the birth. This plan will include what your decisions are for pain relief and the options you would like to have available to you. It can also provide guidance for how the others in the room can help you achieve your goals.

13

THE CHOICES OF CHILDBIRTH

"And it is my prayer that your love may abound more and more,
with knowledge and all discernment."
— Philippians 1:9

The many choices you have when it comes to the birth of your baby can be overwhelming, especially if you are a new mother. This is one of the reasons educating yourself before birth is so important. A Christian approach to birth recognizes that the Lord designed birth, and that it matters greatly. It is important to ask him what he wants in these circumstances with this baby and this birth.

While specific birth choices do not usually involve a moral absolute, we should use the intellect and will God gave us to make the right choices in our own unique circumstances. Two women can make vastly different birth decisions, even though both have discerned well using reason, good information, virtue, and prayer.

Catholic Principles Applied to Birth Choices

So how do you make choices when it comes to birth? Several Catholic principles should be at the root of your decisions:

What is most life-giving in the circumstances?

Which option best protects your life and health and that of your baby? This includes not just physical health but emotional and mental health. Whether you are discerning less significant choices or an emergency life-or-death situation, which option takes the best care of both you and baby? If this is an emergency or atypical circumstance, which option will have the best chance of keeping you and baby safe and healthy? What about openness to life after this baby is born? Will this choice affect the ability to welcome more children into the family later?

Which option does the research and evidence support?

As Catholics we embrace good ethical research, knowing that science, reason, and faith all work together. So which option has true evidence behind it? Unfortunately, in the present day some of the routines and protocols of pregnancy and birth are not actually evidence-based. They are in place as a result of an overly litigious healthcare system or for the ease of the provider. Two examples are the dangerously high unnecessary cesarean rate and the now common practice of a woman's chosen provider not even being present during the birth. Some are the consequence of politicians overstepping their rights and imposing requirements on all, regardless of the real needs of individual mothers and babies. We can think here of the medications given to newborns that are actually unnecessary for most but may still be legally required. You have the right to research and know the true risks and benefits of any decision, and you have the right to ask questions of your provider and receive care that is supported by real evidence in your specific circumstances.

Which option supports what we know about the human body and its design?

In other words: *Which option makes the most sense*? God knew what he was doing when he designed the female body. The way he designed birth wasn't an accident. In making decisions about birth, we want to take God's design into account as the author of our biology. While there are no moral imperatives when it comes to many specific birth choices, we honor God when we choose to make decisions that work with his design to the best of our ability. The more we can allow our bodies to work the way he designed, the healthier we will be, and the less likely it is that complications will result.

Which option most respects your dignity and that of your baby?

With each decision, no matter the scale, it's important to ask which option shows greater respect to your personhood and that of your baby. Does one option respect your dignity more than another? Does one option make you or your baby more a part of a "system" rather than respecting you as unique and valuable human beings? Which option better takes into account the humanity of the mother and the baby and treats them well? The Catholic principle of subsidiarity states that matters should be handled at the smallest, most personal level possible.[84] When it comes to birth, you as the mother are the primary decision-maker for your baby and for your own care. Respect for that should be present in all choices. You have a God-given, natural authority to make these decisions, and your dignity requires that you be truly informed when making them.

Which option seems to be where God is leading you?

God wants you to come to him with your concerns, big and small. You matter to him. You can and should take your birth decisions — big or small — to prayer. Trust the movements of the Holy Spirit, who often gives us a gut feeling to guide our choices. When you're not sure where he might be directing you, simply make the best decision you can and ask him to bless it.

At every single point in your pregnancy, labor, and birth, you have choices, even if sometimes it is merely a response to the current situation. No one should ever force or pressure you into anything against your will. Taking true ownership of your pregnancy and birth for your own sake and your baby's allows you to enter into the sobering and beautiful reality of motherhood. Sometimes, of course, the choices may not be what you would prefer, and it might be that one choice rules out another, but it is important to claim motherhood as a role given by God, making choices based on reason, facts, faith, and prayer.

With our first baby, I really did not make too many decisions; I just sort of assumed everything would go smoothly. In the end, it did in a way ... our baby son was healthy, and I recovered well from the cesarean. But that experience taught me that if I had made different choices, a cesarean might not have been necessary. We realized that if we had one c-section, we might have another and another, and there might come a point where an OB would be telling us not to risk another pregnancy. Our choice to attempt a VBAC [vaginal birth after cesarean] at home was both easy and difficult. In my heart, I believed that I would not be able to fit into the hospital's timeline for a VBAC, and I was right. Our second son was born at home after another long and challenging labor. Our decision to have this home birth led to seven other home births for us. This decision was also difficult because many loving and well-intentioned friends and family were worried about our choice, and let us know. But we had to learn as much as we could and then use our own discernment to make the decisions that were right for us.

Ultimately, I believe that whatever choices we make regarding our pregnancies and deliveries … no matter what they are … prepare us for the motherhood and parenthood that is ahead. Faith, fear, strength, instinct, surrender, and confidence are all tools and qualities that we will need in the journey ahead.
— Lisa H., mom to nine on Earth and one in eternity

BRAIN

BRAIN is a common acronym used in the birth world to help you make choices during pregnancy, labor, and birth. This practice can be useful, especially in situations where an intervention is proposed by a provider or hospital staff. Using the BRAIN technique, with the help of your husband, you can figure out what decision is best for you in your own unique circumstances.

Benefits: What are the benefits of this proposed intervention? How might it help the situation you are in? Why does the provider/nurse want to do it? What does the research really say?

Risks: What are the risks to this option? How could it make the situation worse? What does the real research say? Could this lead to other interventions and complications?

Alternatives: What alternatives are there to this option? Are there other ways to achieve that goal that you can consider or try first?

Intuition: What does your gut say? Is this going against something you really believe concerning yourself, your body, your faith? Is there something inside telling you that this is what needs to happen?

Nothing (or **N**ot Yet): What if you do nothing? Is there a reason you need to make this choice right now? Can you wait on the choice?

The BRAIN method can be helpful during labor and when your will or choices may be more compromised. It helps to take an option and run it through the light of reason, evidence, and your own goals and knowledge of your body and self. Keep in mind that, unless an emergency arises, you can almost always ask for some time to make a decision. Simply asking the provider or nurse for ten or fifteen minutes alone to talk it over and think about it can be extremely helpful, especially if you are feeling pressured to divert from your birth plan. Those few minutes can be the difference between making a choice you are not comfortable with (leading to possible complications, guilt, or even feeling disrespected and depersonalized), and taking ownership of your birth. Even when you decide that the intervention or suggestion proposed is a good one, the fact that you are the one freely making the choice makes all the difference in having a positive birth experience.

Should I Make a Birth Plan?

In recent years, many mothers have taken to writing out a birth plan. This plan is usually a page or two that relays choices made for this birth. There are mixed opinions on the use of a formal birth plan. Some say that your relationship with your provider should be personal and individualized enough that you have already talked through your preferences before the birth. While this is certainly ideal, it's simply not the norm in the current birth culture. Most providers are seeing dozens of patients at a time and cannot remember every single detail for every patient. In addition, if you are birthing in a hospital or birth center, there will be staff and nurses caring for you during your birth whom you likely have never met before and who have no idea of your plans. A simple page or two introducing yourself to the staff and outlining how you have prepared and what your preferences are for birth can be very helpful on all sides.

Write a birth plan and file it with your provider at a prenatal visit. While things don't always go according to plan, having it does make a huge difference. For instance, we've chosen not to give our babies Vitamin K and Hep B — that's on the plan, and they need to abide by it. When you are in pain, you're not in a clear head space, nor necessarily will your husband be. A birth plan increases your chances of things going how you'd like.
— Erin H., mom to ten on Earth and one in eternity

An effective birth plan will be concise, respectful, and flexible. Most staff don't have time to read pages of text and prefer a straightforward page they can quickly scan. A birth plan should always be read through beforehand by your provider at a prenatal appointment and given his or her okay, possibly even signed. Not only do you obviously want a provider who will respect and support your choices, but having that "approval" can quickly diffuse any nurse or staff member who may try to tell you that you cannot do something on your plan.

If you choose to write out a plan, keep in mind that people always respond better to positivity, respect, and kindness. Explaining your plan in a way that will encourage the staff to be on your team will better help you have the birth you want.

It is important also to be aware that things do not always go as planned. There are no guarantees in birth, and sometimes a birth plan needs to change. While it is good and prudent to prepare for your birth as best you can, being aware of the need to make changes and praying for peace and guidance when that is needed is important.

As a childbirth educator, here are my suggestions for birth plans:

1. If at all possible, take a birth class. And if I may be so bold as to suggest it, take an out-of-hospital birth class. Hospital classes are often better at preparing you to accept hospital routines than actually informing you about all your options. There are exceptions, of course, but that's largely been my experience.

2. Talk to your husband and dream up your ideal birth. How exactly would it go? After you've nailed that down, anchor it in reality. Most likely you won't be able to give birth in a seaside resort ... but you may be able to have a birth tub if your hospital offers it. At the very least you can close the blinds and play your favorite music on your phone to drown out the hospital din.

3. Talk to your doctor or midwife and find out what his other regular practices are and about the routine practices at your hospital. Find out how open your OB and the hospital are to your preferences and make concessions if you're able. It's okay to have nonnegotiables, but not everything should be nonnegotiable. Showing some flexibility might earn you some in return.

4. Write out your birth preferences. Follow these guidelines for maximum success:
- Keep it positive. Whenever possible, say what you want, not what you don't.
- Keep it short. One page, maximum, in a font style and size that are easy to read.
- Use bullet points and large, boldfaced type so busy nurses can skim it and know what is on it.

5. Bring the birth preferences sheet to your doctor. Have your doctor sign it and slip it in your file at about 36 weeks, and keep a copy for yourself. Actually, the copy you keep will be more useful as a reference to your husband; you might be a little busy during labor!

6. Prepare yourself for things to go differently than you dreamed up in No. 2. This is real life, after all, and birth is as wacky and unexpected as the rest of it. As Padre Pio said, "Pray, hope, and do not worry."
> — Micaela Darr, mom to seven on Earth and two in eternity, birth educator

---

If you are interested in writing out a birth plan, there are a variety of examples online from which to draw. Some sites even have printable forms that you can fill out.

The following sections will talk about some of the many choices for you and your baby during birth that may be worthy of consideration for your plan. While this book cannot go into every single option you have for each individual birth, we will talk through some of the larger ones most often encountered both during prenatal care and possibly during the labor and birth itself.

Specific Options and Interventions before Birth

Ultrasounds and Prenatal Testing

Ultrasounds have become increasingly common in obstetric care. The use of sound waves to obtain a picture of a baby is an amazing tool for diagnosis. The procedure is now often used to date pregnancies, to assess the baby's health, to help determine baby's position and estimate size, and sometimes just for fun. It has become common in the United States to have several ultrasounds done before a baby is born. It should be noted, however, that there have been no long-term studies on the effects of ultrasound use on the unborn baby. The American College of Obstetricians and Gynecologists (ACOG) states that adverse effects could be found in the future. Because of this, ultrasounds should only be used when medically indicated.[85] There is no requirement to have an ultrasound done, and they should be used with the understanding that they are not foolproof.

There are many stories of women given adverse diagnoses via ultrasound, whose babies turned out to be perfectly healthy. Even more are the stories of women who were given weight estimates of their baby that were a pound, two, or even three off. However, there are times when an ultrasound can indicate an anomaly that may require extra care or intervention for the health of mother or baby. In short, you should weigh the risks and benefits of ultrasound and make the choice for you and your baby that makes the most sense in your circumstances.

The amount of other fetal testing available to mothers continues to rise. There are now blood tests that can be done at eleven weeks that can determine gender and indicate signs for Down syndrome, Trisomy 18, and other conditions. You always have the right to refuse prenatal testing. From a Catholic perspective, *any testing chosen should only be done with the understanding that the life of the baby is not up for debate.* When faced with an adverse diagnosis, the majority of the medical community will recommend abortion, even if the diagnosis is not 100 percent accurate, and even if the condition is not always grave. A review of studies in the United States concluded that the mean abortion rate for babies diagnosed prenatally with Down syndrome was a horrific 67 percent, some hospitals reaching as high as 90 percent.[86] The purpose of any testing from a Christian perspective should only be at the service of the mother and baby. It should be used only to provide prenatal treatment or to identify any extra interventions or medical help that may be required immediately after birth to protect the mother or baby, or to identify where routine interventions might actually be detrimental to you or the baby.

Gender Reveals

If a you opt for the 18- to 20-week ultrasound, or if you have fetal anomaly blood testing done even earlier, you have the option of finding out the gender of your baby before birth. There is, of course, no right or wrong answer to this, and it is a matter of personal preference. Some families feel that it honors their baby and helps them bond with him or her if they know the gender beforehand and may even name the baby. They love being able to pray for and call the baby by name, or to prepare clothes and a gender-specific nursery beforehand, or even to prepare other children for their sibling. Others feel that it honors their baby and the original design of pregnancy and birth not to find out. They often love the surprise in the birthing room, the surprise to family and friends, and the beautiful mystery of it all. For some mothers, it can be a great motivation during labor! Some mothers feel strongly that they or their husband be the ones to announce the gender at the birth.

What *is* important from a Catholic perspective is recognizing the dignity and worth of the baby no matter the gender, and treating him or her as the beautiful and undeserved gift that he or she is. This baby's gender is specifically chosen by God and intrinsic to who he or she is. The Church is very clear on the equal dignity and worth of men and women, and one gender should never be seen as a greater blessing or better than another.

Vaginal Checks

You or your provider may want you to have vaginal checks as you approach your due date. This is done by the provider reaching his or her fingers into your vagina and feeling the position of the cervix, how low or high the baby is (the baby's station), how thinned out the cervix is (effacement), and estimating how open the cervix might be (dilation). While it is very tempting to want to know numbers and "progress," most providers will admit that, especially before labor begins, the state of your cervix at the time of this check doesn't mean a whole lot. You can be completely closed, with baby high and a thick cervix, and birth a baby that night. You can be dilated three or four centimeters with a low, engaged baby and stay that way for weeks. Many providers choose not to do cervical checks on women because of this. These checks don't tell us when the baby will be born, and in many cases can cause an expectation that doesn't come to fruition. Having another person's fingers in the birth canal also increases the risk of transmitting an infection to the mother and is usually fairly uncomfortable. There may be times when vaginal checks before labor are medically indicated or helpful in making decisions, but for the majority of women in a normal, healthy pregnancy, their use is not evidence-based.

During labor, especially in the hospital, providers often want to do vaginal checks to see how close a mother is to being fully dilated and ready to push. One reason for this is to make sure the mom is fully dilated. However, this is not usually necessary, and many providers simply wait until the mom naturally feels the urge to push and then go with that or check at that time. In the case of a woman who has had an epidural, though, a check will likely be more common since she often cannot feel how close she is or the natural urge to push may be compromised.

Another reason providers often conduct vaginal checks is simply to keep track of the mother's "progress." They want to know that her labor is continuing. However, every woman labors differently and not according to a timetable. A woman can stay at three centimeters for hours and then the labor takes off and she shoots up to transition in a half-hour. Or a woman can be at five centimeters when she gets to the hospital and those last few centimeters seem to take forever. As you labor, it's important to ask yourself whether you want to know how many centimeters you are and, if so, what you want to do with that information. What if the number is not what you are hoping for? Will it lead to frustration and an intervention you may not truly want? Vaginal checks increase the risk of infection (not only to mom, but to baby if her water has already broken), are very uncomfortable, and don't always give information that will help. However, they can be a good tool when used in a limited way by a wise provider.

It's important for you to know that you always have the right to refuse a vaginal check. You should also talk to your provider about his or her standard protocol for checks and decide whether you are okay with that, whether you would like to come to a compromise with the provider, or whether the provider is the right one for you.

Group B Strep

When you are close to your due date, your provider will likely do a vaginal culture to be analyzed for something called Group Beta Streptococcus. Group B Strep (or GBS) is a bacteria found in 10 to 30 percent of the population that can sometimes be present in the vagina.[87] If a woman has GBS present in her vagina at the time of birth, there is a small chance that the baby can pick it up through the amniotic fluid (after membranes rupture). When that happens, there is a 1 to 2 percent chance that the baby will contract a GBS infection.[88] In the United States, common protocol is to give antibiotics to a woman with a positive GBS culture during labor to kill the bacteria. Usually this is done with an IV. Other countries simply monitor the baby after birth for any symptoms, unless there are more risk factors present for transmission.

Hospitals usually want a GBS-positive mother to receive at least two doses of antibiotics through IV, usually given four hours apart. The use of antibiotics can lower the rates of transmission, but their use also means that the good bacteria that is present (and that the baby is supposed to pick up to help with digestion, gut health, and lung function after birth) also gets killed. Some women also react poorly to antibiotics, either immediately through an allergic reaction, or later on as it can increase the likelihood of yeast issues, urinary infections, and digestive issues.

Factors that can raise the risk of a GBS infection to a baby are preterm labor, how concentrated the bacteria is, the length of time the water is broken, temperature during labor, vaginal checks, and intrauterine fetal monitoring (where the baby is monitored in labor through a wire and electrode placed in the baby's scalp).[89] It makes sense that a woman whose amniotic sac stays intact longer or who has a shorter pushing phase (meaning the baby was in the birth canal for a shorter time) has a lower chance of picking up the bacteria. A woman who has a labor that is too quick or who doesn't get to the hospital in time may not have time for antibiotics. In that case, the baby can simply be observed for any unusual symptoms. So, if a woman finds out that she is GBS positive, she should know and weigh the risks and benefits of prophylactic antibiotic treatment and decide the course of action that is right for her.

There are also ways to promote good bacteria in the vagina beforehand to help fight against the chance for GBS. Taking a good probiotic during pregnancy helps fill the body and vagina with good bacteria that help control bad bacteria and has been shown to reverse a positive GBS culture in 43 percent of women by the time they give birth.[90] Fermented foods such as yogurt, kefir, and fermented vegetables also help balance the bacteria present in your body. There is evidence, too, that garlic and oregano supplements can help with a GBS colonization.

If you do have a positive GBS culture, consider asking your provider to do another one closer to the time of birth to get a more accurate result. Since GBS is a bacteria that can come and go from week to week or even day to day, we may well be treating women with antibiotics during labor who don't have GBS present (and vice versa). Some hospitals are beginning to test women during the actual labor rather than weeks before, allowing for more informed decisions. In the end, a woman needs to understand what GBS is, assess her risk (if any), know the risks and benefits of antibiotic treatment, and choose the course of action that makes the most logical sense in her situation. If you do have antibiotics during your labor, you should still have the option of requesting a hep lock (or port) rather than a direct IV line. This can then be disconnected in between doses, giving you more freedom of movement.

Gestational Diabetes

Gestational diabetes is a type of diabetes that can develop during pregnancy and goes away after birth. Like other forms of diabetes, it is an issue with the body improperly metabolizing blood sugar. In this case, the extra hormones created by the placenta are what are destabilizing insulin levels. The body creates insufficient amounts of insulin to handle the glucose (blood sugar) coming in, and the insulin/glucose levels become out of balance. Very often, but not always, gestational diabetes can be prevented through diet. Limiting refined grains, carbohydrates, and sugars, and eating sufficient amounts of protein lower the risk of gestational diabetes.

Most providers offer a diabetes screening in a woman's second trimester to assess how her body is metabolizing blood sugar. The common practice is for a woman to fast for a period of time, consume a large amount of glucose drink (the thick orange syrupy drink you may have heard about), and then have her blood sugar tested periodically during and after. Other providers use a much gentler approach and simply have a woman fast for a few hours, eat something high in carbohydrates and sugar (such as pancakes with whipped cream, a bit more delicious than the syrup!), and test her blood sugar after that.

Still other providers will encourage a woman to test on her own for several mornings using a glucometer while keeping to her standard diet. They feel that it makes more sense to base a test on a normal diet rather than artificially spiking her sugars with unhealthy food or drink she wouldn't necessarily be consuming. Some providers are active in helping a woman from the very beginning of pregnancy to choose healthy whole foods and only test for diabetes if there are risk factors or symptoms present. It is important for you as a mother to know that you have options, assess your personal risk, and decide with that in mind.

Gestational diabetes is a concern because it can affect the metabolism of the baby after birth, increase the risk of high blood pressure and even preeclampsia, and/or increase the risk of non-gestational type 2 diabetes for both mom and baby later in life. Primary treatment for gestational diabetes is usually diet. Often a woman who comes back with a "failed" gestational diabetes test will be sent for a longer, more in-depth test or simply be considered positive and sent home with a glucometer and dietary restrictions. Thankfully, most women can effectively control their blood sugar by monitoring sugar and carbohydrates they consume. If a woman is not able to control it through diet alone, she may be put on medication or insulin injections.

How does gestational diabetes affect your birth? Because the chance of a higher-weight baby goes up with gestational diabetes, many women face interventions they might not have otherwise, such as induction, or they may develop preeclampsia due to the diabetes. They may even be presented with the option of a planned cesarean for a suspected "big baby," though weight estimates via ultrasound are notoriously inaccurate. After birth, the baby will often be required by a hospital to have his or her blood sugar monitored. This is done through a prick in the heel that gives a few drops of blood. Thankfully, most babies are just fine, and the diabetes is gone after birth. Nursing their babies as soon as possible often is helpful for mothers with gestational diabetes, as it provides immediate glucose to counter any low blood sugar they may have.

Specific Options and Interventions during Labor

Inductions

It has become more and more common in the last several decades for labor to be artificially induced. While sometimes this is medically warranted, more often than not these inductions are not medically indicated and can increase the risk to both mother and baby. ACOG now admits that far too many women are induced for reasons that are not medically valid. According to ACOG's current recommendations, women should never be induced before forty-one weeks without a strong medical indication.[91] Reaching the due date, easy scheduling, or just wanting the pregnancy to be over are not considered medical reasons. The risks of an artificial induction include but are not limited to: a longer time of labor, harder contractions, anesthesia use (which has its own risk), distress to baby, and an increase in the likelihood of a cesarean section. An artificial induction can also interfere with the hormone interplay present with a natural onset of labor.

A mother presented with the option of induction should fully understand the reasons it is being proposed. She has a right to know whether those reasons are medically valid, what her other options might be (there are ways to encourage labor that are less invasive and without risk), and that she has the right to decline. If she is seriously considering the induction, she can also ask her provider what her Bishop score is and take that information into account for her decision. A Bishop score is a number calculated through a vaginal exam, which assesses the baby's station and the softness, effacement, and any dilation of the cervix. A woman with a high Bishop score (usually about 8) has a much greater likelihood of having a successful induction than a woman with a low score (usually below 5).[92]

There is much more that can be said about inductions, and it is advisable for you to know and research well before submitting to one. While an induction can be used well and wisely for your good and that of your baby, it should be absolutely certain that it is being done for a valid medical reason, and the decision to induce should not be made lightly.

If it is in your best interest or best for your baby that he or she come out sooner, there are a few natural ways with less intervening that you may want to consider. Sexual intercourse is usually the first recommendation. Not only can the flood of oxytocin from orgasm cause contractions, but semen actually has prostaglandins, which help to soften the cervix. Another way is to take brisk walks or get some exercise in. Spicy foods, eggplant, or certain herbs have often been said to trigger labor, though there is not a lot of evidence to cite.

If a woman's cervix is soft and effaced enough, her provider can attempt a "membrane sweep," where the provider sweeps his or her fingers around the inside of the cervix to separate the amniotic sac from the uterine walls. This is not comfortable and also holds risks, but it can release hormones that kick-start labor. Sometimes a few teaspoons of castor oil taken orally can cause abdominal contractions and clean out the woman's system, which may trigger uterine contractions. This often isn't pleasant and should only be considered as a "natural last resort," best done in communication with your provider as it can also potentially increase risk.

"Speeding Up" Labor with Pitocin

Even when birth is not started by a medical induction, often providers or nurses will want to intervene during a labor with extra Pitocin to "speed things up." The use of Pitocin may indeed speed up labor and birth, but it will augment the contractions, usually making them stronger, longer, and more painful. It can also interfere with the natural endorphins released by the brain to handle natural labor. There sometimes may be a reason to do this, but in most cases, unless there is a medical need for the baby to be born sooner, there should be no time limit for labor. If mom and baby are both handling things well, it's often best to let them do things on their own time. The use of Pitocin will also necessitate an IV, extra fetal monitoring because of the now increased risk, and limited movement. The increased intensity of the contractions also makes anesthesia more likely, thus leading to further interventions and risks.

It is good to know beforehand how you would like to approach the subject of augmenting labor to speed things up. Talk with your provider about why he or she would suggest that. Some providers routinely give Pitocin or break a woman's water to hasten birth, while others remain very hands off. The research shows that, unless there is a medical reason to quicken labor and birth, mothers and babies do better when their labor is left alone.[93]

IVs

Some providers and hospitals require that all women in labor have an IV line placed. Sometimes it is because they are actively receiving medication, but other times it is merely a precaution to make administering medication easier should an emergency arise or medication become needed. If an IV is currently unnecessary, however, having it in and receiving unnecessary saline can be painful and also means that you are now unnecessarily tethered to an IV pole during labor and birth. You'll have to drag it with you to the bathroom or to walk the halls. If your provider or hospital requires an IV, you can request a hep lock rather than the direct IV. A hep lock, also called a port, is a line into the hand or arm that can quickly attach to an IV should it be needed. The line is ready to be used if necessary but is not hooked up to anything permanently, so you can still walk around uninhibited, allowing freer movement to get into whatever positions are most comfortable for you. ACOG currently states that an IV is not necessary for most women in spontaneous labor.[94]

Rupture of Membranes

If your water does release before active labor, it is a good idea to let your provider know. He or she may ask if the fluid is "clear" and make sure that there is no meconium (the baby's first bowel movement) or active bleeding present. If the fluid is clear, there is no need for panic or an immediate rush to the hospital. You have the choice to wait for labor to begin or labor at home until you feel active labor is beginning. Many providers may want to "speed things up" or intervene with Pitocin if you arrive before the onset of active labor. Once your water releases, many providers will have you on a timeline in which they want the baby born. For some it is twenty-four hours; for others, thirty-six or more. The reason for this is primarily because the amniotic sac is no longer completely protecting the baby from infection. Most women will go into labor naturally in the first twelve hours after the membranes rupture. When that doesn't happen, according to ACOG, unless there is a reason to intervene, a woman with ruptured membranes and no immediate labor should be given the option of monitored waiting ("expectant management") versus immediate admission and induction.[95]

If there is no sign of infection in you or baby, it is usually fine to let things happen as your body decides. However, if there is anything concerning, such as fever or meconium present, intervention may be of merit. Some providers may want to use antibiotics, some may want Pitocin to strengthen contractions, and some may possibly recommend a cesarean if there is significant meconium present and the baby's heart rate is concerning. Limiting vaginal checks can decrease the risk of passing any bacteria to the baby. If the water has released and labor doesn't seem to be starting on its own, you may want to consider plenty of walking, movement, nipple stimulation, or other natural means of prompting contractions (sex is not recommended if the water has broken). Again, it is wise and recommended to keep your provider in the loop and make the decision that makes the most sense in your circumstance.

If the water hasn't released, sometimes a provider will offer to break your water as a way to start labor or, if labor is well under way, as a way to quicken it. He or she uses a long hook called an amniohook to tear a hole in the membrane. It's important to weigh this carefully. While it can start labor, it also now removes that protection for the baby and starts that timeline, so it's not a decision to take lightly. During labor, while it can quicken birth for some women, a recent Cochrane review showed that the evidence does not support it as a routine practice and that it can even cause complications in a birth.[96] The procedure also removes the cushion surrounding the contraction and can intensify the pain so that a mother who was managing well before has a much more difficult time. This should be a choice made by you, and a provider should never break a woman's water during a vaginal check without the mother's consent.

Electronic Fetal Monitoring

At most hospitals in the United States it is standard protocol, once you arrive in labor and are admitted, to place you and your baby on a continuous monitor that tracks the baby's heartbeat and the intensity of your contractions. Despite evidence that this monitoring does not improve outcomes, often these monitors are required continuously for every birth, regardless of the specific situation of the mother and baby.[97] Two monitors are strapped to the mother's belly and wired to a machine that tracks information. This information is usually then fed to a machine in the room and the nurse's station outside the room. Some hospitals are now providing wireless monitors so they can fulfill their protocol while giving the mother a bit more freedom to move around, use the bathroom freely, or take a shower or get in the tub without worrying about wires. Evidence continues to show that with a normal labor and birth, periodic monitoring via a doppler or fetoscope (monitoring methods) is just as effective in keeping mother and baby healthy as the continuous monitoring. Even ACOG agrees that such intermittent monitoring is perfectly safe.[98] Its newest recommendations state that, for a woman in spontaneous labor, continuous monitoring does not protect the baby more than intermittent monitoring, and a woman should be given the option of that limited monitoring.[99] This periodic monitoring is often the approach used in other countries or home births.

A drawback of continuous electronic fetal monitoring is that it may replace more personalized care. The nurses and staff (and even the mother herself) can become fixated on the monitors. Labor is evaluated by machines rather than by looking at the woman in the room and listening to what she is feeling and the cues she is giving. It is not uncommon for monitors to indicate an issue that is not actually a problem, resulting in interventions that may not be truly needed. In fact, the use of continuous electronic fetal monitoring has actually been shown to increase the rates of pain medications, the use of vacuum and forceps, and cesarean surgery compared with intermittent monitoring, thus actually complicating normal births.[100]

The use of the internal monitor in instances when it is not necessary is also concerning, as it involves a fine needle inserted into the baby's scalp which may cause pain to the baby, and increases the risk of infection to the baby. While the evidence shows that in a normal labor and birth continuous monitoring does not improve outcomes, it is commonly seen as more important for a labor and birth that have been augmented or induced, as the risks to the baby are now higher. If you are hoping for a non-induced, normal labor and birth, you can speak with your provider about the way he or she normally monitors you and the baby and the options you have.

Food and Drink

In a normal labor, there shouldn't be any issue with eating and drinking for low-risk mothers. In fact, it's incredibly important to be well hydrated during such a physical process. Imagine running a marathon without water! However, there are still providers and hospitals who require that a mother in active labor not be allowed to eat or drink (although ice and Popsicles are often exceptions). Their reasoning is that, in case full anesthesia needs to be administered for an emergency, any food or drink could be aspirated and a risk to the mother. However, according to current research, those fears are now unfounded and low-risk women can be free to eat and drink in labor. Many argue that it's a far greater risk to deny a mother food and hydration for hours or even days, compromising her energy and blood sugar, thus increasing the length of her labor, affecting her energy levels for pushing, and increasing the chance of that emergency cesarean happening.[101]

The American Society of Anesthesiologists has even stated that a light meal would benefit most women in labor and that hospital practices should change to allow this.[102] The most recent recommendations of ACOG also state that women in early labor should be allowed to drink.[103] Many women don't want to eat during labor, but it is important to stay hydrated and nourished. A small snack can provide energy needed to keep going when labor becomes exhausting. Talk with your provider beforehand about rules concerning eating and drinking during labor, and make sure they are evidence-based. If you are going with a hospital or provider who doesn't want you eating or drinking during labor, make sure you have gotten some good nourishment and hydration before you get to the hospital.

Walking/Moving Around

Women who have greater ease of movement, unrestricted by IVs and fetal monitors, are able to work with their body, using instinctual movements to stretch the cervix and help the baby rotate and descend down the birth canal. It is only in the last century that women have been routinely required to be monitored. Restricting movement ignores a mother's need to walk, move, dance, and sway however she is compelled, and this can greatly affect her experience and the outcome of the birth. It makes sense to allow a woman as much movement as she needs to help her baby out. If you are birthing in the hospital, do everything you can to maintain the ability to move.

What to Wear

If you are birthing in a hospital, it is usually common to wear a hospital gown when you are admitted and in labor. Some women will have absolutely no problem wearing the gown, while others may prefer to bring their own clothes. If wearing something familiar and more comfortable helps you to relax and feel more "normal" then, by all means, do that. There is no medical need to wear a hospital gown, as long as you choose clothing that can be easily removed. A stretchy knee-length jersey skirt is a popular choice for some women, since it provides coverage but is open at the bottom and easy to move in. At a certain point, you will obviously need to take off any underwear or pants, and it is helpful to have a top that can be removed easily for skin-to-skin contact and breastfeeding after the baby is born. Many moms, whether in their own clothes or in a gown, like to bring their own slippers or socks and a robe to use during and after birth.

Pushing Options

If you are familiar with most popular media portrayals of birth, you would think that the only way a mother can give birth is lying flat on her back, her legs in the air, a doctor between her legs, and pushing until she is purple. But, in a normal uncomplicated birth, a woman can give birth in any position that is comfortable for her at the time. As a doula, I've been at births where women push out their babies on their hands and knees, on a birth stool, using a squat bar over a bed, lying on their side, or even standing with support. There is no intrinsic need for a woman to be on her back, and one of the chief reasons this is most often seen is because it is more convenient for the provider to see what is happening.

Forgive the visual, but consider the logic of trying to have a bowel movement while lying flat on your back. Would that be easier or harder? Does it make sense to be pressured into that position for birth? While some women might prefer that position, a woman should be able to work with what her body is doing and get in whatever position is most comfortable. Choosing the position that works best for you also gives you the benefit of working with gravity rather than against it, putting less pressure on the perineum and decreasing the likelihood of a tear.

If you would like to be able to push out your baby in whatever way you feel is best, make sure your provider is comfortable with that and won't try to pressure you into lying down if you don't want to. You can even practice some of those positions before the birth to see what feels right to you. Many midwives and now even hospitals provide squatting bars that can attach to a bed or a birth stool (a short, u-shaped "chair" that allows you to sit while also giving baby room to come out).

The newest guidelines from ACOG state that unless there is a reason to speed up the birth, the mother should be allowed to wait until she feels the urge to push rather than being forced to push as soon as she reaches ten centimeters, respecting that natural rest that some women are given before pushing.[104] Some women like to be talked through pushing and given direction, but many women prefer not to be coached or "counted" through pushing. The provider should respect whatever way works better for that particular mother.

Episiotomies and Tears

There was a time in U.S. birth practice when women were routinely given an episiotomy just before or during pushing. An episiotomy is a cut made by the doctor into the perineum of the woman (the skin between her vagina and anus) to increase space and decrease the pushing time for the mother. It was defended as a way to prevent tearing of that tissue so that repairs would be easier. However, a growing body of evidence has shown that episiotomies do not prevent tearing and, in fact, can make them much worse, more severe, and contribute to major pelvic-floor dysfunction.[105] Most hospitals and providers no longer do routine episiotomies, but there are still some, so be sure your provider adheres to the evidence and does not routinely give them. An episiotomy should only be used if the baby's life is jeopardized.

Tearing can sometimes happen during the pushing stage of birth. Pushing quickly without giving the perineal tissue enough time to stretch can contribute to tears that will need to be stitched. The best way to prevent tearing is to push gently and slowly, following the lead of your body, not forcing it. Squatting and Kegel exercises while pregnant can also strengthen the perineal muscle and tissues so that tearing is less likely. Different positions during pushing, such as squatting or getting on your hands and knees rather than lying on your back, can also prevent tearing. Some providers may try to prevent tearing by using massage or hot compresses and counter pressure on the perineum while the baby is crowning. That can help, but you have the right to decide if you would like those measures taken or not.

If you do tear, you may need to have stitches placed after the birth. The provider will often use lidocaine or something similar to numb the area (if you do not have an epidural) and do the repair. Your perineum will be tender with the stitches and will need extra care during recovery. Herbal baths, witch hazel, and ice packs can help heal the area. A squirt bottle with warm water, sprayed on the area when you need to urinate, will make things much easier. Your midwife, doctor, or nurse should help you know how to take care of the stitches and skin properly so that it will heal well.

Cord Clamping

One of the routine interventions that has been slowly changing in the current model of birth is when the umbilical cord is cut. Standard practice for decades was to clamp and cut the umbilical cord as soon as the baby landed in the hands of the doctor. Many providers still do this, but there are several compelling reasons to consider delaying the cutting of the cord. In fact, ACOG has recently changed its position due to the evidence and is now advising that the cord not be clamped until at least thirty to sixty seconds.[106] The World Health Organization (WHO) recommends even longer, saying that it is optimal to wait "more than one minute after the birth or when cord pulsation has ceased. Delaying cord clamping allows blood flow between the placenta and neonate to continue, which may improve iron status in the infant for up to six months after birth."[107] Most people advocating for delayed clamping wait anywhere from three to ten minutes, or simply watch and cut only when the cord is completely limp.

The umbilical cord pumps blood into the baby from the placenta, and at the moment of birth there is still up to one-third of the baby's blood held in the placenta. Cutting right away thus deprives the baby of up to one-third of his or her own blood. This blood is rich in stem cells, oxygen, and iron. Babies whose cords are not cut right away have higher iron levels immediately and up to six months compared with babies who did not get that blood.[108] Another reason to wait to clamp and cut the cord is because the baby, after birth, is in the midst of transitioning to breathing air. Until that moment, the baby has received all of his or her oxygen through the umbilical cord. The cord supplements that oxygen until the transition to lung breathing is completely made. This can be vital to babies whose birth was more difficult or whose breathing has been compromised. Other countries have developed emergency carts for these babies that sidle right up to the bed of the mother, allowing the cord to remain attached to the mother while baby is given extra medical help.[109]

Yet another reason many mothers choose to wait to clamp and cut the cord for a few minutes is because it is rich in stem cells. Scientists are only beginning to understand the potency and power of stem cells. In fact, stem cells have such power that there are companies in the business of freezing and banking the cord blood of the baby on the chance that it can help cure the child of future potential diseases. Many mothers and providers feel that perhaps it is best to allow the baby to have all of his or her stem cells at the moment of birth, as he or she was meant to, increasing long-term health and vitality and maybe even preventing diseases, though that has yet to be proven.

Delayed cord clamping usually means waiting until the cord stops pulsating (until there is no longer a pulse felt in the cord pumping blood to the baby). As the blood pumps into the baby, the thick, almost gelatinous cord becomes thinner and thinner, and the pulse weaker. The pulsing usually stops five to ten minutes after birth, although many parents prefer to wait until the cord is completely limp and void of almost all blood. One side benefit of waiting to cut the cord is that it slows down the rush at some hospitals and among some providers to take the baby for weight, measurement, and cleaning. Since the baby is still attached to mom, he or she can stay with her on her chest, and other non-vital exams and procedures wait.

If you do decide that you would like to wait on cutting the cord, make sure your husband, doula, and provider know about this beforehand. You will be busy in the tremendous work of having your baby, and it can be their job to remind the provider not to cut the cord right away.

Skin-to-Skin

Evidence now overwhelmingly supports the practice of placing a naked baby directly on his or her mother's chest for skin-to-skin contact immediately after birth (provided, of course, that there are no concerns with the baby or mother). Most home births have always done this, and many hospitals are now taking steps toward helping more babies and mothers receive this "golden hour" of uninterrupted time together. The first few moments and hours after birth are incredibly complex physiologically for both mother and baby, and we don't fully understand much of what is really happening in those precious moments. We do know that the more immediately the baby can be placed right up near the mother, and the longer he or she can stay there, the better. This provides for a less distressed baby (he or she knows and recognizes your smell, your voice, your heartbeat) as his or her temperature and breathing is naturally regulated by yours.

Having your baby given to you immediately not only respects your natural right as his or her mother, but enables you to release more oxytocin, bonding you to baby and working to release your placenta, contract your uterus, and control bleeding. Baby is able to nurse as soon as he or she can, and that additional oxytocin works to help you with the third stage of labor and in recovery. Babies who are given to their mothers and held skin to skin are calmer and feel safer. There is no need for baby to be whisked away for weighing, shots, full exams, footprints, washing, or anything else during this time. All of that can wait as you and baby get to see each other for the first time. The midwife or nursery staff can simply and easily assess the vitals of the baby while he or she is on your chest and make sure that everyone is healthy. Your choice to have this time should never be interfered with unless the baby's health or yours is truly in jeopardy. This skin-to-skin contact is not only important in those first few hours, but human touch is vitally important for the baby's overall development for days, weeks, and months after birth, and it has been shown to have long-term importance for premature and low birthweight babies.[110]

The Placenta

More often than not, the hospital or your provider will take the placenta of your baby and dispose of it in whatever way they see fit, either incinerating it, selling it, or donating it. However, many mothers are choosing to keep their placenta to consume, either by encapsulation or ingested in other ways. Their reasoning is that every other mammal on Earth consumes the placenta shortly after birth, and there may be physiological reasons why it is beneficial to human mothers and babies as well. It is thought to replace iron and restore the balance of hormones to the mother, giving her an easier recovery and warding off postpartum depression. There are professionals who will take the placenta and encapsulate it in pill form to be taken postpartum, or saved for menopause. Some may never be comfortable with this idea, but it is an option many mothers are taking, which they certainly have the right to do. It is important to know, though, that there is little research on benefits and possible risks of this practice.

Other mothers choose to bury the placenta rather than have it burned or sold to pharmaceutical and cosmetic companies, which many hospitals do. While this is not required, it is certainly in line with Catholic teaching on respect for the body and its parts. When possible, burial is the preferred way to treat amputated limbs, so it seems fitting that the placenta, with its crucial role, be treated similarly.[111] A mother may also choose to donate her placenta for legitimate and moral research purposes in accord with the Church's teaching on organ donation.

Should I Choose Medicated Pain Relief?

While the option for narcotic or anesthetic pain relief during labor in a hospital is valid, a growing concern is that most women are not fully informed of all the benefits and risks of the decision. Yes, you sign a lot of papers when you get to the hospital, many of which say that you give assent to treatment and understand there is risk involved, but often that is simply a legal formality. Rare is the mother who (while in labor or otherwise) chooses to read through all the paperwork. Unless you have taken the time before birth to inform yourself of your options, it is difficult to give truly informed consent, yet it is imperative to a positive birth experience to know the options and make a truly informed choice.

If you make a well-informed decision for medicated pain relief, there is no need for guilt or shame. While there are many benefits to a completely natural labor, there are most certainly times when a well-timed epidural or the use of medication can be a useful tool for a birth. There is no moral implication from the decision to use medicine for pain relief if you discern that it is best for you in your situation.

The Epidural

In the United States most women who desire pain medication during birth choose an epidural. An epidural is a line of medication inserted between the disks of the spine that numbs the lower body. You may feel some pressure and sensations but, depending on the strength of the epidural as well as the skill of the anesthesiologist, you will no longer feel most of what is happening. While that brings relief from the pain, it also means that you can no longer walk around and are tethered to the epidural line and the IV line. With a full epidural, most common in the United States, you will not be able to get out of bed. It is then much harder to work with instinct and the natural sensations of the body that help get the baby out. This restricted movement means that you are less able to work with gravity or get into different positions and move around to help dilate the cervix. An epidural can often slow labor, leading to Pitocin use, and increases the chance of baby being put in distress.

Some Benefits of the Epidural
- Partial to full pain relief
- An exhausted mother having a long labor can get a chance to rest and even sleep
- For a mother struggling with severe tension or fear during labor, it can sometimes help her body relax enough to dilate

Some Risks of the Epidural
- Sharp decrease in blood pressure for mom (which in turn, can affect blood supply to the baby)
- Allergic reaction to the medication
- Increase in the use of oxygen
- An ineffective epidural where the anesthetic does not relieve all pain
- The need for a catheter, which increases the risk of a urinary-tract infection and bruising and soreness of the urethra
- Baby's heart can respond poorly (the reason for continuous fetal monitoring)
- Prolonged labor
- Shivering
- Nausea
- Increased risk of cesarean section
- Longer pushing stage since the mother can't feel how to push and often pushes ineffectively
- Higher use of forceps or vacuum on the baby during pushing
- Increase in use of episiotomy during pushing
- Increased time until mother is able to get up and walk around after birth
- Spinal headache after birth caused by a leakage in spinal fluid
- Permanent nerve damage at the site of the epidural catheter
- Long-term back pain[112]

Some mothers may have none of these issues upon receiving an epidural, while others can check off almost everything on the list. The important thing to know is that the risk is present, and it is only by having the information and applying that information that you can make the best decision for your personal circumstances.

If you decide to have an epidural, your nurse and the anesthesiologist will be the ones with you as it is administered. Often you will need to receive a bag of IV fluids beforehand. In most cases, all other people are required to leave the room as you get it, including your husband and doula, and it normally takes twenty to thirty minutes to complete. You will be asked to remain completely still and curve your spine as the anesthesiologist inserts the needle, and through that, the tiny tube will be inserted that will keep the medication flowing into your body. Once you have the epidural, you will be almost completely numb from the waist down. Your uterus will still, hopefully, be contracting, but you won't feel it. It is extremely helpful for the nurse, your husband, or your doula to help you flip from side to side every so often to help facilitate the descent of the baby and the opening of the cervix. They can also help by keeping you well hydrated with water. It is helpful to place a birth peanut (like a big exercise ball but in the shape of a peanut) between your legs to keep your pelvis open while you are in bed.

Because of the added risk, an epidural requires continuous monitoring of the baby's heart to ensure that he or she is tolerating it well. Depending on your circumstances, you should still have the option of turning the epidural down or off, should you so choose. Some women like to have the epidural turned down when they are ready to push in order to better feel and work with the contraction. Shortly after the baby is born, the epidural will be turned off, and it usually will take an hour or two to regain feeling in the waist and legs.

Narcotic Pain Relief

Another option for medicated pain relief in the hospital is through IV medications. The reason epidurals are usually offered before these is because these other drugs carry a greater risk to the baby. A greater amount of these medications cross the placenta and reach the baby, resulting in babies that are born with these drugs still in their systems. Babies who have received drugs such as Nubain, Stadol, and others during labor are more likely to have breathing issues after birth, be lethargic, and not nurse well.[113] Some mothers choose this option because it does work to dull the pain but affects the actual labor less than an epidural. They can still move around and have less risk of causing more interventions. However, many women report that the drugs make them feel "high," nauseated, or in a fog, and the drugs can even cause hallucinations.

Laughing Gas (Nitrous Oxide)

While not in common use in the United States, women in Europe and Canada often have the availability of nitrous oxide, or laughing gas, during labor. Breathed in through a mask, this option does not pass to the baby and provides some pain relief for the mother. It is less risky than other methods (though there is concern if a mother has a genetic MTHFR mutation). It does not interfere with the mother's movement or labor, though it does cause the mother to feel a little "high." The effect wears off more quickly but is easily re-administered.

Sterile Water Injections

Another not very common practice, used in other countries and sometimes in the United States, is sterile water injections. This is most commonly used for a mother who is experiencing difficult back labor. A provider or anesthesiologist uses simple sterile water and injects it into four spots in her lower back. These injections, done correctly, can greatly relieve back labor with nearly zero risk to the mother or baby.

....

While we've talked about a lot of decisions to be made before or during birth, this is not meant to be a comprehensive list, nor is it meant to replace open and evidence-based discussion between you and a good provider. There are many other options and choices available during your pregnancy and birth that are worth thinking about but fall outside the scope of this book. Again, a good birth class or a doula who knows the local scene in your community can help you walk through those choices and make decisions that are right for you and your baby.

No matter what, know that you have dignity and worth, and your provider and anyone else working with you during your pregnancy and birth should always respect your freedom and ability to make your own choices. You always have the right to say no, and you always have the right to good, factual information. Your consent should be of highest priority to the people you are asking to be present at your birth.

Our choices in birth matter. A lot. Of course they do.
Every choice has a consequence, and we should make
the best ones we can in our own circumstances and have
accurate information to make them. The moms I teach
and doula make all different choices, but what's most
important is that they know what options they have, take
into account their values and personal situations, and
have the support and correct information needed to make

the choices right for them. Know your options, learn about them, pick a provider who will truly respect them, and remember that you have the natural right to make these choices for yourself and your baby.

— Lauren G., mom to five on Earth and one in eternity, birth doula, and educator

14

GRACE-FILLED BIRTH: INVITING GOD INTO THE BIRTH ROOM

"I appeal to you therefore, brethren, by the mercies of God, to present your bodies as a living sacrifice, holy and acceptable to God, which is your spiritual worship."
— *Romans 12:1*

Whether you birth at home or in the hospital under the care of a midwife or obstetrician, or whether the birth is surgical or vaginal, natural or medicated, you have the opportunity to bring your relationship with Christ and your faith into birth. His grace is always available, perhaps especially in these transformative moments of womanhood. It is a beautiful thing when he and his work are openly recognized in the birth room. As we meet our little ones for the first time, this fruit of our union with our husband, this baby whom we've grown and loved for months, we see not only our child, but a child who is even more so God's.

We can ask God to be profoundly present in this work of birth, allowing the Holy Spirit to cover the room and work actively within us as we birth. There are many ways that we as mothers can tangibly do this. There is no requirement to do any of this, and each woman's unique relationship with God will manifest differently, but I hope some or all of the suggestions here will be helpful as you enter your unique birth experience.

The Prayer of Birth

Before we talk about "extra" ways to bring prayer into the birth room, remember that your birth itself can be a deep and powerful prayer. Our bodies are designed to give glory to God, and they speak a language on their own. Your act of birth, however you experience it, can therefore be a prayer and offering to God. You simply need to will it, offering this act of birth back to him as an act of surrender, worship, and praise.

This "willing" of birth as a prayer doesn't necessarily mean that you will undergo heightened spiritual awareness or ecstasies. It is important to be careful of accepting the lie that holiness is supposed to look or feel a certain way. The power of our prayer lies in our trust and faith that God's promises and revelation are true. Our bodily prayer of birth can be offered in union with the suffering Christ, who laid down his life and knows the spiritual and physical test that these moments can be. Our Lord made a choice, willed to offer his life, and even agonized beforehand. He didn't feel all warm and fuzzy about it, and certainly not through it. For our births, we don't need to feel a certain way before or during to make birth a beautiful sacrifice and prayer. Simply making an act of the will turns our births into something holy.

Still, there are ways to be even more intentional about your time of birth. Below are a few specific ways you can enter it even more fully.

Prayer Intentions

As Catholics we believe we can offer up our pain and suffering as a prayer, uniting it with Christ on the cross. Childbirth visibly shows — as no other bodily work can — that the fruit of suffering is new life. The time of labor and birth is a wide-open invitation from Christ to take a share in Christ's sufferings and use it to bring new life, not only to our babies but to the world.[114] Imagine the incredible fruit for the world if every mother intentionally united those powerful moments of birth to the sufferings of Christ!

Before birth, some women make a list of prayer intentions. You can choose to assign a prayer intention to each contraction, maybe listing them in the order of importance so that as your labor intensifies so do the needs. Your doula or husband can go down the list and read each new intention with each contraction, you can simply look at it yourself, or, if things are very intense, just unite your will with whatever is on the page. God knows. If you have one big intention on your heart, offer the entire labor up for that. A cesarean birth also gives plenty of opportunity during and after for the same type of offering. A doula or your husband can read your intentions before and during the surgery, and you can have the list close by, referring to it during the extra moments of pain and recovery that a cesarean entails.

With my first two, I viewed the natural childbirth process as a physical challenge to be conquered. Run a marathon, check. Natural childbirth, check. It wasn't until I was expecting my third that I began to think of it in terms of an opportunity for suffering that I could offer up for myself and others. And, really, what better opportunity could there be? Childbirth is an intense physical suffering, but for a finite amount of time and without lasting trauma (for me, so far). Plus, you get an extraordinary payoff at the end.

Even with my first two births, before I had a concept of redemptive suffering, I willingly endured the physical pain of childbirth in order to (a) have a baby and (b) not be pregnant anymore. But with my third, I was able to prayerfully add another dimension to the experience that really made it richer and more meaningful for me, even though I would point to that as my most painful birth experience. I have been blessed with excellent physical health. Pregnancy and labor are my big chance to attempt to unite my suffering to Christ on the cross.

— Kendra Tierney, mom to nine

Praying the Scriptures

There are plenty of Scriptures that are powerful in the birth room. Consider printing out several verses that speak to you and reading them or having them read to you during the birth. Or choose one verse that becomes your "birthing verse" to return to over and over during the birth. (There is a list of appropriate birth Scriptures included in Appendix B.) You can also have an entire list ready during birth, and your doula or husband can choose which one might be most helpful at the time. There are Scriptures that speak to the times when we are afraid, when we need encouragement, when we need to refocus, or when we ought to pray in thanksgiving. There is a unique and mighty power in the Word of God that can give us the strength we need when things become difficult, and these verses offer extraordinary graces to sanctify or even change the course of a birth.

Every week we hear the words "This is my body given up for you," and those words touched my heart in a way I could never have imagined before and during my cesareans, when I chose to offer my body, to take on so many risks and unknowns, all for the love of someone I had yet to meet.

— Molly W., mom to two on Earth and four in eternity

Calling upon the Saints

Our brothers and sisters in heaven, who are able to see things from an eternal perspective, are united with us, praying for us and our babies during this precious time. We can unite with them more fully by praying a litany of saints during labor, having images of our patron saints in the birth room, or calling upon specific favorite saints for help. There are dozens of women saints who experienced labor and birth and who can be especially helpful. In Appendix A is a link to a Litany for Laboring Mothers that includes a long list of sisters in heaven who experienced childbirth and can empathize and intercede for us while we birth. The Communion of Saints extends to all who are already in heaven or in purgatory awaiting heaven. Based on this teaching, we can also ask prayers from family and friends who have died or even from previously miscarried children. This connection can be especially poignant to a mother during her birth.

When active labor begins, I run like a little girl to the Blessed Mother. My husband leads me in a Rosary and I pray, "Mama, please wrap me and baby in your mantle and carry us over the waves when they come." Then I'm ready to cross the sea to meet my little one.

— Melody Lyons, mom to eight on Earth
and one in eternity

The Rosary, Chaplet, and Other Traditional Prayers

Many moms appreciate praying the Rosary or even just holding one during birth. The Joyful and Sorrowful Mysteries are especially appropriate during birth. I vividly remember praying the Rosary with my husband while I was in labor with my third baby. As the labor intensified, I was less and less able to pray out loud, but he compensated and prayed through the parts I couldn't. It was such a beautiful moment in our marriage. As soon as we were done, the midwife arrived and soon I was pushing out a baby. Looking back, it was as though the whole event was sanctified by those prayers prayed together. The nice thing about the Rosary and other memorized prayers during labor is that you don't have to think much about what you are going to say. Your heart and soul can mean the prayers, and the words still have meaning while your physical energy is absorbed in the work of labor.

While on the way to the hospital, I shared on social media that prayers were needed and asked that everyone please pray for trust and peace in his will for us. One friend, whom I've never met in person but have connected with via social media, thanks be to God, sent me a private message and shared the Prayer to Our Lady of La Leche, which was exactly what my heart and soul needed. Reading and praying this prayer while sitting in a hospital bed waiting for my OB-GYN helped me to get to a place of prayer and trust rather than fear, anxiety, and frenzy. Forcing myself to read these words forced my soul to look up to find him, who has never left me in life before. I needed those words. I needed this prayer.

— Amanda Perales, mom to three

The Divine Mercy Chaplet is another option. It's prayed on rosary beads, but the prayers are much shorter. For both the Chaplet and the Rosary, the repetitive nature of the prayers can help you meditate and foster the relaxation that is more conducive to labor and birth. Another choice is to have an audio rendition of the Rosary or Chaplet playing in the background as you labor. Then you can enter into it as you are able, and, even if you cannot pray, it clothes the birth room in that prayer.

I definitely benefited from listening to Fr. Benedict Groeschel's audio recording of "The Rosary Is a Place." Not only was the prayer comforting and his voice so peaceful; there is also a song that repeats throughout that goes, "I can't do it alone, but I can do it with you," and that really helped to focus me.

— Amanda D., mom to four

Music

Many women love to listen to music when in labor. Some hospitals even offer the option of music playing during a cesarean birth. Music has power to change the environment and move our souls (either positively or negatively). While any music that helps you relax and feel more comfortable is beneficial and worthy, choosing sacred or praise and worship music can become a vehicle for prayer. For some, singing or simply listening and meditating upon the songs that stir our hearts is a favorite way to pray, and that certainly can apply during labor and birth. If that resonates with you, consider making a playlist of your favorite songs that could provide help, beauty, and focus during birth. And don't forget to bring whatever player you may need to make it happen.

During three of my pregnancies, there was specific music that I would listen to during the third trimester. Once it was Gregorian chant, another time it was the soundtrack to the Saint Bakhita movie, and most recently it was from a Christian pop artist. I made sure to bring that music with me when I was in labor, and it really helped me focus during hard contractions near the time of transition. The music had a very powerful way of bringing me mentally and prayerfully into a focused state.

— Janelle Horn, mom to six on Earth and four in eternity

Spontaneous Prayer

Prayers during birth don't have to be planned or organized, or even very elaborate. These are the spontaneous movements of our hearts to God during birth. Sometimes it's the whispered words of a husband over his wife as he asks for strength and blessing and help. Sometimes it is the words mumbled throughout a contraction or at a moment of decision. Most often it is words that spring naturally to your lips or heart as you near the end and find yourself silently or loudly begging for God's help and strength. As Saint Thérèse said, "For me prayer is an upward leap of the heart, an untroubled glance towards heaven, a cry of gratitude and love, which I utter from the depths of sorrow as from the heights of joy."[115]

It's worth noting that it is quite common for women, even atheists, at some point during a natural labor to call upon God. Most often during transition, many women will begin to chant or moan through the Lord's name — either "Oh, God" or the name of Jesus. Granted, it may not always be with the most willed reverence, and sometimes (on the outside at least) it appears exactly the opposite. But I believe it tells us something about what happens when we feel our weakest and are near our breaking point. These prayers, in their simple beauty, are a profound testimony to the spirituality of birth, for they come without prompting or thought as we almost instinctually reach out for help from something greater. If you find these holy words springing to your lips, you can intentionally make them a beautiful prayer, surrendering yourself to the need for his help and strength.

It would be impossible for me to endure the pain of childbirth if I saw it as only that: pain. I know some women take prayer requests to pray through as they labor. I'm a little too simple for that. When the pain got serious, I clung to the small and the simple. As I passed in and out of each contraction I found myself saying simply, "Jesus on the Cross, Jesus on the Cross" and allowing my mind to explore the suffering of my Savior.

And it's amazing what strength I drew from this! The pain was terrible, but as I meditated on the wounded body of Christ, I felt empowered and often thought, "I would suffer this and more for you!" and suddenly my pain gave way to joy. Of course, this short sequence of events happened over and over as the contraction passed, I slipped into sleepy rest, and then another contraction came on, and I resisted the pain until once again I was gazing up at my Savior on the cross.

I am an imperfect sinner, and I'm not going to claim I was some saint as I labored, just as I don't claim to be tougher than anyone else. I'm not. But acknowledging that suffering is meaningful, and offering it as a gift to the Lord makes the act of having a baby so much more beautiful, pain and all.

— Nancy Bandzuch, mom to four

Using Sacramentals in Pregnancy and Birth

We discussed sacramentals in Chapter 11 on preparing for birth, and they are also powerful channels of grace in the birth room. God works through our use of physical items, and we see this even in the Old Testament — think of Moses' staff in Exodus or the bones of Elisha (see 2 Kgs 13:20–21). In the New Testament, physical items are also vehicles for God's grace — the hem of Jesus' garment (Lk 8:44), mud and even the spittle of Jesus (Jn 9:6–12), or the handkerchiefs and aprons of Saint Paul (Acts 19:11–12). Using sacramentals more fully disposes us to receive the effects of the sacraments (grace), and the *Catechism* states that through them "various occasions in life are rendered holy" (1667). Considering that birth is one of the most powerful and life-changing moments in a woman's life, what better time is there to use sacramentals?

Blessings received during pregnancy, especially if from official rites of the Church, will remain with you and provide grace in the birth itself. As the primary sacramental of the Church, these previously received blessings are effective and powerful within birth, extending their grace into the birth room and beyond. Your husband, doula, or other member of your birth team can also offer words of blessing during the birth, laying their hands on you and blessing you, praying over you, and extending that grace further. In some Eastern Catholic rites, a priest is actually called when a mom is in labor so he can be ready to bless the baby and mother as soon as possible after the baby is born.

Holy water or oil can be brought into the birth room and used to bless you and baby as you labor. A simple Sign of the Cross made with water or oil on your forehead or womb is a beautiful and easy way to anoint the time of birth. Having a few reminders in the birth room that can lift your heart and mind to God can be powerful — it could be a crucifix or statue of Mary, images of your favorite saints, Scripture verses printed out, or even simple holy cards.

During one of my own labors, I had a crucifix in my hand during transition, and as I clutched it and the force of the metal impressed itself on my palms, the power of the moment and opportunity I was given became apparent. The only word I could utter was "Jesus." Looking back, I see just how present God was during that time and what an invitation it was to enter into his life-giving love, a love that requires complete sacrifice of self. The crucifix was a tangible reminder during those intense moments.

Many moms choose to wear a blessed crucifix, medal, or a scapular. Popular choices include the Miraculous Medal, images of Saint Gerard, Saint Brigid, Saint Gianna, Saint Anne, or a patron saint (either mom's or the baby's). Even in the case of a cesarean, there should be no problem with a mother wearing or at least holding one of these during her birth.

Candles provide a sense of peace, warmth, and safety, and are popular even in secular birth circles. As discussed in Chapter 12, there is a physiological reason why laboring women prefer dim lighting. You can take this natural idea to a supernatural level and have a blessed candle on hand to light during birth. If you are birthing at a hospital that doesn't allow lit candles, have someone you trust light a candle for you at their home or church as you birth, or light your candle while you labor at home before you go to the hospital. You could also bring a vigil candle that has a plastic or glass enclosure and place a battery-powered tea light inside to mimic the idea.

....

Again, these tips for bringing grace into your birth are mere suggestions. Every woman's relationship with God is different, and every woman's individual birth is going to be different. God gives us a multitude of ways to avail ourselves of grace precisely because each one of us is unique. Use what speaks to your heart and resonates with you, and be open to whatever the Lord is asking of you for this particular birth. Make no mistake that he is stirring in your heart and inviting you to draw closer to him through this birth. He longs to be there with you, his precious daughter, as you enter into your own paschal mystery and bring this new little life into the world.

15

THE CESAREAN BIRTH

*"Upon you I have leaned from my birth; from my mother's womb, you
have been my strength. My praise is continually of you."*
— *Psalms 71:6*

An atypical issue that presents itself before birth or during labor may indicate the need for a cesarean birth. A cesarean, also known as a c-section or surgical birth, is when the baby is born via surgery, through an incision in the lower abdomen and uterus. It is always performed by a surgeon.

A necessary cesarean can be a beautiful and even life-saving event. The ability to have a skilled medical provider perform a necessary cesarean is truly a gift and an example of God working through the gifts of the people he has created. Cesarean births are without doubt part of his plan and should be considered an amazing gift to the women and babies who need them. In the case of some placental or cord issues, physical infirmity, some breech presentations, sometimes preeclampsia or other situations when the birth needs to happen yet induction is not deemed ideal, and in many other situations, a cesarean may be the safest way to get the baby out.

God never intended childbirth to be a painful experience.
The pain of childbirth is a direct result of sin. God is
so good that he allows us to turn pain into something
beautiful for his kingdom. Whether we are laboring
naturally with our children or recovering from a major
surgery, we glorify God through the pain we undergo for
the sake of our children.

God does intend us to be open to life and children. He
likes when we are born. He likes to be present when our
children are coming into the world. He gives us helpers,
prayer partners, and wonderful people to aid us. For

some, that might look like a husband holding a woman up in a birthing tub in a family room. For others, it might mean a room full of doctors and nurses, communicating with each other and you to ensure a safe delivery. Each of these people is a gift. Each of them is equally given to us to aid in the process of our children greeting the world.

Mary W., mom to five

There are three "types" of cesarean: planned, unplanned, and emergency. A planned cesarean is usually the result of a situation that presents itself during pregnancy, known about beforehand and often scheduled well ahead of time. Mom goes in at the scheduled time, is not in labor, and surgery is performed. A cesarean is considered unplanned when it is the result of a situation at full term or during labor that, while not an explicit emergency, makes a cesarean preferable to the planned vaginal birth. An emergency cesarean is when a mom is in labor, is expecting to birth vaginally, and a situation suddenly presents itself that directly compromises the life or health of the baby or mother.

What Happens in a Cesarean

Exactly what happens in a cesarean will depend somewhat on whether the surgery is planned, unplanned, or an emergency. In a planned cesarean, you will likely determine and schedule the date with your provider days or even weeks before it happens. However, some women who know they will need a cesarean opt to go into labor and come in then for the surgery. This way, baby and their body can determine the birth day, which helps them feel more at ease that the baby is truly ready to be born. Some providers, however, may be uncomfortable with or very unused to this idea, and in some instances it may not be safe. For a planned cesarean, you are not supposed to eat, usually from midnight until after the baby is born. When you go in, you will go through hospital intake and be prepped for surgery.

In an unplanned or emergency cesarean, you will most likely be transferred from a normal labor room to a surgical room. Most cesareans now use a complete epidural to numb you from the waist down, keeping you awake for the birth. If the situation is a serious emergency, providers may choose to give immediate and full anesthesia, since it is quicker, which will make you unconscious for the birth. In the case of full anesthesia, often the father is not allowed to be present for the birth. With all types of cesarean, most providers require that the mother's arms be outstretched and strapped down to avoid the possibility of movement, though many are now changing that protocol, believing it is better for mom to have her arms free to hold the baby right away. An IV with fluids, pain medications, and possibly antibiotics will be necessary, as will a urinary catheter.

The surgeon will make a cut into the lower abdomen along the bikini line and into the uterus. You will typically feel a lot of tugging, pulling, and possibly nausea, and often it is a little difficult to breathe since you are lying on your back and there is pressure from the surgeon's movement. If the baby is head down, there will be an attempt to bring the baby's head out first, mimicking a bit of a vaginal birth. The baby will then be completely pulled out by the obstetrician.

In a cesarean birth, there is still usually the option for delaying the clamping of the cord, immediate skin-to-skin contact, and the father or mother announcing the gender of the baby, but this isn't the protocol many doctors were trained under, so it may be something you need to request and push for if you want it. Once the cord is cut and the baby has been assessed and introduced to you, usually the baby goes either to the father or nursery staff so your incision can be sewn up. This may take anywhere from thirty to forty-five minutes, depending on the incision and the skill of the doctor. It is important at this point that the doctor use a double-suturing process that stitches the incision up in two layers. A double-layered stitch gives you a much stronger scar and uterus, should you become pregnant again. Not only does that protect your next pregnancies and babies, but it gives you a much safer and higher chance of a vaginal birth with subsequent births.

Once you are finished in surgery, you will be brought into a recovery room, where, hopefully, you will be able to be with and hold your baby again. It will likely be difficult to move and hold the baby comfortably, and you may feel extremely tired or groggy from the anesthesia and pain medications. The father and/or a doula are invaluable at this point because they can help with holding the baby, helping you nurse the baby, and with diaper changes. Recovery from a cesarean will most likely be more difficult than from a vaginal birth, and it's important to let your body heal, so avail yourself of any help you can. It is critical to rest and not put too much strain on your stitches, but it is also helpful for healing to stand up and walk a bit as soon as you are able. Mothers who have had repeat cesareans will tell you that walking and moving around as soon as possible makes a huge difference in the speed of healing and the overall ease of recovery.

Your nurses will teach you how to care for your stitches and will monitor your bleeding and the cramping of your uterus just as they would after a vaginal birth. Some women need heavy-duty medication to handle the pain after the surgery, while many are able to get off stronger medications within a day or two and switch to something like ibuprofen. Your nurses and obstetrician will be monitoring your pain levels and making sure you show no signs of infection or other complications.

On the whole, babies born via cesarean section are more likely to exhibit breathing difficulties.[116] While this isn't always the case, it is helpful to know beforehand, and this is one of the reasons the neonatal intensive care (NICU) staff will be in the room and monitoring the baby during and immediately after the birth. While there is no need for them to step in unless the baby shows some signs of difficulty, they are there as a precaution and should only be used when necessary.

Babies born via cesarean also tend to have a bit more difficulty breastfeeding. Many times there is no problem, but because the baby is often taken by the staff right away for assessment, increasing the time it takes for the baby to get to his or her mother's breast, this can interrupt the physiological instinctive response of the baby immediately after birth. This will not break a breastfeeding relationship, by any means, but you may need to push through and persevere a bit more than you otherwise would have. There are ways to hold the baby for nursing (like the football hold or nursing while lying on your side) that are more comfortable post-cesarean. If you have any difficulties, don't hesitate to get the help of a good lactation consultant, doula, or experienced friend.

The Rise in Cesarean Births

While a cesarean birth can be a wonderful gift to a mother and baby who truly need one, there is much concern that in the last several decades cesarean births have increased at an explosive rate. The World Health Organization has stated that a healthy cesarean rate for a country is approximately 10 to 15 percent.[117] In 2014, the total cesarean rate in the United States was 32.2 percent, and in Canada it was 27.5 percent.[118] Whether that is from poor prenatal practices or because of poor birth protocol, that means that some 50 percent (or more) of the mothers in the United States who have a cesarean may not actually need it, placing those mothers and babies at greater risk.

You deserve to know that a surgical birth has inherent risks to you and your baby not present in a vaginal birth. All else being equal, a cesarean is riskier and should only be performed when a complication arises and the risk of a vaginal delivery is determined to be greater than the risk of the cesarean. The risks include:

- Hemorrhage
- Infection in the uterus or at the site of the incision
- Negative reaction to the anesthesia during surgery or pain-management drugs used afterward
- Baby responding poorly to the medications
- An increase in the rate of NICU stay for the baby
- An interruption in the natural hormone interplay that happens during spontaneous vaginal birth
- The lack of transmission of good bacteria to the baby that happens in the birth canal (research is now showing that the transfer of good bacteria to the baby plays a role in long-term gut health, colic rates, lung function, and immune support of the baby)
- A higher rate of complications with breastfeeding
- Longer recovery
- Increased risk of uterine rupture during a subsequent birth
- Accidental injury to the baby
- A greater risk for postpartum depression
- Increased risk for placenta issues, such as placenta accreta or placenta previa, in subsequent pregnancies
- Increased risk of amniotic fluid embolism
- Increased risk of maternal mortality

Ideally, you should consent to a cesarean only after you understand the risks involved and have agreed with your provider that this is the best way for your baby to be delivered.

Mortality rates for the mother in cesarean births are almost four times that of vaginal births, and the risk of an amniotic fluid embolism is about five times as high.[119] Anytime we place poor science or personal preference above what is in the best interest of the health and well-being of mothers and babies, we compromise their dignity and health. This is why it is important to know your provider's cesarean rate and to have honest conversations on the reasons he or she would recommend or perform one.

Sometimes after one or perhaps multiple cesarean births, providers tell mothers to wait to conceive again for at least a year so their uterine scars can heal sufficiently. Many women who have had several cesareans are told they should take measures to never get pregnant again because of the risk another pregnancy and surgery imposes on a compromised scar. The concern is not only that the stress from a new pregnancy on the incision site can put the mother at greater risk for a uterine rupture before or during the next birth, but also that the risks to mother and baby for placental issues go up significantly with each subsequent cesarean.[120] The decision to perform a cesarean can have lifelong implications not only for a mother but for future family size, sexual life, and fertility decisions.

Again, a cesarean birth may be warranted and a tremendous blessing. But no woman should be forced to limit her ability to welcome future children or increase risks to her or her baby because of cesareans that are not truly necessary.

Ways to Reduce the Possibility of a Cesarean

There are very real ways you can reduce your chance of needing a surgical birth. None of these is guaranteed, of course, but the following are a few ways to reduce the possibility of a cesarean:

- Go into spontaneous labor. Medical inductions in some circumstances can increase the chance of a birth ending as a cesarean.[121] Sometimes this is because the mother's cervix and body were just not ready. Other times it is because the strength and intensity of augmented labor through Pitocin or other drugs are too intense for the baby and the baby goes into distress because of these harder contractions. The use of epidurals is increased with induced births, so the baby or mother may also respond poorly, necessitating a cesarean.

- Choose your provider well. Don't be afraid to ask potential providers what their cesarean rate is and listen well — not only to what they answer but how they answer. Choose a provider with a low cesarean rate and a low induction rate.

- Make sure your provider gives evidence-based care. A suspected "big baby" is not considered a valid medical reason for a cesarean. According to ACOG, cesarean "delivery to avoid potential birth trauma should be limited to estimated fetal weights of at least 5,000 grams (11.02 lbs.) in women without diabetes and at least 4,500 grams (9.92 lbs.) in women with diabetes. The prevalence of birth weight of 5,000 grams or more is rare, and patients should be counseled that estimates of fetal weight, particularly late in gestation, are imprecise."[122] In fact, studies have shown that the expectation of a large baby (and the provider treating it with more interventions) is more dangerous than actually having a "big" baby.[123]

- Stay active and eat well. Exercising and eating a quality diet high in protein and low in refined carbohydrates can lower your risk of gestational diabetes, preeclampsia, and obesity, all of which can raise your chance of a cesarean.

- Take a good birth class. A good birth class will go into greater detail on valid reasons for a surgical birth as well as reasons that providers may give that either are not in line with their own medical body (ACOG) or are highly subjective. The more information you have, the better your decisions can be.

- Move around during labor and avail yourself of non-pharmacological pain-relief options. The more tools you have to handle labor, the faster your labor will move and the less likely you will be to request intervention with epidural use that can increase the chance of a cesarean.

- Hire a doula. Studies show that women who have a doula have a lower risk for a cesarean section.[124] Since doulas are nonmedical professionals, that says a lot both about birth practices in the United States and the important role support and advocacy can play during birth.

- Consider a midwife or family doctor as your provider. If you are in a low-risk pregnancy, consider using a midwife rather than an obstetrician for your birth. Midwives are overall more skilled in and familiar with normal birth. Obstetricians are highly trained in and have a specialty in surgery. There are some who even say that makes them more likely to default and recommend, or see the "need" for, a cesarean when there may be simpler methods that should be tried first.

We had a cesarean for our first child, and the other eight were delivered at home. For the cesarean, I wish I had understood more that each measure the hospital uses to "help" the delivery along may sometimes help, but sometimes these interventions can also complicate the birth process. It is very hard to refuse the interventions when in the throes of labor and struggling. I wish I had known more about the consequences of procedures like induction, breaking the water, taking a sleeping pill, etc., before I was in the intensity of labor and birth.

— Lisa H., mom to nine on Earth and one in eternity

Entering into the Cesarean Birth

If it turns out you need a cesarean birth for your own health or that of your baby, you can thank God that the option is available. This can be an opportunity to surrender and enter deeply into the passion of Christ. Some women will have no problem accepting and celebrating that this is the way this child should enter the world. Others may have a more difficult time coming to terms with the decision.

One step toward making peace with a cesarean is being fully informed and playing an active role in the decision. If the mother is educated in the birthing options, can see the reasons why a cesarean may be optimal in her situation, and makes the decision freely, she can have much more peace that this is the right decision. Not only that, but her inherent dignity, intelligence, bodily autonomy, and role as mother of the child are respected. A woman who feels pressured into a cesarean, feels the cesarean option is the result of poor birth practices, or has misgivings that it is the best option in her circumstances will understandably have a harder time making that decision. This can also lead to more difficulty in processing the birth experience later.

From a spiritual standpoint, a necessary cesarean birth is an opportunity for a mother to surrender herself to God and to her baby in a beautiful and unique way. How Christlike it is as she offers her body, cut and opened, for this precious new little life! She gives completely of herself, often abandoning her will for the sake of her child. In her longer recovery, she will have ample opportunity again to offer her body as a sacrifice. And the visible scar will remain on her body from that beautiful self-gift.

I'd hoped to have all-natural births, but it wasn't wise to attempt in my case. Naturally, with every pregnancy came the concern of the outcome of these c-sections — anxieties which seemed to creep up each time regarding the surgery itself and spinal blocks — not the new little lives I was so ecstatic to meet.

In all three instances, as I was strapped to a T-shaped bed, very aware of all the possible complications that come with this type of birth, I was reminded of the cross, the dying to self in order to bring forth new life. Not gonna downplay it, I was scared, really scared, but the cross was most recognizable to me in these circumstances as I found myself lying upon that cold table in the middle of the OR. I was stretched to my limits, pumped with pain meds, unable to move, opened and stitched back up. There were even small and seemingly insignificant crosses in the process, such as the inability to scratch a tickle on my nose or brush away an eyelash. I was completely at the mercy of the attentiveness of my husband and the doctors and nurses present, and it was there that I felt the culmination of what self-sacrifice was: "No one has greater love than this, to lay down one's life for another" (Jn 15:13). In this case, I was then inspired to reflect upon the symbolism in my situation, with my own limited understanding, and what it must've been for Jesus to be on that cross, laying down his life for us. With this, the anxiety would leave as an influx of peace would arrive, and soon thereafter, so would the little beloved one for whom I'd been sacrificing.

— Marchelle G., mom to three

A mom undergoing a cesarean often deals with a variety of emotions before, during, and after the surgery — fear, surrender, anxiety, doubt, grief, and anger are a possible few. And these, of course, are mixed with the joy, elation, and relief (along with the fluctuating hormones) of welcoming the new baby into the world. It is certainly a time to ask for and rely on the grace of God to carry you through.

Even if you look back and think that your cesarean was possibly unnecessary, you can still find beauty and meaning in the process. For whatever reason, this was the way this baby was born, and God was working in and through that situation and experience. While it isn't true that "all that matters is an alive baby," you can and should thank and praise God for the gift of this baby, healthy or otherwise. However, you should also be allowed the freedom to express any grief, disappointment, or anger you may experience, especially if you were treated poorly or feel as though you were lied to or manipulated. You have every right to process that in your own way without fear of being judged or shamed.

I hope that people grow to understand that the emotions surrounding a cesarean vary from woman to woman and can range from mourning to relief, depending on the situation. While a safe delivery of our babies is key, it does not do to discount the way our emotions are tied to our births. Walk with the mothers in your life and allow them to feel the range of emotions, whether it is relief or sadness or fear or confidence; honor our choice as brave, beautiful, and just as full of sacrificial love.

To a mother being faced with a planned cesarean or healing from an emergency cesarean, I want to remind you that you are fearfully and wonderfully made, and it is not how you give birth that defines you as a mother — your love and ongoing sacrifice for your children is what makes you a mother. Your birth, no matter the route, the location, the interventions, or the medications, is beautiful because your unique experience was an act of true love.

— Molly W., mom to two on Earth and four in eternity

Options in a Cesarean Birth

In the case of a cesarean birth you still often have options to help it be the best birth it can be. As discussed earlier, if planned, and it is a safe option, some mothers prefer not to schedule the surgery but rather to go into natural labor and then proceed with the cesarean. This allows her the peace that both she and her baby are physiologically ready, and it may allow her to ask questions about and make decisions that will suit her needs better. Just as in a vaginal birth, her voice and concerns should be respected and addressed, and she should always be treated with the utmost dignity.

More obstetricians and hospitals are moving toward a "gentle cesarean" model. Here, rather than the opaque screen that shields the mother's view of the birth and is meant to protect the sterile area, a transparent screen or even no screen is used. This way she can see the baby being born. In a traditional cesarean, the mother's arms are often strapped down in a crosslike fashion to limit movement. While this is stunningly symbolic, many doctors say it isn't necessary. In fact, some argue that keeping her arms free not only decreases anxiety and helps her feel more in control; it also lets her hold her baby as soon as possible.

You have the right to ask that there not be extraneous conversation among the staff during the birth and that any talking be kept low and at a minimum. Some operating rooms offer the option to have music playing. There is also usually no reason (unless baby is in distress and needs emergency measures) why a cesarean baby cannot have his or her cord clamp delayed. It is even worth pushing for, especially since the cesarean baby is at risk for a harder start and will benefit from as much blood from the placenta as he or she can get. Often, even after a cesarean, dad can still cut the cord when it is done pulsing. In a gentler cesarean, mom's chest can be kept bare so the naked baby can have skin-to-skin contact right away. Some mothers ask that they be talked through the procedure so they can understand what is happening.

If you are having a cesarean, you may also ask to have your doula present along with your husband. Usually, this is the decision of the obstetrician, but it may be influenced by hospital policy. Not only can a doula help keep you calm and explain what is happening; she can stay with you as a support person while your incision is sewn back up so that dad can be with and hold the baby.

If you know that you will be having a cesarean or find yourself needing one unexpectedly, know that God is with you and that he still invites you to make this a beautiful and holy birth. You can still receive the rites of blessing sometime before the birth, and if it is a planned cesarean the anointing of the sick can also be received beforehand. Your husband can pray over you before and during the birth. Often, mothers will hold a rosary or crucifix during the surgery. Your husband or doula (if allowed to be present) can still whisper words of Scripture over you or remind you of intentions that you wanted to remember during the birth.

It's a monumental act of surrender to be essentially not in control of what's happening to you. During each surgery, I've had the choice to bemoan my circumstances or to prayerfully transform them into an exercise in virtue. I've often prayed during my c-sections, reflecting on the fiat of Mary for strength. I've said "yes" to bringing a new life into the world, and then I must surrender myself and my baby entirely into the care of another. I give myself entirely over to the medical professionals around me and trust that they have my well-being at heart. Total trust. Total surrender. Totally offering myself and my little one up to the care of another. Sort of sounds like how I'm supposed to be with God every day, huh? I surrender myself entirely — hand my very life over in complete faith — and though I've been poked, and prodded, wounded, and humbled, the result is overwhelming — the result of surrender and trust is new life.

One of the biggest sacrifices a c-section mom may have to make is not holding her baby immediately after birth. It's heart-wrenching to hear your baby cry but not have held her yet. It's so bittersweet to have your baby brought over to caress your cheek on the surgery table, but you're not able to reach out and draw him near. I could waste my energies and emotions on how it's not fair and how much it hurts, or I can choose to embrace it as another of the sacrifices I offer in my circumstances. I offer it up in union with all that Mary suffered when she could not hold her Son when she must have so desperately wanted to. And I offer it up for the little one I'm waiting to cuddle — her health, her sanctity, her everything.

— Theresa Blackstone, mom to six on Earth
and two in eternity

Vaginal Birth after Cesarean (VBAC)

The prevailing wisdom used to be "once a cesarean, always a cesarean" when it came to future births. Some providers still practice this way, but the evidence clearly shows that a vaginal birth after a cesarean is a valid and safe option for most women. In fact, the American College of Obstetricians and Gynecologists now officially states, "Attempting a vaginal birth after cesarean (VBAC) is a safe and appropriate choice for most women who have had a prior cesarean delivery, including for some women who have had two previous cesareans."[125] Just as with many other birth practices, conventions are slowly changing as the data is shared, women speak up, and more providers acknowledge and practice this way. Every post-cesarean mother should be uniquely assessed and considered for a VBAC, and she should make the choice based on the best evidence and information. The mother and provider should take into account the reason for the primary cesarean, the normalcy of this current pregnancy, the type of incision and suturing that were made, the mother's determination, as well as other factors when it comes to assessing the probability of a successful VBAC. Thousands of women have had successful VBACs, and many have had a vaginal birth after two, three, or even four previous cesareans.

According to ACOG, a successful VBAC "avoids major abdominal surgery, lowers a woman's risk of hemorrhage and infection, and shortens postpartum recovery. It may also help women avoid the possible future risks related to having multiple cesareans, such as hysterectomy, bowel and bladder injury, transfusion, infection, and abnormal placenta conditions (placenta previa and placenta accreta)." Moreover, "a successful VBAC has fewer complications than an elective repeat cesarean while a failed TOLAC [trial of labor after cesarean] has more complications than an elective repeat Cesarean." The risk of a uterine complications with a trial of labor after a cesarean is 0.7 percent to 0.9 percent.[126]

In short, if you have had a previous cesarean, you should be encouraged and supported in assessing whether a VBAC is a good option for you and weigh the benefits and risks. If you are planning one, you may have more emotional and mental hurdles to overcome. For this reason, it is often recommended that you hire a doula and get support from a post-cesarean VBAC-friendly group, such as a local ICAN (International Cesarean Awareness Network) chapter. The site vbacfacts.com is also a great resource for help in making that decision. It is also very important to make sure your provider is truly VBAC-supportive and knows proper evidence-based protocol for VBAC. Knowing your provider is completely on board and wants this for you, too, rather than simply "allowing" it, can make a big difference in your confidence and success.

I truly didn't realize how upset I still was about my first birth until I found out I was pregnant with my second child. At one point, someone asked me how I felt about being pregnant again and I started sobbing, completely out of nowhere. I knew that I wanted this birth to go differently, and I was determined to give myself the best chances to make that happen. I put myself in the care of some highly skilled midwives, hired a doula, and read everything I could get my hands on about natural childbirth. I was basically a poster child for preparing for a VBAC (vaginal birth after cesarean).

What I wasn't prepared for was the feeling that I experienced when I walked into the hospital. All of the trauma and grief that accompanied my first birth came flooding back, and I felt paralyzed by the weight of it. In that moment, walking down the hall to the maternity wing, my husband glanced down at his watch and commented, "It's past midnight ... it's your birthday." And with that, I was able to feel God's presence and a courage I hadn't felt before. I felt prepared, ready, and fearless. A few hours later, our little girl was born via VBAC, guided out by my own hands and snuggled onto my chest. I felt awe at not only how much love I had for my girl, but also in my own body, and how God had designed birth with such intense beauty and love. Whereas before I felt like my body had somehow been "broken," this time I was able to stand in awe of what a gift my body actually was. This appreciation of my body as a gift carried over into the rest of my experience of motherhood.

— Christina Kolb, mom to three

As with any birth choice, you should always be treated with respect and given accurate information to make your decisions. You should never be bullied into a decision and should feel free to ask your provider any questions and expect solid and honest answers so that you can make the most educated and informed decision that is best for you and your baby.

16

OPTIONS FOR YOUR NEWBORN

*"I do not know how you came into being in my womb.
It was not I who gave you life and breath, nor I who set in order the
elements within each of you."*
— 2 Maccabees 7:22

There are many decisions to make when it comes to your newborn baby. It can be overwhelming, especially if you are a first-time mother, to claim these options and make these decisions. Just remember, God has entrusted this unique baby to you and has made you his or her primary caretaker — and that means you have all the grace you need to enter in and make these choices. These decisions can profoundly affect you, your baby, and your family. While we can't go through all of them here, we will touch on a few big ones you will need to make for your baby in the first hours and days.

First, if you are giving birth in a hospital, once the baby is born, the baby is considered a unique patient. His or her care is now transferred to the jurisdiction of the nursery staff and not the labor-and-delivery staff. It also means that, while you are the mother of the baby, some of the decisions regarding the baby may now be legally fuzzy, or the baby may be subject to government- or hospital-required treatment whether you want it or not.

Rooming In or Nursery Care

If you are in a hospital, you should have the choice of either keeping the baby with you the entire time (rooming in) or using a nursery, where the nurses provide care for your baby. The benefits to rooming in are many, not the least of which is you finally get to meet and hold (in your arms!) this little human being you've been thinking about for nine months. Rooming in also allows you to nurse your baby on demand right away and as often as needed, which is important in bringing your milk in and establishing a good supply for the baby's needs. Babies are shown to do better when they are closer to their mothers, exhibiting less stress and less crying, and taking good advantage of those first hours and days when babies and mothers are designed to be learning how to nurse.

There are benefits to nursery care, however, especially if you have undergone a cesarean and are not physically capable of taking care of the baby right away. Often after a cesarean, mothers are not able to turn over to pick up the baby, or pain medications make it unsafe to try. If you have had a long and difficult vaginal birth, you may also feel some relief at having the nursery staff available to take care of the baby for a few hours while you rest. However, if at all possible, it should be made very clear that the baby will be brought to you immediately if he or she is showing signs of wanting to nurse (rooting or unrest; crying is considered to be a late indicator of hunger), or if you or your husband change your mind. Any expectations or plans for the baby should also be made clear to the nursery staff, such as what tests the baby will get, any injections, decisions on breastfeeding or bottle use, baths, etc.

Vitamin K

An injection of vitamin K is often given to newborns to help with any blood clotting after birth and for up to six months after. If babies have experienced bruising due to a long labor and malpositioning, if they for some reason need to undergo surgery after birth, or if they have any internal bleeding, their limited stores of vitamin K are not adequate to control it. Babies' vitamin K levels do not match adults until about six months old, and breastmilk does not contain adequate supplies. In some states, this injection is a legal requirement and parents do not have much of a say in whether their babies receive it or not. While some believe there is a yet unknown reason babies are naturally born with lower levels of vitamin K and that it shouldn't be supplemented without clear reason, there is compelling evidence that the vitamin K shot helps prevent dangerous bleeding in young babies.[127] Some parents choose the option of an oral vitamin K supplement given to the baby because it contains fewer preservatives than the injection, though it is hard to attain in most hospitals and has a lower effectiveness than the injection. It is definitely worth looking into the evidence for vitamin K supplementation and, if you have a choice, making your decision based on that evidence as well as the individual circumstances of the birth. A baby who has had a difficult birth, has bruising, requires surgery, or whose parents are choosing circumcision has a more pressing need for vitamin K supplementation.

Erythromycin

Almost immediately after birth, most babies in the United States receive an antibiotic ointment called erythromycin squeezed over their eyelids. The reasoning behind this is that if a mother has an active and untreated case of syphilis or gonorrhea, it can pass to the baby during birth, infecting the baby and potentially causing an infection or even blindness. The standard of care in almost every hospital now is to give the ointment regardless of whether the mother has tested negative, even if the baby has zero risk for these infections, and even if the baby was born via cesarean and was not in contact with the birth canal.

In some states this is legally required, and trying to refuse it or the vitamin K can even result in a call to Child Protective Services. In other states, parents can make the choice to refuse the ointment if there is no reason for it. While erythromycin is important for a baby who has been potentially exposed to these infections, it is not necessary for a baby who has not. Some argue that the ointment irritates the babies' eyes and interferes with their vision as they first open their eyes, especially as they are designed to make eye contact with their mother while nursing. There is also a growing and valid concern about the consequences of antibiotic overuse.[128]

Bathing the Baby

The newborn bath seems to be a protocol that varies greatly depending on the hospital. In most cases, there is no medical need to bathe a baby after birth or even in the days after for the baby's sake. They've just been living in a sterile environment after all! If a baby is especially messy after birth, some mothers prefer to have them cleaned off, but that can often be done with simple wiping. There is also a protective factor that vernix (the creamy coating that babies sometimes have on their skin before and after birth) provides to the baby's skin. Vernix can simply be rubbed into the baby like lotion. Waiting to bathe the baby has even been shown to have a major impact on breastfeeding success and on lowering hypothermia and hypoglycemia rates.[129] Vernix provides temperature control, infection defense, and helps the baby pick up the mother's scent, which in turn assists the baby's instinct to latch at the breast. The primary reason baths are often insisted upon in a hospital setting is for the protection of the staff, since the remains of the mother's bodily fluids may still be on the baby, and for aesthetic reasons. If the nursery staff is pushing a bath for the baby, you do have the right to refuse, or you have the right to do it yourself. If you decide to bathe the baby, avoid using any soaps or strong lotions, as they are too harsh for the baby's delicate skin and the scents can interfere with baby and mom learning each other's smells and the resulting hormone interplay that bonds them and helps with breastfeeding in the weeks after birth.

Formula or Sugar Supplements

If you are planning on exclusively breastfeeding, you will often need to be vigilant if baby is in the nursery and not rooming in with you. Make clear that you do not want any supplements (sugar water or formula) given to your baby without your consent, and that you want the baby brought to you at the first signs of rooting (where babies turn their head and are looking for food) or hunger. If you are breastfeeding, take advantage of lactation consultants if available. Formula or other supplements can interfere with the baby nursing at the breast and establishing your breastfeeding relationship and supply. There is also concern over how formula or other supplements will affect the newborn's virgin gut and intestinal health.

Glucose Testing

After birth, preterm babies, babies under and over a certain weight, and babies born from a mother with gestational diabetes are usually required to have their blood sugar tested via a heel prick. Blood-sugar protocol varies greatly from hospital to hospital, provider to provider, and even staff member to staff member, and it often changes. The concern is that a baby with low blood sugar will become hypoglycemic, and if that occurs for long periods of time the baby has a small risk for developmental delays. The best way to get good and healthy blood-sugar numbers is by nursing as soon as possible and nursing often.[130] Waiting to bathe the baby can also help reduce hypoglycemia. If blood sugar needs to be tested, you can request that it be done while nursing or when the baby is in your arms, to help soothe the baby.

Hepatitis B Vaccine

The Centers for Disease Control (CDC) currently recommends that every baby receive the hepatitis B vaccine at one day old. Hepatitis B is a disease that is transmitted through infected blood, semen, or other bodily fluid entering the body of a person who is not infected. Unless a mother has a case of hepatitis B herself which can pass to the baby during birth, or the child will for some reason be exposed to the blood or bodily fluids of another person with hepatitis, it is highly unlikely that a newborn would be at risk. For this reason, and because many parents are concerned with the additives included in the vaccine and with the idea of challenging the baby's new immune system so early, many parents refuse this vaccine completely or until later. The vaccine is effective in preventing transmission for those babies who may be at risk.

Vaccines are certainly a hotly debated topic, and parents are encouraged to research well and make the choice that is most appropriate for them given the risks. As the parent, you have the right to make this decision, and the vaccine is not required by law. The decision should be evidence-based and should take into account benefit versus risk in each individual family and circumstance and be free from manipulation or coercion.

Circumcision

If you have a boy, you will need to make the decision about whether or not to have him circumcised. This topic is highly controversial and very personal. As with all big decisions for our children, the decision to circumcise or not should be made with full information, consent, and a proper understanding of the human body and the dignity of the human person. It is one to be made based on scientific evidence, natural law, an understanding of our faith, and with discernment and prayer. Since it is not a procedure that can be undone, and one that has real consequences, it should be discerned well.

In other parts of the world, infant circumcision is usually only done as part of the religious tradition for Muslim and Jewish people. It is important for Christians to note that the Church has actually spoken about circumcision. We are forbidden by the Church and Scripture to circumcise for religious reasons. We believe that baptism now takes the place of the rite of circumcision. The Acts of the Apostles relates how the first Church council, the Council of Jerusalem, led by Saint Peter, decided authoritatively and definitively that circumcision is no longer the means of salvation and should not be undertaken as such.

Saint Paul makes the issue of the Old Covenant requirement of circumcision clear: "Now I, Paul, say to you that if you receive circumcision, Christ will be of no advantage to you. I testify again to every man who receives circumcision that he is bound to keep the whole law. You are severed from Christ, you who would be justified by the law; you have fallen away from grace. For through the Spirit, by faith, we wait for the hope of righteousness. For in Christ Jesus neither circumcision nor uncircumcision is of any avail, but faith working through love."[131] Pope Eugene, at the

Council of Florence, issued a papal bull stating that the Church "strictly orders all who glory in the name of Christian, not to practice circumcision either before or after baptism, since whether or not they place their hope in it, it cannot possibly be observed without loss of eternal salvation."[132] While circumcision may be morally permissible for a valid medical reason, it is not permitted as a practice of faith.

Currently in the United States, the rate of circumcision has been steadily decreasing. The most recent statistic from the CDC in 2010 says that 54.6 percent of newborn boys are circumcised.[133] From a health perspective, the WHO states that only one in three boys worldwide is circumcised. It is not officially recommended by any medical institutions in the world and is considered a nontherapeutic cosmetic procedure.[134] According to the WHO, there is a 1.5 percent risk for complications resulting from circumcision. These include death, hemorrhage, infection, accidental removal of too much of the foreskin, adhesions, and more.[135]

There is no current consensus in the medical community whether routine circumcision has any significant health benefit, though there is some evidence that circumcision may lower the rates of sexual transmission of HIV. Some studies suggest that urinary-tract infections may be lower for circumcised boys, but others are inconclusive or state that risk of infection because of the circumcision makes that argument void. Medicaid in some states and a growing number of health insurance companies will no longer cover the cost because it is not considered necessary. There is conflicting personal testimony from adult males on whether the circumcision procedure affects their experience of sexual intimacy.

Circumcision is hotly debated and can be an emotional and personal decision. Reflecting on the dignity of the baby, we can say that it is important for the decision to be well researched and made with correct reasoning and intention by both parents (not just the father) with a proper understanding of the dignity of the body. Some Catholics argue that the prohibition of medically unnecessary amputation in the *Catechism* applies to circumcision, while others believe that is a stretch.[136] As the child has no say in this matter that affects him forever, and since it is a procedure that cannot be undone and has risk, it should only be made with proper discernment and information.

If you do not choose circumcision, there is no special treatment for the penis. The foreskin is intact and adhered to the glans of the penis for a few years. It should never be forcefully retracted by you or a physician or nurse. There is no special cleaning in the infant years. When the child is older and the foreskin naturally retracts, he can easily be taught to retract the foreskin in the shower and rinse the penis with water. If you do choose to have your baby boy circumcised, be absolutely certain that appropriate anesthetic is used and try to nurse or soothe the baby immediately after. You will need to take precautions for a few days after, treating the penis with vaseline and gauze to control bleeding, prevent infection, and keep the wound from adhering to the diaper or the scrotum.

Other Tests and Procedures

There are several other tests and procedures that may be offered or suggested for your baby, depending on the place and state of his or her birth. You may need to decide on hearing tests, blood screening for genetic diseases, jaundice treatment, and more. A birth class or doula will be helpful for learning what other newborn procedures may be common practice in your state or from your hospital or provider. As always, remember that you are the parent and can research and discern what tests and procedures have merit in your circumstances.

NICU Care

If there is a significant concern for your baby, he or she may need extra care and intervention in the neonatal intensive care unit (NICU). This is when it is especially important that you have a provider you trust and are birthing in a place that you trust, so you can have peace that any separation of mother and baby and intensive intervention during that precious time is truly best for your baby. While it is outside the scope of this book to go into every instance where this is a possibility, even there you have choices and should work with the circumstances to make the best decisions for your baby.

Being with the baby as much as possible, giving colostrum and breastmilk to the baby either through nursing or pumping, skin-to-skin contact, researching concerns, and advocating for the best evidenced-based care possible for your baby are often all still possible. It is an incredibly difficult and draining process to have a baby in the NICU, but God is still present and his grace is abundant for the taking, perhaps especially in these circumstances. Drawing support from other NICU parents, developing relationships with the staff, and prudently deciding when you need to intervene in the care and when you need to let things go and trust are all important.

Choosing a Pediatrician

At some point during your pregnancy you will also likely want to choose a pediatrician or family doctor for your baby. If you have a hospital birth, this doctor (or, most likely nowadays, a whole practice) will be responsible for discharging your baby or will delegate that role to the hospital's resident pediatrician. Many of the same principles you use to choose your care provider will be used to choose your baby's pediatrician.

- Does the pediatrician treat the baby and you with dignity and respect?
- Does he or she use evidence-based practices?
- Does he or she recognize your God-given authority as the parent, and will they respect informed choices you make for your children even if they may disagree?
- Is the pediatrician competent in staying up to date on current knowledge regarding breastfeeding, growth charts, and antibiotic use?
- Does he or she help prevent illness and foster true health?
- Does he or she use outdated information or practices?

Just as with your own provider for pregnancy and birth, you have the right to switch pediatricians if you have concerns about the quality of care offered. Your doula, friends, and online mom groups can be great places to find worthwhile recommendations for pediatricians that will fit well with your preferences, your philosophy of health, and your faith.

My husband and I have learned to ask questions about everything along the way. We are the ones in charge of our baby, not the hospital staff. For us, it's important to know that we have the right to decide and say no to things, from wearing the hospital gowns (I hate those things!) to the choice of vaccines for our baby. We can educate ourselves and are responsible for making the best choices for me and for our baby.

— Megan Lyons, mom to four

17

PROTECTING THE POSTPARTUM PERIOD

"Come to me, all who labor and are heavy laden,
and I will give you rest."
— Matthew 11:28

The days immediately following the birth are usually emotionally charged and exhausting. They can be thrilling and ecstatic but also physically and emotionally draining in ways never before experienced. Especially if this is your first baby, those first days and weeks are a huge learning experience. You are meeting your baby. You are caring for a completely dependent newborn. Your body will be doing things it has never done before. It still has work to do as it heals and recovers and is likely feeding this new little person it created. And it's likely all this happens on less sleep than ever before. Your whole world is dramatically changed. This is the postpartum period.

Practical Postpartum Care

After birth, you will need lots of rest and comforting, nourishing food. Most women find that they are ravenous in the hours and days after birth. You've just run a marathon, and now your body is gearing up to produce milk. You will need those extra calories to replenish and to produce that milk for the baby. Those first few days after birth should be nothing but rest, nursing, eating, drinking lots of water, and welcoming this new little person into your family. Any other activity beyond that should be done slowly and only insofar as it doesn't interfere with that primary responsibility of a mother to heal, recover, and bond with her baby. The care and support of a husband and extended family and friends is critical to this postpartum time. It is a beautiful testimony to a Church that values life when a postpartum mother is completely provided for with meals, housework, baby watching, or any other necessary chores or child-care.

You will most likely be tender, and if you had a surgical birth, you may not be able to move well for several days. If you had stitches with a vaginal birth, your perineum and bottom will likely be sore for several days, too, depending on the degree of the tear. If you are at a hospital, they will probably give you iced pads that will help with any swelling and healing. If you are at home you can make something similar by spraying some witch hazel or merely water on a pad, washcloth, or cloth diaper and putting it in the freezer. For a cesarean scar, the nurses at the hospital and your doctor will check it several times to make sure it is healing properly and will give you instructions for keeping it clean. Herbal baths and creams can be a help in healing during the days after birth, but be sure to check with your provider that what you use is helpful in your situation.

During the hours and days after birth, nurses or your midwife or doctor will be checking vaginal bleeding to make sure it is controlled and gradually lightening. They will also most likely want to feel your uterus and even massage it a little bit to make sure it is contracting and shrinking to its normal size. This is not comfortable and can be quite painful the first few times, but it is helpful to make sure your body is healing well and is controlling the bleeding. You can even feel it yourself with your hands and do some of the massaging. You may especially feel postpartum contractions as your baby nurses and oxytocin is released. These afterpains actually get more intense with each subsequent birth, as the uterus has more work to do to contract to its normal size. Many women opt to take over-the-counter pain relief or herbal remedies to help with these contractions.

Whether the birth was vaginal or surgical, you will have a period of bleeding that can last from one to six weeks. This is called lochia, and in many ways it can resemble a very heavy period, though often the blood is mixed with mucous and other fluids. It is normal, especially after you rise from sitting or lying for a while in those first few days, to pass some small blood clots, but if you pass anything larger than a golf ball, or any time you think something is off, you should consult your provider. The bleeding should gradually lighten in the first day or two, decreasing from heavy, to medium, to light, to spotting. The placenta that detached from your uterus and caused this big "wound" needs time to heal. Bleeding sometimes becomes the barometer of whether you are getting adequate rest or whether you are doing too much. If at any point in the days or weeks following birth you experience very heavy bleeding, chest pain, shortness of breath, severe headache, vision changes, a temperature higher than 100.4°F, seizure, or a red or swollen leg that is sensitive to touch, call your provider immediately — these can all be signs of dangerous postpartum complications.

If you birthed at home or at a birth center that released you right after birth, you will likely receive a visit the next day and a few days later from the provider to check in on you. If you are in a hospital and have had a vaginal birth, you will most likely be released two days or so after the birth. For a cesarean, you usually have three or four days.

It often comes as a surprise for mothers in the hospital that they don't get a whole lot of uninterrupted rest. There are a lot of interruptions for all sorts of reasons and usually at all times of the day — blood pressure checks, uterus and bleeding checks, the janitor emptying your garbage, the cafeteria person wanting your food order, the pediatrician making rounds, the nursery staff wanting to check the baby's blood sugar or temperature, the hospital photography service, the nurse giving you more paperwork to sign, and more. (For some mothers of many, they still find this more relaxing than being at home!) Consider seeing if the maternity ward of the hospital has a "do not disturb" option so that both you and your husband, if he is there, can get some rest, which is the most important piece of recovery. Some hospitals will be more amenable to leaving you alone to sleep if there are no concerns. Some hospitals will only "allow" you to sleep if your baby is in the bassinet next to you and not in the bed, and some require a light on at all times if the baby is in the room.

The postpartum period is always a roller coaster for me, no matter how well prepared I have felt before delivery. Each new baby presented new joys, new considerations, different dynamics within the family, health issues for mom or baby … some things I could just not prepare for! What works best is to expect the unexpected, to rest as much as possible, not to get up "just to do a few things." All of these little lessons with each new baby have helped as I continue in the motherhood ahead!

— Lisa H., mom to nine on Earth and one in eternity

Protecting and Honoring the Postpartum Time

As much as possible, you should rest for at *least* two weeks after the birth. God designed there to be a period of recovery after birth. This is just as much for your baby as it is for you. There is certainly much practical wisdom contained in the Old Testament provisions and rules surrounding the postpartum seclusion time of a woman after birth. Having no plans, staying on or near the bed or couch, and having no other chores or obligations besides taking care of and nursing this newborn is best for both of you. You will heal faster and your milk will come in easier for your baby — and you likely won't get this chance again.

At about two or three days postpartum, the colostrum that your breasts have been producing, which is incredibly important for the baby's health, packed with nutrients and antibodies for his or her immune system, will change to beautiful, nourishing breastmilk. You may feel extremely full and engorged, and you are likely going to leak a lot of milk as your body figures out just how much to produce for this baby. The best thing to do during this time is to nurse whenever the baby needs to. It may feel as if you are nursing constantly, but that is exactly what both of you need.

Nursing often helps your body heal and forces you to rest, building up your milk supply for your baby to provide him or her the optimal nutrition for the days and months ahead. Resting, drinking, and eating enough is vital in helping your milk supply meet baby's needs. At birth, the normal newborn's stomach is about the size of a marble, so it makes sense that newborns digest that milk quickly and need constant fill-ups! All of this biological interplay is part of God's original design for our bodies. All of these events work together amazingly well for the good of not only mother and baby, but also the whole family. Trust your baby's cues and your body's cues. They are there for a reason.

The care you receive and give yourself during the postpartum period is also important for your own emotional and mental health. Your body just went through one of the most difficult physical feats humanity endures, not to mention the nine or so months of pregnancy that preceded it. It needs time to heal and recover! Your hormones are also adjusting, and postpartum can be an incredibly emotional time.

The immediate postpartum period is usually thought to be about six weeks long, but most experienced moms know that the healing and adjustment time varies tremendously depending on each baby and the circumstances and family dynamics surrounding the birth. Six weeks is usually about the time when you may feel somewhat back to normal physically — your body is usually done with the immediate healing and recovery from the birth. But just as with pregnancy and birth, every woman is different, and even each postpartum time for that woman is different. You may feel great within a week or two of giving birth, slowly getting back to normal. However, emotionally and mentally it can take months to even years for some women to feel "normal" again. Do what you can to give yourself room for that recovery.

Women in today's culture have a huge disadvantage when it comes to care during the postpartum period. We often feel (or are) expected to bounce right back within a few days of birth. This can be downright dangerous. In almost every other time and culture prior to today's, there was a period of confinement and recovery surrounding birth.

Pregnancy and birth is a tremendous work, and the body and mind need time to recover. But today's culture has mostly moved away from that model of care. Women are often expected to get right back to work, laundry, other children, making dinner, and hosting visitors far too soon. In the United States, the Family Medical Leave Act now provides that a woman's job is protected for up to twelve weeks after birth. For many women, though, that time is partially or totally unpaid and they cannot afford to lose that income, forcing them back into the workforce sooner rather than later. Take whatever steps you can to ensure that your primary job after birth is healing your body and feeding your baby. Extended family, the Church, and the community should take the lead in doing what they can to support families during this time, especially for women who desire to stay home with their babies but feel economic, social, or personal pressure to return to work.

Because we have been taught to value independence so highly, sometimes it can be difficult to ask for or take help, even during this important time. If this is you, consider it an act of love on your part to let others help you. You're giving them an opportunity to extend love and mercy. Even if you feel great, it is still an opportunity for others to honor the amazing work that you've done and the new life that is here. Those who value womanhood, motherhood, and new life should be doing their best to honor this sacred time for you and your baby. So let them! Take help that is offered, receive meals graciously, and if someone offers to pick up some groceries for you or help in some other way that would be good for you, let them.

If you don't have a strong support system around you, do your best before the birth to set things up so they will be conducive to your rest and recovery after birth. Consider making freezer meals and stocking up on lots of groceries as a future gift to yourself and your baby. See if there are any ministries or groups of older women at church who could help. There are an increasing amount of grocery stores offering delivery and companies providing meal delivery service. This is a great time to give yourself that luxury. Get any big chores out of the way that you know will need to be done so you don't have to worry about them postpartum. If you have the ability, hire help if needed, whether in the form of a housekeeper, a few nights of take-out food, or a postpartum doula (a doula who trains specifically in helping mothers through the postpartum time).

God designed this time for you and baby to be sacred and powerful. Yes, those first days for many women can be very difficult, but there is a profound grace present. Don't rush through it. Honor the work you've done and the design of God in creating children this way. Take the time to heal and to sink into these days. You have done something beautiful and important. The world and its obligations will come soon enough, but days with this newborn will never be here again. This season will pass; do your best to enter it and allow it to be.

The flood of hormones most moms experience and the "getting to know you" time with your newborn in the first few weeks is often now referred to as a "babymoon." Just as you and your husband may have experienced the innocent, awkward, romantic, and hormone-fueled weeks after your wedding day as a "honeymoon," there is a similar aspect to the time right after having a baby as you get to know this new person and form a relationship. Embrace that time and enter into it as best you can. With each subsequent baby, it might feel a little crazier managing the house during this time, but the repeated experience also brings with it the deep knowledge that these days don't come back.

The postpartum family should not be expected or obligated to entertain visitors or houseguests, and any visitors who are welcome should be willing to serve however they are able. Don't be afraid to set limits on what is good for your family or to say no to visits that will be stressful. This is a good opportunity for husbands to protect their wives and children and be assertive about what is best for their family. While it is incredibly exciting and fun to introduce the baby to relatives and friends, the health needs (both emotional and physical) of the mother and baby for bonding, healing, rest, and feeding need to come first. No one who is sick should be near the baby in these first few weeks. For many parents, their first outing with the baby is appropriately to Mass or to the baby's first pediatrician appointment.

Something you may want to consider in the postpartum period is seeing a pelvic-floor specialist. Whether you had a vaginal or surgical birth, a pelvic-health specialist can be a huge help in assessing whether the muscles and organs in your pelvic floor are healing correctly. Unfortunately, most doctors and midwives are not adequately skilled in this area, and many women suffer with incontinence, diastasis recti (a split in the abdominal muscles that doesn't heal after birth), organ prolapse, sexual difficulties, and more because the pelvic floor was weakened by pregnancy and birth and never properly healed. This is especially poignant for women who have had multiple pregnancies and want to be open to a large family. Problems with the pelvic floor can cause debilitating issues in subsequent pregnancies and can compromise that hope. Your doula, a midwife, local birth groups, or an internet search can help you find someone local to help you make sure that you are healing properly in every way.

The Reality of Postpartum Depression

Postpartum depression (PPD) is defined as depression and extreme sadness suffered by a mother following childbirth, making it difficult to care for herself or her baby.[137] Fortunately, more awareness has been developing in recent years about the reality of PPD as well as the causes and treatment of it. The postpartum period can be extremely difficult, and the difficulty is exacerbated by a society that doesn't properly respect or reverence this time. We expect mothers to live up to standards that are unhealthy (even dangerous) after they have a baby. It is safe to say that most women struggle to some extent or have specific issues to overcome during the postpartum days and weeks. Fluctuating hormones, sleep deprivation, the emotional stress of not feeling like "yourself" or being able to do what you were able to do before, having to accept a completely different body, can all contribute to bouts of sadness, anger, frustration, or feeling out of control.

For some women, the physical, emotional, and mental stress can trigger a deeper PPD. Even with the best of help and support, many women find themselves struggling and suffering greatly during these postpartum days. According to the National Institutes of Health, the symptoms of PPD include:

- Feeling sad, hopeless, empty, or overwhelmed
- Crying more often than usual or for no apparent reason
- Worrying or feeling overly anxious
- Feeling moody, irritable, or restless
- Oversleeping, or being unable to sleep even when the baby is asleep
- Having trouble concentrating, remembering details, and making decisions
- Experiencing anger or rage
- Losing interest in activities that are usually enjoyable

- Suffering from physical aches and pains, including frequent headaches, stomach problems, and muscle pain
- Eating too little or too much
- Withdrawing from or avoiding friends and family
- Having trouble bonding or forming an emotional attachment with her baby
- Persistently doubting her ability to care for her baby
- Thinking about harming herself or her baby[138]

While some of these on their own may merely be the signs and symptoms of normal postpartum difficulties, if you are experiencing several of these symptoms, or if you feel as if something may be off, talk to your provider about your options. It's a beautiful gift you can give your family to recognize that there might be something wrong and to work to fix it. It may be enough simply to figure out if there are certain triggers you have that exacerbate symptoms and then work on addressing those. For example, for some women, chronic intense sleep deprivation from the baby's wakings, along with not being able to make up for that with daytime naps, or having an unhealthy amount of obligations and expectations outside of the baby and family, can trigger PPD. For some women, the 24/7 needs of a newborn are a new experience and a shock to their normal lifestyle, and they might not have much practical help or emotional support. Some women are so busy that they don't get the chance to eat, take care of themselves in a healthy way, or heal physically before they are expected to fulfill unrealistic obligations and outside demands. All of these can trigger PPD, and it is especially so in women who have a history of depression or who do not have a strong support system around them.

Additionally, a woman's hormone levels shift so abruptly immediately after birth that there can be a hormone deficiency (usually progesterone) also contributing to potential PPD. Your provider may be able to check hormone levels and recommend a natural supplement to regulate things (like a progesterone cream or vitamin/enzyme supplement), or may prescribe synthetic progesterone. There is also the option of prescription medication that may be a good answer for women with severe symptoms of PPD. Talk with your provider, ask trusted friends for their experience and advice, research on your own, and pray about whether those might be an appropriate and safe answer for your situation.

Like most mental illnesses, diagnosis and treatment of PPD can be subjective. It's also difficult to know the exact causes, which are often a combination of factors. We do, however, know that several things contribute to an increased risk. A history of depression, bipolar disorder, or other mental illness creates a higher risk for the mother, as does a stressful life event surrounding the pregnancy or birth, such as a job loss or death of a family member. A baby with medical issues can also increase the risk, and a mother without a strong support system surrounding her after birth is also more likely to exhibit signs of PPD. A traumatic or difficult birth, or a birth experience that may have interrupted the normal hormonal interplay of the body, can also be a trigger. Recent research has shown that the use of Pitocin during birth also increases the risk of anxiety and PPD.[139] Mothers who are not able to, or choose not to, breastfeed are also at a statistically higher risk, as are women in poverty.[140]

It's interesting to note that some countries tend to have much lower occurrences of PPD, though hard statistics are elusive. What is different in those countries? Well, according to a study cited by the National Institutes of Health, there are six characteristics in those cultures markedly different from our own.

- These cultures maintain a distinct postpartum period of recovery.
- They maintain protective measures reflecting the new mother's vulnerability (cultural rituals proper to the care of the postpartum mother).
- They expect social seclusion (a period of being home for recovery and definitely not entertaining).
- They mandate rest for the new mother through cultural or religious tradition.
- They mandate functional assistance (practical help) either in the form of legally provided or culturally expected help after birth.
- They promote social recognition of her new role and status.[141]

Much of this stands in contrast to our typical expectations and treatment of new mothers in our society. While PPD certainly exists everywhere and looks to be increasing everywhere, according to more recent research, adopting some of these cultural attitudes toward the postpartum time could help curb the rising trend of PPD in our culture.

Knowing the factors that can contribute to postpartum depression is incredibly important in helping mothers, babies, families, and society as a whole respond to the problem. Some of the factors may be unavoidable in certain circumstances, but it is still helpful to know if you may be especially prone to PPD so that you, your provider, and your family can be proactive in preventing or responding to it. There are certain factors that can be addressed and treated beforehand so that women, babies, and families can truly thrive.

In my experiences with postpartum depression, I felt completely alone. Not because I didn't have loving friends and family who supported me, but because I knew no other women who had been through serious PPD, too. Which meant to me, in my less than rational state of mind, that I must be the only one in the world who ever felt this way.

Right before I began medication during my second round of PPD, I finally learned that another close friend had experienced depression for some time after the birth of her first child. We talked briefly about it for ten minutes over the phone, and then didn't speak of it much again. Depression, especially when it revolves around something so beautiful as the birth and care of a baby, is hard to talk about. We don't want to be labeled as someone with a mental illness. We don't want to be thought of as a weak or incapable mother. We're in a dark and sometimes ugly place, and it's excruciatingly painful and embarrassing to bare our souls — so we do everything we can to smile and pretend there's nothing wrong. And we just don't talk about it.

Postpartum depression, along with other maternal mental health disorders, is a complex illness that affects both the mind and the body; it's not a mood that can be switched off by sheer willpower. So, if you're suffering from PPD, stop demanding this of yourself. And if your loved one has PPD, don't expect this of her. Instead, speak to a doctor about options to help yourself or your loved one to overcome PPD.

This dark time will not last forever, but while it does,

sometimes just showing up makes you a hero. And if you can, take it a step further. Once you acknowledge that you have PPD, you're already on the path to a better life again. Now, reach out for physical, spiritual, and professional help (aka medication, counseling, and/or therapy), because you can't do it alone.

— Lydia Borja, mom to five

18

CLAIMING YOUR STORY: PROCESSING THE JOY OR PAIN OF YOUR BIRTH

"We know that in everything God works for good with those who love him, who are called according to his purpose."
— Romans 8:28

(Because of the intense nature of parts of this chapter, please use your own discretion in reading, especially if you are currently pregnant.)

We've talked a lot now about statistics and research, choices and ideals for your birth. But let's remember again that we are talking about real and unique people in real and unique circumstances. Every woman's life, personality, needs, fears, hopes, and situations are different. Every birth is going to look different. Your birth may end up exactly as you hoped, or it may turn out nothing like you expect. While it's good and important to plan for and work toward what we consider the best possible and most ideal birth, it is also important to remember not only that birth is unpredictable but that women's choices are going to look different depending on unique perspective and needs.

God made *you* the mother of this baby — not any other woman, not your friend, not your husband, not your provider, not your doula, not your mother, and not the author of that book on birth that you read. This is primarily your story and your baby's story. Other people will play a part, but it is not their birth. Let's be clear: There is grace and beauty available in every birth, whether surgical or vaginal, medicated or natural, planned or unplanned, whether you end up alone in your backyard or with every medical intervention under the sun. And God is ready, and wanting, to be a part of your unique story.

As you make decisions and process your birth afterward, keep that perspective. Other people can be there to help, but it is not their birth. It is for you to own and do. If you are making the best decisions you can using real science, truth, and love, aware of your personal situation and asking the Holy Spirit for guidance, then there is no reason to let guilt or judgment (from yourself or others) rob you of peace. You are the mother of this baby, and this birth is yours.

There is a tremendous learning curve when it comes to birth. As much as you can and should prepare, nothing but going through it yourself will teach you exactly what it is like. And no one else will know exactly what going through birth for you will be like. With each subsequent birth, you gain a little more insight, a little more wisdom about what you need and would like. That's why we need to process our births, which involves claiming them as our own and sometimes sharing them with others.

I hope your birth was incredible, that it helped you tap into your feminine genius and was a beautiful and profound moment in your womanhood, that you felt empowered and respected, and that it was exactly what you hoped for (or better). You deserve to celebrate the work you did, to honor how God worked through you to bring this beautiful baby into the world. Processing the birth — the beautiful parts, the hard parts, the funny parts, the difficult parts — by talking it out with friends or your husband, through prayer, or through writing the story down can help you chronicle this life-changing event, and it can also be a help for any future births.

How you understand and process your birth experience can have a profound impact on your emotional health as well as your confidence entering into motherhood. Birth is written deeply on our psyche and memories. That's why it can be such a tricky subject, triggering defensiveness, tears, judgment, or pride — precisely because it is so personal and intrinsic to who we are as women and mothers.

Each birth we go through changes us. The history of humanity shows that women (when they feel safe) share their stories with one another, and especially in recent years it has become more common for women to write down their birth stories. This trend speaks not only to how powerful the experience of birth is, but also to the long-term impact it has on the woman herself and the sisters around her.

Even if you don't remember every minute detail, birth leaves its imprint on you. The experience your husband, doula, or provider has of the birth may even be different from what you internalize, and it is important for you to honor that. As best you can, it's helpful to remember how things happened, how you felt, how you responded internally, and what that means for you now. There is a power that comes from claiming and owning your story.

It is important to be honest with yourself about how the birth affected you and what, if anything, you would do differently. Every birth, even those that go far off the plan and don't meet our hopes, can teach us something about ourselves and be vital to our personal story and growth.

Your story doesn't just serve you. It can also serve the women around you. For many women, it helps, as they prepare for birth, to read or hear other women's good birth stories (not to be confused with horror stories!). Knowing that other women have done it lets us know that we can, too. Reading how someone worked through labor and catching a glimpse of the triumph experienced at the end has an incredible effect on our own confidence and mindset. Just as a marathon runner or athlete can gain advice from others who have done it before and be encouraged by stories of triumph, so, too, can a mother find herself encouraged during pregnancy, realizing that her training, sacrifice, and work will be more than worth it.

Sharing your story in an appropriate setting can be an encouragement and help to the sisters around you. Also of help can be what you learned from your birth. Are there things you wish you had done differently? Do you regret any of your decisions? Can you recommend something that helped you? Respectfully and prudently sharing those parts of your story with other women can be an amazing gift, contributing to the rebuilding of the collective memory of birth and womanhood within our culture.

The birth of my third child was a beautiful spiritual encounter for my husband and me. Although we had delivered our first two children naturally, just like this one, I don't believe that we had consciously invited Christ to our birth in the same way that we did with him. This baby was our first home birth, and so I had been more intentional about the environment that I was creating for the birth. Christ showed up in the most moving way, and my beliefs about birth shifted in a way that I hadn't expected. I was so humbled by the beautiful birth that I had experienced, and I was truly grieved that societal beliefs and culture have robbed so many mothers and fathers of the exquisite joy that can be present when welcoming their child into the world. Oh, yes, it's difficult work to give birth! But that work leads to a precious joy that is all the greater because of the pain; it reminds me of the beautiful prayer of the Church, "O happy fault that earned for us so great, so glorious a Redeemer."

I spent some time pondering this realization that birth is more holy and sacred, more important to the life of the family, and more impacting on the bonds of holy marriage than I had ever realized. I thought about the fact that families and society are being negatively impacted by being so unaware of the immense graces that are available to us during birth. I think I subconsciously believed that natural birth and even home birth are more open avenues of these graces, because in my own experience, that had been true. However, my fifth baby was a home birth transfer during labor for a cesarean section; yet again, I had a powerful spiritual experience of birth. I have come to believe that the attitude with which we approach our births is much more important than the details of how and where the birth happens. We must make decisions about birth based first and foremost on prayer. Every birth story is different. But what makes them all the same is that for each and every birth, Christ awaits our invitation to attend.

— Katie W., mom to six on Earth and four in eternity

Complications, Regret, and Trauma during Birth

There are times during birth when things don't go as planned, when plans are ignored, or perhaps only in hindsight do we realize the choices we would have made differently had we had more information. Because birth is so innate to the design of woman, a bad birth experience can profoundly affect our heart, mind, soul, and body. For some women, birth can actually be a traumatic experience, especially if the innate desire to be respected, informed, and safe is threatened, or if circumstances beyond anyone's control bring fear and chaos.

Perhaps, even with all the best information and circumstances, you or your baby had a bad or traumatizing birth experience mentally, emotionally, or physically. Certainly, sometimes it is no one's fault when a birth isn't ideal or becomes traumatic. Perhaps you were not well prepared for the reality of birth, or perhaps an emergency arose. Even if no one is at "fault" for a bad birth experience — or even a tragedy — you as a mother and woman still need to process that experience and work through the effects of it. It is not at all helpful to brush the experience aside, or for others to belittle what happened. When such an important moment in your life becomes an episode of shock, fear, sadness, or tragedy, it can affect every part of you deeply.

If this is you, know that it is right and good to acknowledge this and give yourself the space to work through it. It is not helpful to shut up valid emotions, thoughts, and effects of a birth because, "at least the baby is healthy." You can thank God for the health of your baby (if that is the case), but it is still okay to be sad about parts of the birth that were not ideal, not what you wanted, or that were, in fact, traumatic to you or the baby. Recognizing the loss when things don't go according to God's original design honors him and reinforces your personal dignity and that of your baby.

In some instances of traumatic birth, women feel they were manipulated into choices or not given any respect or choices at all. There are cases of legitimate physical and emotional abuse during births. Far too many women have birthed under circumstances of fear, coercion, abuse, and, in some instances, even direct refusal to honor their choices and requests. "Birth rape" is a very real thing, where women in the birth room are directly violated by someone giving them an exam or violating their consent for treatment by force, and often these measures are deemed acceptable simply because the one doing it is in a position of power. Providers have recently begun to be prosecuted and sued for such instances.

In one of the most vulnerable moments of her life, it is absolutely essential that the mother always be treated with dignity and respect. This should never be at the expense of the baby, of course, but violating a mother's reasonable wishes, her autonomy and dignity, forcing or coercing her to accept treatment, or performing exams or procedures without her consent is never acceptable. This is a violation of her dignity as a woman and her God-given role as a mother. Taking advantage of a woman in the most vulnerable moments of birth is shameful and an affront to God, the mother, the father, and the baby.

If you have experienced what you would define as a traumatic birth, please know that it is okay to recognize and talk about it. You did not deserve what happened to you. You have the right to grieve, be angry, sad, disappointed, and to process your birth experience. Find a safe place to share where your experience won't be belittled, judged, or brushed aside, and also where it won't possibly cause unnecessary fear in other women before their own births. If the situation is severe, know that you could even be dealing with post-traumatic stress disorder; consider finding a good counselor who can help you work through the issues surrounding your birth.

Pray for healing from wounds created by the experience and ask God to redeem that birth for you somehow. Perhaps it will be through helping others have better births; maybe it will be through refocusing and healing the memories of the event; or perhaps you can simply learn from that experience and apply those lessons to your next birth. Maybe it will simply (and importantly) be through finding peace despite the suffering and pain you endured. Part of your healing may be in directly addressing anyone you feel may have played a part in that trauma and drawing their attention to how their actions abused your dignity. If the situation is grave enough, you may have recourse legally or within the hierarchy of a provider's or staff's place of work or professional organization.

Ignoring the effects of a traumatic birth can be dangerous emotionally, mentally, spiritually, and even physically. It can contribute to anxiety disorders, depression, eating disorders, anger issues, marital issues, and even physical illness. If, for whatever reason, you were denied a positive birth experience, there is not something wrong with you for being sad about that and acknowledging that loss. It is an honest and healthy assessment and demonstrates maturity and acknowledgment of God's beautiful design. He can and wants to heal and redeem those moments for you, and it is a gift to yourself and your family to let him. Our Lord knows what it is like to be abused, mistreated, mocked, and shamed. He knows what it is like to go through physical and emotional trauma. He wants to take even the difficult moments, the painful moments, the choices we regret, or the situations that were beyond our control and draw us into his Sacred Heart. There we can lay the pain down and, in return, find freedom, healing, and peace. There, we can allow him to speak directly to our hearts: "Behold, I make all things new" (Rv 21:5). He has the power to redeem even the most painful situations and somehow bring beauty out of them.

My first pregnancy was a huge learning experience for me. I wasn't familiar with pregnancy and birth, and living far from my family left it largely up to my husband and me and a few close friends to navigate the normal ups and downs. I spent a lot of time scrolling on BabyCenter, asking questions at my OB appointments, and wondering what birth would really be like once the big day came.

While the first labor and delivery was peaceful, it wasn't until about a year later when we started discerning future children that I realized that as much as I loved our little one, the birth experience itself was less than ideal. I had often felt belittled for asking so many questions and treated with little respect. Prenatal visits almost always included checking my cervix or some other invasive checkup. They were painful, and no one explained why they were doing them. But I figured it was just how things were. I didn't know better to question.

At the hospital, while in labor, I was given the same treatment. Placed on my back while laboring, hooked up to many unnecessary machines and IVs, and given round-the-clock cervical checks without much respect or communication. At one point my doctor came in and without discussing it with me walked past the nurse and said, "If she doesn't speed up, put her on Pit [Pitocin to augment labor]." At that point, I had only been on the bed for two hours and was progressing fine. But the process seemed to be doctor directed with the one goal just to speed labor along so we could get it over with. When pushing finally came, I was given an episiotomy without my knowledge which led to a fourth-degree tear. (I was told it was third degree several times until I read my medical record.) The recovery took weeks and weeks, and, again, I believed this all to be a normal part of birth at the time.

When I started researching on my own and reading blogs and books on birth, I was amazed to find out that birth didn't have to be this overly medical. Some women actually birthed without medication or tearing, and some even recovered with minimal pain. Babies bonded well, mothers were treated with dignity, and there were less invasive ways to chart progress and health in a pregnancy and labor. After this discovery, and when we conceived our second, I planned to birth naturally, declined additional exams to check dilation unless truly necessary, and tried techniques to prevent tearing while pushing. That pregnancy went well, and I felt a world of difference in respect with a different provider (a certified nurse midwife in a hospital setting). I felt prepared mentally as well for the first time after reading *Ina May's Guide to Childbirth* and some Bradley birth books and resources.

At forty weeks, I began having very early contractions as I showered for my regular checkup that day. I wondered if I might be on my way to birth! When we arrived at the appointment, I received an ultrasound and everything looked great. At the checkup, my midwife offered to see how far dilated I was and I agreed, curious to know if the contractions I was feeling were doing anything. That was when all my preparations and plans changed in an instant. As she checked me and said "about three-and-a-half to four centimeters" I felt inside of me a strange pop that wasn't my bag of waters. My midwife pulled her hand out and I felt a fast, warm gush. Then another. And another. I looked down and I was bleeding everywhere. So much so, that the nurse and midwife who've been working in the birth setting for decades were visibly shaken and rushing as fast as they could to get me over to Labor and Delivery. His birth ended in a very necessary cesarean. The bleeding was caused by a marginal placental abruption that happened as I began contracting in the office visit. It was the last thing I wanted, and several times I wondered if I might lose the baby or my own life.

That night was the loneliest night of my life. My husband had to go home to care for our three-year-old, and since I was post-op I couldn't care for the baby in [the] room alone, and the nursery had to take him. I remember feeling so empty in my body and my heart. I was shocked holding my baby for the first time several hours later and not feeling bonded or connected to him. There was no surge of oxytocin and everything seemed forced and difficult. I mothered him and loved him from memory of my firstborn. That was something I hadn't expected at all, but I can understand now because of the nature of his delivery. Two days after the birth I received a blood transfusion because of the sheer blood loss and my numbers still so low. Breastfeeding was difficult and I had to fight with the nursery to get a syringe to formula feed at the breast rather than bottle. My milk took days to come in, and overall it was a very trying experience for our whole family.

Emotionally, I experienced birth PTSD symptoms for months after, often having nightmares about being laid on the operating table and trying to escape. I also experienced anxiety and panic attacks, always wondering when the next bad thing would happen to our family. Driving by the hospital produced high levels of anxiety and flashbacks as well. That birth opened my eyes to the suffering that is part of so many stories. I tasted a place that I didn't know existed in both births at that point — one of intense joy with my first and one of intense pain with my second. Both formed me as a mother and taught me more than any book could.

When we conceived my thirdborn, the second we found out, I had a deep and lasting peace, knowing that this birth would be completely fine. I had come a long way from the past two births and sought out a provider that would not only have our safety, but our emotional well-being, in mind and treat us with dignity. I was able to find a wonderful midwife, and we had a smooth birth at home. It was vastly different from my first two, and for the first time I had a provider that spoke to the baby in utero as a person with dignity. There was so much reverence and respect for both me and baby the entire time. I wasn't forced into any procedures without discussing things first, and the safety of me and baby were still the priority. The sheer pain of an all-natural and fast birth was incredible, but being able to birth how my body dictated without much intervention made a world of difference. Although this baby was bigger than my first, I tore very little. I had one cosmetic tear stitched up and everything else was perfectly fine.

With our fourth, I had on-and-off contractions for over two weeks. Each night I'd go to sleep contracting, and then they would be gone by morning. It was mentally challenging to wonder each day if and when she would arrive. The last few days before her birth were especially challenging. Finally, the night of my thirty-first birthday, I had contractions that stayed and woke me up. They were short and well spaced, however, so I didn't take them seriously. That morning, I had a few that were just intense enough that I felt I wanted my midwife there — more for emotional support than anything. I even apologized when she arrived that I may have called her too soon. This labor was so different from my last because I was able to relax my entire body and breathe through each without them getting too intense or close together. I had no indication birth was very close. So, my midwives and I sat in my room chatting and hanging out. I had one contraction that felt really strong, and after that one my water broke all over my carpet. Still, we thought it might be at least several minutes until things progressed. It appeared I hadn't even reached transition yet with how I was acting. Five minutes after my water broke she was born.

Shortly after the placenta was birthed, I began bleeding too much and felt a little spacey, so I was given Pitocin and herbs, which worked wonderfully. However, the bleeding and quickness of everything seemed to have triggered past birth trauma, and I began having mild panic and anxiety attacks for the following hours. It was the smoothest and quickest birth, but the hours after were challenging emotionally as I worked through my body's response to such a quick birth and also the emotions it all brought up.

As I reflect on all four births, I find that birth brings with it inexplicable suffering and joy. There is a beautiful mix of pain and bits of heaven as we come close to the thin veil that separates time from eternity. It's a taste of something that truly has no words — whether the birth goes perfectly as planned or disastrously as feared. I've had such a variety of births, and no matter how different the circumstances have been, they have all left my heart and my entire being very raw to something I sense only mothers truly understand.

— Angie W., mom to four

19

LOSS

"The Lord is near to the brokenhearted, and
saves the crushed in spirit."
— *Psalms 34:18*

(This chapter will approach a sensitive and delicate subject. Please use your own
discernment in reading, especially if you are currently pregnant.)

My prayer is that you never need this chapter. The sad reality is, though, that even if you have not experienced this loss, you probably know someone who has experienced the loss of a baby before, during, or shortly after birth. Far too many families have gone through the grief of losing a little one without information about what to expect during a miscarriage or stillbirth.

It may seem out of place to have a chapter on loss in a book about birth. Yet every life has value, even those who never make it into this world, and these babies also have their own story. In the case of the death of a baby, the mother will often still need to go through a form of birth, be it natural, surgical, induced, or otherwise. It is important for women of childbearing potential to know what to expect, as well as their rights, when it comes to having a miscarriage — before it happens.

If you are reading this because you have experienced or are experiencing the death of your baby, I am so very sorry. Know that even in the midst of this grief you, as mother to this baby, can make choices that will honor the dignity and reality of the precious little person you mourn.

Your Rights during a Loss

We believe that a unique human person is created at conception, as science shows and our faith confirms. So the death of that person, no matter how early, should be treated as such. Whether the loss is your own or that of someone close to you, being a people who value every human life means that when it comes to miscarriage, we need to respond accordingly. Mothers have the right to evidence-based care that respects their dignity as well as that of their child, not only in birth but also in miscarriage and stillbirth.

Regrettably, this is not always the case. In the midst of shock, fear, grief, and ignorance, a mother suffering a miscarriage can get swept into a medical system that may or may not be providing proper individualized attention and care. She often might feel as if she doesn't have a choice in her treatment or course of action, or doesn't receive valid answers to her questions. Because she is in the midst of grief, she may not even think to ask any questions. Rarely are options presented to vulnerable moms so that they can make the choices that are best for them in their circumstances. There are countless mothers and fathers who, looking back on the loss of their baby, wish they had done things differently.

The following is a list of important points to know when it comes to miscarriage and stillbirth, all of which should be clearly emphasized during a miscarriage.

You have the right ...

- ... to ask to be tested for progesterone levels and receive an immediate prescription for supplements if there is a chance it could save your baby.
- ... to have another ultrasound to confirm beyond any doubt that your baby has passed before making any decisions.
- ... to request a copy of an ultrasound picture.
- ... to opt to deliver the baby's body at home.
- ... to ask questions.
- ... to trust your instincts.
- ... to not have any concerns dismissed.
- ... to always be treated with respect and dignity, and, at any point, to change providers or ask for a new staff member.
- ... to know all short-term and long-term risks of a D&C procedure. For some women a D&C may be the best option; however, you deserve to know that it has the risk of causing infertility or compromising a future pregnancy,[142] weakening the cervix, resulting in a future premature birth,[143] or complicating a future birth because of scar tissue.[144]
- ... to refuse a vaginal exam. If the baby is still alive, it can increase the risk of a membrane rupture and preterm labor,[145] compromising the life of the baby. These exams also carry the risk of infection to the mother.
- ... to have the father, a doula, and/or another support person present

during any medical exams or treatment.

- … to call a priest to come pray with you and bless the baby's body.
- … to say no to any treatment.
- … to choose to do nothing.
- … to hold your baby's body and not be rushed.
- … to choose some sort of pain relief.
- … to have a funeral for your baby.
- … to bury your baby. (If the baby's body passes in the hospital or the remains are removed via a D&C procedure, you have the right to your baby's remains. Be aware that in some states there may be laws governing how his or her body is released.)
- … to take personal time from work.
- … to name your baby, grieve your baby, and talk (or not talk) about your baby.

Especially when a mother and father are grieving, they deserve to be treated with compassion, have access to evidence-based care, and have their voices heard and respected. Maybe, slowly, as more and more people share their stories, know their options, and demand better care, we can make a difference, not stopping until all mothers and babies receive the care they deserve during this heartbreaking time.

Going through a Miscarriage

There are several ways a miscarriage can occur. Sometimes a miscarriage happens quickly, in the very early weeks — you've had a positive pregnancy test and a few days later begin to bleed. This is what is referred to as a chemical pregnancy or sometimes a molar pregnancy. It is just as much a miscarriage as if it happened further along, but, unfortunately, it is treated as routine and there are no visible remains of the baby. Sadly, this can even happen without your knowledge, since it often occurs right on or after the time that you would be expecting your period. When a miscarriage happens further along, sometimes the bleeding or cramping begins first and indicates a problem. Other times it happens that at a routine ultrasound a couple is shocked to find that the baby has no heartbeat and has passed away.

If you are pregnant and begin spotting or cramping in the early weeks, call your midwife or doctor. Usually an ultrasound is ordered to figure out what is going on. If the ultrasound shows the baby has no heartbeat, the doctor or midwife will inform you and estimate at what week the baby stopped growing. The bleeding is the beginning of passing your baby. If there are no signs of dangerous hemorrhaging, you will often be sent home to complete the miscarriage.

If the baby is still alive, find out if it can be determined what is actually going on and what you can do, if anything, to help protect the life of your baby. Testing and, if indicated, supplementing progesterone may be vital to helping save your baby's life. Go home, get rest, hydrate, pray, and do as little as possible physically. Spotting can also be caused by a small bleed in the uterus (which often clears up on its own, though it depends on the severity), intercourse, vaginal checks, or placenta issues.

Whether an ultrasound was routine or ordered because of bleeding, if it is clear that your baby has passed, it is strongly encouraged that you make sure to have the ultrasound technician print a picture of your baby for you. This picture will be the only photograph you may ever have of your baby. This shouldn't be a problem, but there are women who are denied this simple and easy request because the baby has passed. If, for some reason, this happens, fight for that picture. Having even that one photograph of your baby can be a tremendous comfort later on and a valuable reminder that he or she is part of your family and not forgotten.

If you discover at a routine ultrasound that your baby has died, you do have the choice to go home and wait for the miscarriage process to continue naturally. This may take a few days or weeks. As long as there is no sign of infection or hemorrhage, you do have this option. It is incredibly difficult emotionally and sometimes physically, but for some women it can be a preferable option to having the remains manually removed, which we will discuss below.

Our eighth pregnancy resulted in a miscarriage. It was very difficult for me, but God was so present to me, too. I literally felt held and carried by God and by all those who I knew were praying for us through the time when we were waiting for the miscarriage to take place and after as we buried the remains together as a family in a cemetery. He was with us all along that way.

— Lisa H., mom to nine on Earth and one in eternity

The Miscarriage Labor

Often, if the passing of the baby begins on its own, it will feel like a mini labor. There will be cramping and intermittent contractions that grow in intensity until the baby, the yolk sac or placenta, and the tissue are expelled from the uterus. It is likely there will be bleeding, possibly a lot, during all of this. It may seem weird, but to help ensure that your baby's body does not get flushed and receives a dignified burial if possible, you can use a bowl to catch anything that is passed. You may be able to see the baby's body, which is a tremendous blessing, but it may be too small or have already begun to break down, and you may not recognize anything. Either way, you can still treat the remains with respect. This is a reason that many women prefer to miscarry at home rather than at a hospital or doctor's office, so they can ensure that the remains are saved and treated with dignity.

Once the baby has passed, the cramping should mostly subside and your bleeding should ease a bit. It is normal to bleed for a few days afterward, and you needn't worry too much, as long as it is not heavy. You should be in communication with your doctor or midwife, and he or she will likely want to examine you to make sure the miscarriage is complete to avoid complications or the possibility of infection.

If you go through the miscarriage at the hospital, they will often want to take the baby's remains to pathology. You will have to undergo exams and questions and are vulnerable to the beliefs and procedures of hospital staff who may or may not understand how difficult this is for you. If you decide to go to the hospital, a Catholic hospital may be a better option if there is one in your area. Most Catholic hospitals recognize that the remains are yours and will turn them over several days later for burial if you desire, though there are sometimes restrictions due to state laws and guidelines. Some Catholic hospitals also provide a general burial place for the remains of babies within a diocesan cemetery for those who don't claim their baby's remains. Don't be afraid to ask questions. You may feel weird or uncomfortable, but if it is possible, a proper burial is a beautiful gift to your baby. If you want to bury your baby on your own, know that individual states have different laws regarding the release of the remains. In some, you may not be able to claim and take the remains of your baby without the interjection of a licensed funeral director, who will actually come pick up the remains from the hospital on your behalf. If you were not able to save the baby's remains for whatever reason, it is okay to grieve that, and you can still have a Mass prayed for your child.

If the baby has died but labor doesn't seem to be starting on its own, you will likely be offered medical intervention. This is a time when it is very helpful to have or know of a solidly pro-life doctor to ensure that you and the baby are treated with dignity and respect. The methods offered if your body is not yet going into labor are a D&C (which stands for dilation and curettage) or a D&E (which stands for dilation and evacuation). Both of these are methods to remove the baby and tissue from your uterus surgically. The cervix is dilated and in a D&C your baby's body and the uterine lining are removed by the doctor with surgical instruments. In a D&E, the baby's body and uterine lining are suctioned out. In both these instances the remains are usually sent to pathology labs to ensure that everything was removed. You should have the option for anesthesia since these procedures can be painful, and they do run the risk of scarring your uterus or cervix, which can cause complications in future pregnancies or births.

If you decide that this is the best option for you, *make sure that you have at least one more detailed ultrasound and are absolutely, 100 percent certain that the baby has died.* There are many instances of women who refused a D&C and discovered later on that their baby was okay, or that there was a twin, or that their dating was simply off, or that there was a mix-up in the blood-testing paperwork. A D&C or D&E may be the best choice, but should only be used when you are absolutely certain that the baby has died.

After your miscarriage, you may still feel pregnant for several weeks. It feels cruel, but it sometimes takes a while for the HcG hormone that you produce while pregnant to be out of your system.

The Remains of the Baby

One of the corporal works of mercy for Christians is burying the dead, and this mercy certainly extends to unborn children. If you have the body of your baby, you have several choices. You can buy or build a simple wooden casket. This doesn't have to be fancy or even a "real" casket. It can be a simple box or container large enough to hold the baby's remains. Unless the baby's body is refrigerated between the time of the labor and the burial, know that it will start to break down. If the hospital has the remains, arrange to pick them up, unless you have a Catholic hospital that will be burying the remains for you and you prefer that.

It is possible to have a funeral Mass offered for your child, and, in fact, the Church encourages it. A priest can offer a funeral Mass as well as the burial prayers by the graveside. For both, the Order of Christian Funerals specific to the death of a child is used. Call your priest and ask to schedule something. The priest may also offer a special blessing for the parents after a miscarriage.[146] You may bury your baby at a cemetery or simply in a special spot in your yard (there may be state laws to consider). As mentioned, many Catholic dioceses have an area set aside in their cemeteries for unborn children, often free of charge. This is a wonderful option, but you may not be able to place a marker, and the baby is usually buried with other little ones who have died. If you would like a plot unique to your baby, you will need to purchase that from the cemetery (though some offer it free for children) and arrange for burial.

Can You Baptize Your Miscarried Baby?

As Catholics we know the importance of baptism for our children. We can find peace in knowing that for those babies for whom baptism was not possible we "entrust them to the mercy of God" (*Catechism of the Catholic Church*, 1261). However, if we are able to perform a baptism on a miscarried baby, we should do so. If you are able to identify your baby's remains and are not sure whether the baby is alive, you can use water and offer a conditional baptism: "If you can be baptized, I baptize you in the name of the Father, Son, and Holy Spirit." If the baby is clearly alive but in danger of immediate death, you can and should perform an emergency baptism. While we cannot perform an official baptism while the baby is in utero, if we suspect that the baby is in danger or has already died, we can cover that baby with the baptism of desire, trusting that God knows our intentions for the baby and our desire for that baby to receive the grace of baptism.

The Church teaches that we can have "hope that there is a way for salvation for children who have died without baptism."[147] In *The Hope of Salvation for Infants Who Die Without Being Baptized*, the Vatican's International Theological Commission writes, "Our conclusion is that the many factors that we have considered above give serious theological and liturgical grounds for hope that unbaptized infants who die will be saved and enjoy the Beatific Vision."[148] We can pray and hope that we will see our little ones in heaven.

Our plan involved an induction the next day. It was long,
it was painful, and yet it was so special, that time with
just my husband and baby, creating her own birth story.
We were blessed to have a friend, a Catholic midwife,
with us; she conditionally baptized our babe as she

physically entered this world. A few weeks previously I had experienced a strong feeling, I had contemplated that something was wrong, and I recall consciously handing her to God. I prayed, "Thy will be done" and covered her by the baptism of desire.

Our hearts were broken, and yet in sorrow there is joy; there are precious moments. That day, as we waited for labor to start, every member of the nursing staff sharing their own stories of loss, they truly extended their hands in love, they nurtured and prepared us. They forever have a place in our hearts.

We took our wee babe home in her little shoebox coffin, and we rang our priest, who was very good to us. He came and conditionally baptized her again and buried our baby in a burial ceremony on our front lawn. This was incredibly consoling. We are forever grateful to that priest and to the Church for her sacraments.

— Erin H., mom to ten on Earth and two in eternity

Going through a Stillbirth

A baby who has died after twenty weeks is technically considered a stillbirth rather than a miscarriage. If it is close to the twenty-week mark, the birth may go similarly to what we described above for a miscarriage. However, if later, chances are higher that you may need to be in the hospital or in the care of a midwife at home for what will be more similar to a full-term delivery. If the baby has died and you and your provider have determined that you should not wait for natural labor to begin, rather than a D&C or D&E, you will have to be in the hospital for an induction of labor, usually using Cervidil (a prostaglandin gel applied to the cervix to prepare it for labor) and Pitocin for a vaginal birth, though sometimes a cesarean may be required.

Needless to say, this is incredibly difficult emotionally and physically. The presence of your husband, of a doula with experience in loss (sometimes called a bereavement doula), or of any other support you need will be helpful. Thankfully, many hospitals now have perinatal bereavement workers to work with you and walk you through the process of birthing your baby. You still have many of the same rights as you do with a living child when it comes to how you labor. You are free to choose or not choose different interventions or pain relief, and you can still have your choices respected during this time. You should get time after the birth to hold your baby's body for as long as needed. Many parents choose to take pictures of their baby and invite other family members to come see the baby. It is encouraged that you call a priest who can come and anoint and pray over the baby.

Because of the age of the baby, it is legally required in almost all states that a funeral director be involved and handle the burial. They will be responsible for taking care of the body and will walk you through the steps of the funeral planning and burial.

Carrying to Term after an Adverse Diagnosis

Another particularly heavy cross is receiving a difficult diagnosis in utero, whether because of a significant medical condition or one in which the baby will not survive after birth. Many mainstream medical professionals now recommend and expect mothers to abort their babies upon such a diagnosis. It is a strong and beautiful testimony to the dignity of every single life and the preciousness of this child when a mother and father choose to carry their baby to term, despite adverse diagnoses. Couples who make this choice leave room for a miracle and also recognize that even the best fetal screenings have a failure rate. Moreover, their witness underscores the eternal truth that every child is infinitely valuable, and that God is the author of all life, not us. Whether a person lives for a few moments or a hundred years, each is equally valuable.

Carrying to term a baby not expected to live is incredibly heart-wrenching. During a pregnancy like this, some parents find that a midwife or doctor who shares their faith (or at least truly respects it) can be an important part of their child's story and their own experience. If that is not available to you, though, know that your witness to the sanctity and value of every life can be powerful to a medical system and staff that may view it differently. Nowadays, thankfully, there is usually more support and help available in the hospital setting for parents who choose to carry their baby to term. There will usually be as much time as you need spent with your baby, funeral and baptismal arrangements will be aided, and often bereavement support is provided by the hospital. While individual circumstances will vary, parents will usually still be able to have a birth plan and have the birth they desire for their baby.

My first loss occurred after I had two healthy babies. This miscarriage shook me to my core. I had to develop coping mechanisms on the spot because it was my first real experience with loss. I desperately wanted to get pregnant again, and I did, with my Benjamin. At seven months pregnant, my doctor told me that they had not checked my ultrasound from twenty weeks until now. They told me at twenty weeks that he was a boy, but not that he had anencephaly, a condition "not compatible with life." We were shocked and angry and devastated. The doctor here in Michigan told us to induce the baby now. We were so confused. Wasn't that an abortion?

We called our priest. He came to our house and listened to our sad story. He anointed us and told us to embrace life even though we may want to stop the pain. He was a guide through the darkness. From that moment on we did embrace our dear Benjamin. We switched doctors to a wonderful Catholic doctor in another state near extended family, which was our best decision. We chose to carry our baby to term and then deliver him there so that our extended family could be part of his life. That was the second-best decision we made.

Our doctor there prayed with us on his knees before Ben was born. Our family visited us in the hospital as we waited for Ben to join us. Actually, he was acutely with us. We didn't wait for his birth to celebrate his life. We cherished every single minute.

Benjamin was born into love.

It was important to us, and therefore our doctor, that he was baptized right after birth. A dear priest friend was called when Ben was close to being born, and he was waiting in the hall as Ben came into the world. His baptism was so special. Then my family poured into the room. Smiling and tearful. The Holy Spirit filled the room with joy and grace. My precious baby was alive in my arms. But, it was clear that he couldn't survive on this Earth. I held him as he died in my arms the very next morning.

Of course, that is not the end, because we have our faith. Benjamin is at my side as I volunteer to care for the dying at hospice. He comes with me to my pregnancy loss support group meeting that I lead. And he gave me the courage to donate my kidney to my brother last month. Through the Communion of Saints, love is eternal and our bond is not broken.

Margaret Swedene, mom to six on Earth
and two in eternity

Mourning Your Baby

Remember to allow yourself time to grieve. The loss of your baby at any age is a big deal. It's not just a lost dream or an unfortunate health issue. It is truly the death of your child, and you deserve to mourn it as such. It's okay and right to be sad. It's okay and right to take a while. It's okay and right not to feel like yourself for months or even years. You will heal, but you will never forget your child. The rawness will likely wear off (and that's okay and right, too), but it's acceptable to feel that there is always someone missing. It's okay to talk about your baby and accept help from those who love you.

It is helpful for many families to name the baby, no matter at what age he or she died. It can be comforting to know that your baby has the dignity of a name and to be able to ask that baby's intercession for your family. It is also helpful for siblings to have a name to connect with their brother or sister in heaven. You can pray to that member of your family, even if it has been years since you lost him or her. If you do have other children, talk about their sibling. They have a right to know about their sibling and, if needed, to grieve that loss as well.

God is so near to you during this time, though it may not feel like it. You may feel angry with him or rejected by him, or experience profound desolation during your grief. Hold on to the fact that God is walking you through it. We may never fully understand why things happen the way they do, or why this child died, but remember this wasn't a part of his original plan, either. If it is hard for you to connect with God during this time, consider reaching out to Mary. She held her lifeless Son after his agonizing and undeserved death, and she can be a tremendous comfort. She gets it. Saints such as Zélie Martin, who lost four children herself, can be great intercessors for us as we mourn.

Be sure to allow time to heal physically. Remember, you just gave birth and likely lost some blood. Give yourself time to rest, stay hydrated, and take care of your health. Some women bounce back right away, but others may take several weeks to feel normal physically. Give yourself room for that.

There are several other ways to honor the life of your baby. You can have a Mass said for your baby at your parish. Pro-life offices in many dioceses offer special Masses for grieving parents. There are also countless other personal ways to remember and honor your child:

- Display his or her ultrasound picture in your home.
- Keep mementos of your child, such as the ultrasound picture, the positive pregnancy test, or cards in a special box.
- Hang a Christmas ornament or a stocking in the child's memory.
- Plant a tree or flower in the child's memory.
- Participate in Pregnancy and Infant Loss Remembrance Day on October 15.
- If you feel called, share your experience with others.
- Make a donation in your child's memory to a crisis pregnancy center, your parish, or any charity that is personal to your family.

Each parent's way of grieving will be unique. Provided we are acknowledging the dignity and personhood of the unborn baby who has died, there are a multitude of ways to grieve that are healthy and deserve to be respected. There is a tremendous amount of healing that can come from acknowledging the reality of the son or daughter who has died and doing everything in our power to recognize that loss within ourselves, our families, our communities, and our Church.

Pregnancy after Loss

Experiencing the loss of a baby, or even having a living child faced with a difficult medical condition, can significantly impact every pregnancy afterward. Losing a baby can also bring loss of trust in your body and pregnancy, and loss of joy during future pregnancies. While not every mom experiences this, it is certainly common. Especially in the case of multiple losses, mothers can struggle with questions and doubts. Will *this* baby live? Even if there was no found cause for the previous loss, it can be difficult to rejoice fully in the life of this new baby. Those mixed feelings can then be compounded by guilt over not feeling the "right" away about this new baby.

Those six short weeks that we had with our baby were so happy. I still possessed a slice of innocence that I'll never recover. The pregnancy was very desired, the baby was so very loved, and we were so, so excited. Miscarriage never even crossed my mind, but I would miscarry our baby at home on the night of October 10 after only a minor warning that something might be wrong. And I'll never quite know that kind of hidden delight during a pregnancy again. I can still remember exactly what it felt like, having the secret of a new life inside you, imagining the future with that little one laid out before you, the anticipation of bringing a new person into this world, picturing little toes and a tiny button nose. The term "expecting" has always been one that has appealed to me so much more than "pregnant," because it captures a bit of those fluttery feelings of excitement and anticipation and joy.

The last few pregnancies though, I've expected a miscarriage, not a baby, and there is nothing but dread in that. Even though my pregnancy with my son after my four losses was healthy and without any major complications, I was convinced my baby would not live until the moment my husband placed him on my chest after his birth. Seeing his face for the first time was honestly a bit of a shock because, despite being forty-one weeks pregnant, I was not expecting a living, breathing child.

So much more than a baby is lost during a miscarriage. It's the loss of hopes and dreams, innocence, joy. For me, it changed every pregnancy after. I'm glad I got those weeks of happiness with that baby, and I mourn the fact that the three subsequent babies I lost after that first loss didn't get a moment of joy or expectation from me. My son who lived didn't either until his birth.

— Mandi Richards, mom to three on Earth
and four in eternity

———————————

It can feel so bitter to not only have to endure the loss of one or more babies but to then have our experience forever changed. There is no easy solution to this without the grace of God and his healing, in which we strive to embrace this difficult cross. Know that your experience has the potential to make you better appreciate the mystery and miracle that is each new life, and the precious and unique dignity of each child. You are now more keenly aware of the fragility of life and the fact that no matter how many days your baby lived, and regardless of his or her abilities, gender, size, or health, every life is precious. Take heart that your vulnerable, beautiful openness to life and your pain and heartbreak are part of transforming your heart and soul, and can be a powerful witness to the world.

20

BREASTFEEDING YOUR BABY

"Yet you are he who took me from the womb; you kept me safe upon my mother's breasts."
— Psalms 22:9

While a detailed and complete overview of breastfeeding and its many facets is beyond the scope of this book, any book about birth would be incomplete without addressing this final biological interplay between mother and baby. Breastfeeding is designed by God, and it is holy and good. Just as Christ, after his death and resurrection, continued to feed his Church in the Eucharist, so too a mother can continue her gift of self as she feeds her child from her very body. Throughout Scripture and in the tradition of the Church, the breastfeeding relationship has been honored and considered beautiful, and breastfeeding should always be supported, never shamed.

We need only look at the few thousand portrayals throughout history of the Blessed Mother unabashedly nursing the baby Jesus to see that breastfeeding is designed by God and be reminded of its beauty. Whether struggling with other people's perceptions, reflecting on our own decision, working to overcome breastfeeding difficulties, or suffering from exhaustion because of the difficult work involved, we can find strength and inspiration from Mary. In fact, La Leche League, a world-renowned breastfeeding information and support group, was founded by a group of Catholic mothers and named in honor of Our Lady of La Leche (Our Lady of the Milk). Their work helped transform the modern world's view of breastfeeding, enabling countless women to successfully nurse their babies.

Breastfeeding is so highly regarded that even popes have encouraged mothers to breastfeed their babies (though it is important to note that it is not a moral requirement). In his October 26, 1941, *Allocution to Mothers*, Pope Pius XII said: "Except where it is quite impossible, it is most desirable that the mother should feed her child at her own breast. Who shall say what mysterious influences are exerted upon the growth of that little creature by the mother upon whom it depends entirely for its development!"

Pope Saint John Paul II said breastfeeding is a subject of interest to the Church and called for greater support, training, and encouragement for mothers to be able to nurse their babies:

> From various perspectives therefore the theme is of interest to the Church, called as she is to concern herself with the sanctity of life and of the family.... In practical terms, what we are saying is that mothers need time, information and support. So much is expected of women in many societies that time to devote to breastfeeding and early care is not always available. Unlike other modes of feeding, no one can substitute for the mother in this natural activity. Likewise, women have a right to be informed truthfully about the advantages of this practice, as also about the difficulties involved in some cases. Healthcare professionals too should be encouraged and properly trained to help women in these matters.[149]

Immediately after birth, your body is designed to create colostrum (many women begin producing it months before the birth). Research has found that colostrum is filled with life-giving nutrition that helps the baby immediately and has long-term health benefits. The medical and pediatric world calls it "liquid gold" because of its powerful ability to protect the baby's immune system, provide antibodies, protect and develop the baby's digestive health, and give the baby the healthiest start possible. The baby only receives teaspoons at a time, but those tiny drops are transformative for the baby's health.

A few days later, your body will begin producing milk, which is perfectly formulated for the specific needs of your baby. More and more is being discovered about the tremendous complexities and benefits of mother's milk. We've long known that breastmilk lowers the risk of colic, allergies, ear infections, hospitalizations, illnesses, SIDS, possibly obesity and diabetes, and provides the complete and perfect source of nutrition for babies for up to a year.[150] It's also a perfectly designed conduit for the necessary touching and bonding that baby needs. It greatly lowers the risk of breast cancer for women and helps with postpartum healing.[151] We now know that the milk is specifically designed for your baby's age, and that the nutrition and components vary, depending on how old the baby is. Scientists have also discovered that any germs you pick up when holding and kissing your baby are taken into your body, and your body responds by creating antibodies in your milk against that particular germ. What an absolutely incredible design! (The fact that it is completely free is also a huge benefit to many families.)

Ideally, the baby should be brought to the breast as soon as possible after birth and allowed and encouraged to nurse as much as he or she wants. Not only does the baby need the colostrum, but this helps your uterus contract and heal, and assists your body in creating milk. The nursing relationship works in a supply-and-demand type of way. The more baby nurses, the more your body is signaled to create milk. When the baby nurses less, it signals your body to create less. In order to make sure your supply will be adequate, you need to respond to the baby's signals. Some will want to nurse almost constantly after birth, which is okay. That's how they ensure there is the milk supply they need.

It is currently recommended for babies who aren't so ravenous that they still be encouraged and allowed to nurse every two or three hours. The evidence overwhelmingly shows that it is impossible to "spoil" a newborn, and that frequent holding and feeding on demand — whether breast or bottle — is best for their health.[152] The skin-to-skin contact of breastfeeding also has significant developmental importance.[153] Breastmilk, perfectly designed, is easily and quickly digested. Additionally, because the baby's stomach is so tiny, he or she will want to nurse often. As the baby grows, feedings will space out, though most babies go through occasional stages and growth spurts when they may still want to nurse every hour or two.

Because of that supply-and-demand relationship, if you are worried about your milk supply, nurse often. The more the breast is emptied, the more milk you will create. If you find you are making too much, make sure the baby is completely emptying a breast before switching to the other side. Pumping out milk will signal the body to keep replacing that milk, so while it may sometimes be necessary to express or pump out a bit for comfort or to avoid too much engorgement or a clogged duct, continually pumping out milk will trigger your body to produce more.

Breastfeeding is not always easy. A few babies may latch on right away without struggle, nurse well, and mom never experiences any pain or struggle. Then there are the rest of us. A good lactation counselor can help address problems and help you and your baby learn a good latch, so you aren't in pain and the baby is able to get milk effectively. A wide-open mouth with tongue extended and lips flared on the breast is a good latch and should not be extremely painful. There may be some initial discomfort, especially for the first-time mom, but it shouldn't be excruciating. That type of pain indicates a bad latch on the baby and should be corrected. It can take a while for you and baby to figure it out. For some, it requires a good deal of patience.

More and more is being learned about the problem of tongue-tie in babies and how that can affect the ability to latch well and drink enough milk. Inverted or flat nipples, separation at or after birth, medical issues with the baby, and underlying supply or medical issues for you can also create a challenge for nursing. If you are struggling, *get help*. Almost all of these can be overcome with proper information and support. A good lactation consultant, an excellent provider (either yours or your baby's pediatrician) who is experienced in breastfeeding, or advice and help from friends who have had successful breastfeeding experiences can be a lifesaver. There are also a few good resources in Appendix D to help with support, encouragement, or troubleshooting concerning breastfeeding.

In recent years the practice of milk donation and milk sharing has begun to take hold in communities and hospitals. Just as with the wet nurses of the past, women who for whatever reason are unable to breastfeed or produce enough milk are being supported by other women around them so babies can thrive. This is a beautiful and good thing for both babies and mothers. Milk sharing seems to be expanding, helped on by groups on social media, and hospitals are even opening milk banks so premature babies can receive donated breastmilk vital to their health. What a beautiful gift it is for women to feed the hungry in this way.

Just like birth, baby-feeding choices can be intensely personal, emotional, and, sadly, even divisive. We mothers care so desperately about our babies that anything that even hints at questioning our choices can provoke us to become defensive and/or combative about our choices. Every mother deserves to be respected, and you should never be shamed or guilted into one choice over another when it comes to feeding your baby. You deserve to have all the information and support you need to make the right choice for you and your baby. It is possible to recognize that breastfeeding is the objective ideal even while realizing that it may not be possible or best in your unique circumstances.

If you are in a position in which breastfeeding is not possible or ideal, know that giving your baby the nutrition he or she needs in the best way you can is a beautiful and loving act. It's okay for you to acknowledge the loss if it wasn't working, and you may even need to grieve that nursing relationship if it was important to you. Breastfeeding is not a moral obligation of the Church, and we can be profoundly thankful for the gift of other ways to feed and nourish our babies when needed. Whether we feed our hungry baby at our breast or through a bottle, we can lovingly heed the call of the Lord to feed the hungry in our very home, and that is a beautiful and holy privilege.

> After having such a terrible, horrible, no good, very bad experience with breastfeeding and creating a secure attachment with our firstborn when I was working full-time, I was determined to do it differently for round two. When I was pregnant again, I started looking into ecological breastfeeding. I fell in love with this practice of mama and baby togetherness, and when I used it as my model for caring for this baby, I was amazed at how natural, liberating, and stress-free it was.
>
> We have such a strong and secure attachment, and I have never seen a calmer, happier, more independent, or more flexible baby. Now, I believe that her temperament is simply calmer than our firstborn's and she would be an easier baby regardless. But, I truly think ecological breastfeeding has helped.
>
> God created women's bodies with the ability to nourish their babies. Until recently, when pumping became an option, breastfeeding meant that a mother couldn't be away from her baby longer than a couple of hours because her baby would soon be hungry and need to nurse. It makes sense to me that this lack of separation between mother and baby serves other positive purposes and is a natural way I can choose to parent.
>
> — Haley Stewart, mom to three

21

NAMING AND CLAIMING
YOUR BABY

*"For this child I prayed; and the LORD has granted me my petition
which I made to him. Therefore I have lent him to the LORD; as long as
he lives, he is lent to the Lord."*
— 1 Samuel 1:27–28

No Catholic book on birth and babies would be complete without talking about the importance of names. Naming your baby is one of the most fun, sobering, overwhelming, and important tasks as a parent. That name will be with your child for all eternity! It is important that the name be chosen with discernment, and with that perspective in mind. While trendy, unique, or catchy names may be tempting and fun, a name with meaning and depth should still remain a greater priority from a Christian perspective.

The power of names is of paramount importance in Scripture. Dozens of times in the Old and New Testaments, God tells parents what to name their baby or changes someone's name to reflect a new reality or position. Eve, Abraham, Sarah, Israel, Samuel, Benjamin, Peter, Paul, John, Jesus (and many others) are all names given by God at or before birth, or at a turning point in the person's life. It is abundantly clear in Scripture (as well as in other traditions and cultures) that a name truly means something, strengthening a person in a certain characteristic or mission. Many priests and religious follow this tradition when they take a new name as they receive their habits or make their vows. In fact, Pope Benedict XVI said, "Knowing someone's name implies a kind of power over that person because in the biblical mentality the name contains the most profound reality of the individual, it reveals the person's secret and destiny. Knowing one's name therefore means knowing the truth about the other person."[154] In almost every other culture, even from a non-Christian perspective, the name given to a baby has profound power and meaning to the child and to the family. When we take a name and it is sealed in baptism, that name becomes a part of who we are.

Choosing an obviously Christian name used to be required for baptism. In 1983, canon law changed to require only that parents, godparents, and pastors ensure that the name chosen not be foreign to Christian sentiment (Canon 855). Names such as Lucifer or Adonis, or something along those lines, would thus be forbidden. While earlier restrictions are no longer in place, their existence can help us understand the Christian importance of a name.

Many Catholic parents choose the name of a saint who is important to them. The child is then gifted with lifelong prayers from that patron in heaven and can grow in relationship with that saint, learning from and modeling his or her own life after the saint's. Some choose names that directly reflect some virtue or reality of the Christian life, such as Joy, Faith, or Emmanuel — a word they hope will live itself out in the life of the child.

That isn't to say that there is not room for unique or new names. In fact, a faith-filled perspective can provide even more creativity as you seek a name that best fits this new child, your hopes for him or her, and one that respects his or her dignity as a child of God. The list of saints to choose from or words with deep meaning that can be turned into a name is exhaustive! And, of course, many choose to honor their family by using a family name.

It can be helpful in this important work to pray with your spouse that God will provide insight and inspire you with a right and fitting name. Doing so not only gives room for the Holy Spirit to move within your hearts, but it is a reminder to both of you that the child first belongs to God and is ultimately a gift from him. It is a powerful act of faith and love to name our babies with that in mind.

The Obligation and Importance of Baptism
"Fatherhood and motherhood represent a responsibility which is not simply physical but spiritual in nature."
— *John Paul II*, Letter to Families

As Catholic parents, not only do we have the tremendous and sobering responsibility of our child's physical well-being, but we recognize that our child's soul is in our care, too, and is of utmost importance. After the baby is born, we are required as Catholic parents to get our babies baptized. We have cooperated with God in giving them the gift of physical life, and now we cooperate with him by giving them the gift of spiritual and eternal life, claiming them now for Christ and his kingdom. Baptism is "the basis of the whole Christian life, the gateway to life in the Spirit ... and the door which gives access to the other sacraments. Through Baptism we are freed from sin and reborn as sons of God; we become members of Christ, are incorporated into the Church and made sharers in her mission."[155] Baptism allows our children to partake in the divine nature of God with souls prepared for heaven. What better gift could we give them?

Catholics take baptism very seriously. Because of the profound power of this sacrament, the Church says that children have the right to have their parents bring them to baptism, and to do so as soon as possible. "The Church and the parents would deny a child the priceless grace of becoming a child of God were they not to confer Baptism shortly after birth. Christian parents will recognize that this practice also accords with their role as nurturers of the life that God has entrusted to them."[156] In fact, canon law says that parents are required to bring their babies for baptism within the first few weeks of the baby's life, going to their pastor as soon as possible before or after birth to request baptism. And, of course, babies in danger of death are to be baptized without delay and can be licitly baptized by anyone as long as the proper form is used.[157] Proper form includes pouring water on the baby while speaking the words, "I baptize you in the name of the Father, and of the Son, and of the Holy Spirit."

As a Catholic, the Sacrament of Baptism should be a priority. Having all the relatives present for the baptism is wonderful and good, but this should not be given higher priority than the requirement to baptize within the first few weeks. The occasion is worthy of a celebration, but perhaps planning and hosting a party can be taken over by grandparents or godparents so you can bring your baby as soon as possible to the font without the mental and physical stress of party planning. A simple, humble celebration is also a beautiful thing and may be more realistic and less stressful. Consider planning what you can before the birth so that less needs to be taken care of after. Deciding on godparents, taking any required baptismal classes, choosing what baby will wear, and completing any party plans can make scheduling the baptism after baby is born that much easier.

The role of a godparent is a serious spiritual responsibility within the Church. The godparent is expected to be a role model in the Faith, assisting parents in sharing the Gospel with the child, and taking a role in his or her spiritual upbringing. Therefore, a godparent must be someone in good standing with the Church, who believes all that the Church teaches, has received confirmation, and has the ability and desire to fulfill this spiritual role for the child. Only one godparent is required for baptism. If two are chosen, they must be one male and one female. Individual dioceses or other rites outside of the Latin rite may have other specific requirements that your priest can discuss with you. A non-Catholic baptized Christian may be chosen as an accompanying "Christian witness," but this is not technically a godparent. A non-baptized person may not fulfill either role.[158] Contrary to some belief, the godparent is not necessarily the person who will be practically or legally responsible for a child if something were to happen to the parents, but he or she does have an even more heightened spiritual responsibility in that case.

The godparent, then, should be chosen with great care and discernment. Aside from being an active and devout Catholic, this person should ideally be an active participant in your child's life. The godparent should be especially supportive during sacraments, in sharing and encouraging the child in the Christian life, and in praying for that child.

There is also a Church custom that has been mostly lost in modern times called "churching" for a new mother. This blessing, since ancient times, is given to the mother the first time she is able to return to church after the birth of a baby. Its purpose is for the mother to render thanks to God for her birth and ask for blessing as she actively takes on the important role of motherhood. It can be given by any parish priest. However, because it has fallen out of custom, it may be difficult to find a priest who is familiar with it. Some priests who do offer it do so in conjunction with the baptism. The blessing involves the mother kneeling with a lighted candle, specific Scriptures and blessings prayed over her, and then being led into the church by the priest. Churching is a beautiful and holy custom, should a mother desire it.[159] At the least, it is another example of how the Church so highly values motherhood and the gift of a newly born baby.

Never have I felt the full weight of another person's soul until becoming a mother. This little person, whom I co-created with my husband, by God's grace and goodness, mattered everything, and needed to someday be united with Our Lord in heaven for eternal happiness. On that day, our little one was calm throughout Mass, and upon being baptized, our sweet boy drifted off into a sweet slumber. It was beautiful and filled with grace — grace that moved my soul to tears of joy, thanksgiving, and happiness. In those moments, during the gift of holy Mass and the Sacrament of Baptism, nothing else mattered.

— Amanda Perales, mom to three

22

BORN IN GRACE: BIRTH STORIES FROM CATHOLIC MOMS

*"Let us consider how to stir up one another to
love and good works, not neglecting to meet together, as is the habit
of some, but encouraging one another, and all the more
as you see the day drawing near."*
— Hebrews 10:24–25

It can be profoundly helpful to read and be encouraged by the positive and empowering stories of other mothers as you prepare to give birth. These stories are powerful reminders that birth can be beautiful, healthy, and holy. God has a unique and beautiful path for every woman, so every birth will be — and should be — different. I pray that within these stories you will find some hope and encouragement that God is at work in and through birth. May you and your precious baby have an amazing and grace-filled birth.

....

The Birth of Nathaniel Patrick
By Jill K., mom to two

After struggling for a couple of years with infertility, my husband and I finally conceived our first child. My first pregnancy was very difficult. I experienced terrible and almost constant sickness for much of the pregnancy. I struggled to celebrate the gift we had been given because I was so ill all the time. I wish I knew then what I know now; it is all so worthwhile! During the second half of my pregnancy I was diagnosed with gestational diabetes, which was also a struggle. It was not easily controlled, and I began to feel as if my body was a failure. I was not feeling very confident about my ability to get through labor and delivery successfully and without interventions. This scared me, so I decided to hire a doula for help. I didn't know much about what this would entail, or how helpful it would be, but I was sure I wanted the extra support. After a little bit of research and (I believe) a lot of divine intervention, I found someone who fit my personality and spiritual needs very well. I was already starting to feel a little bit better.

Due to my gestational diabetes, I was being monitored more closely than with a typical pregnancy. During the last month, I went in for an ultrasound (this is pretty routine with gestational diabetes), and it was discovered that my son had a major congenital birth defect that would affect him for the rest of his life. We were shocked, devastated, scared, and heartbroken. With only a few short weeks left in the pregnancy, we found ourselves trying to figure out what this would all mean for our child, and grieving the loss of the child and life we anticipated having. I could not see God's plan, and I felt so betrayed by him. This was not in *my* plan. This was not what I asked for. Why my son? Why me?

A couple of weeks later, at yet another ultrasound to monitor my pregnancy (and just a few days shy of my due date), the doctor decided that we needed to induce labor due to low amniotic fluid levels. Once again I found myself in a position of helplessness and fear. I was extremely uncomfortable with the idea of being induced, especially for a reason like low fluid. What should I do? The first thing my husband and I did was call our doula for support. We wanted to feel as if we had someone in our corner who understood our fears. Ultimately, we decided to go ahead with the induction. Although I was uncomfortable with it, I felt that I had to take into account the special circumstances at play and decided it was more appropriate for me to trust medical advice than call my own shots.

Shortly after arriving at the hospital and getting situated in my room, my husband asked our doula to come for support. Although I was not in true labor yet, we were desperate for a familiar face with some expertise. During the course of that night I experienced pain and fear as I had never felt before, and have never felt since. Despite being induced, I still felt strongly about having as "natural" a birth experience as possible. For me this meant I was not interested in pain meds. I made this decision for a number of reasons. I felt strongly that in my situation this was the safest way for me to bring my son into the world and reduce the probability of further complications. I also felt betrayed by my body and wanted a chance to regain confidence in my ability to do this on my own. After infertility, a difficult pregnancy, gestational diabetes, and a devastating diagnosis for my son, I needed to know that I could do it. Although none of these things were my fault, I needed to renew trust in my body's ability to do what it was made to do.

I also felt strongly that I did not want to waste the pain of childbirth. I had some pretty major things happening in my life (both with the baby and otherwise) that needed some deep prayer. I knew, as a thirtysomething American woman living a comfortable life in the suburbs, that this was an opportunity to offer up suffering that I might not get otherwise. I saw it as my duty and privilege to accept it openly and harness it for God's glory, or (due to my brokenness) at least his mercy.

I was blessed to have a doula who shared my Catholic faith, and that proved invaluable. With each contraction she coached me (and my husband) through pain management and prayer. She read a prayer intention for each contraction, helping me make the most of each one and giving me a sense of deeper purpose. My husband heroically held me up when I couldn't stand anymore (I insisted on standing through almost the entire labor). He was my rock. This continued until I wasn't capable of much of anything anymore. The pain was too much, and all I could do was exist and succumb to each passing second. *Lean into the pain.* As with life, I found that the key was to ride the wave instead of fighting it. *Lean into the pain.* Acceptance was better than denial. Denial never really works in the end, anyway. *Lean into the pain.* The only way to beat it was to allow it to happen.

Mary said yes to God. She accepted the pain, fear, and loss of control that would inevitably envelop her life with that simple but terrifying "yes." Could I? With grace all things are possible. "Leaning into the pain" was my yes, perhaps one of the few chances I would ever have to enter into the mystery of the Passion and offer up suffering in such a profound way. Equally important was embracing the support I was being given. Much as with God's grace, I needed to be open to allowing others to enter into this intimate and personal moment. At my most vulnerable I needed to embrace community. As an introvert this was counterintuitive but necessary. My husband and doula were amazing. I truly could not have done it without them. In addition to that, nurses and other medical personnel were in and out of my room. Not only did I have to be open to their help, but I also had to cooperate with it. While this might seem like an obvious thing to point out, there are moments during the throes of labor when the last thing you can imagine is having to listen to anyone's suggestions, even if they're right.

Eventually, the time came to push. For many women this is the point during labor when their body takes over and tells them what to do. Not for me. I did not have the urge to push. I was at the mercy of my support system. All I could do was rely on them to guide and encourage me through the process. *Mercy.* I couldn't take much more, but I was determined to get my baby out without further intervention. Hours passed and progress was slow. Eventually, the time had finally come. My son was about to enter into the world, but I was scared. I didn't want to push. I was afraid of how much it would hurt. *Lean into the pain.* With my doula at my side, the midwife ready to go, and my husband in position to help catch the baby, I gave those last few pushes and my son was finally here. Praise God he's here. Praise God it's over. *But was he okay?* Yes. After some testing we would learn that, yes, he was affected by the condition they found in the ultrasound. In time, I would learn that despite this he would be fine. Life would be very different for him, but he would be okay. *Lean into the pain.* God is mercy.

I pray that God will help my husband and me teach him the lessons so beautifully illustrated through my labor: that we need to do more than be open to God's grace; that we need to actively cooperate with it; that community matters and without support none of us can handle this whole life thing on our own; that we can't control what cards we are dealt, but with help from God and others we have some say in how we're going to play them. Through pain comes beauty, redemption, and strength.

....

The Birth of Collin John Paul
By Carolyn Svellinger, mom to five
WWW.SVELLERELLA.COM

Friday evening, the fourteenth, I began feeling mild contractions — like heavy menstrual cramps for the ladies who've never experienced them. Also, I experienced a sudden congestion in my sinus cavities before each contraction. Strange, I know, but relevant, now that I think about their location in relation to my body's central blood vessels and nerves. The morning came and they persisted. I knew that my labor had officially begun. How exciting! I'd been preparing for this for nine months and was anxious to put my knowledge and research into practice. The playoffs had arrived, and this was the championship game. My husband and I called and texted my parents, who took our boys for the day so that I could labor peacefully at home.

It made such a huge difference to labor in the quiet comfort of our home.

Instead of my previous two births (basically panicking and hustling out the door for my epidural), I eased my way into each contraction. For the better part of the day, I was able to shuffle about, crocheting my blanket project, napping and lightly snacking as each contraction came and went. I mostly experienced one or two every half-hour.

The contractions slowly increased in intensity throughout the day. After a long afternoon nap, my husband and I took a tour of the grounds on our property. That's saying something for me, as I never take "tours" or hikes or walks outside. I'm not the outdoorsy type. Walking is supposed to help gently encourage the baby further into the birth canal (gravity). I really enjoyed just slowly walking with and being by my husband, talking, joking, and laughing.

So, after a relaxing, restful day, the intensity of my contractions picked up at 4:00 p.m. I remained in our living room with our orange medicine ball, hanging over it, sitting on it, kneeling over it while crocheting the blanket I'd been working on through each contraction. I decided to upload a contraction timer app for my phone, which helped a ton. My children have a little Pottery Barn Kids chair that I moved to and started leaning over for support. As the contractions picked up in intensity and frequency, I didn't want to move from the chair. My husband made a joke that I normally would have laughed about, but as another contraction began, I told him, "No, no, no, that isn't funny; this is serious right now," and I began to breathe through the throbbing wave.

I realized we needed to head to the hospital when I found myself in a meditative rest — almost sleeping — in between each contraction. Though the contractions were three to four minutes apart, I knew I would absolutely refuse to get into a car for a thirty-minute ride to the hospital if I waited any longer. I had probably ten contractions that I had to work through in the car, in the parking lot, and into the emergency entrance.

Of course, we entered, and I had a large audience in the waiting room, silently watching me work through the one contraction I had at the desk. Seriously, why were there twenty people in the waiting room at 9:30 on a Saturday night? I refused a wheelchair, and my husband and I walked our way to the labor-and-delivery floor. It was difficult, and I began to become emotional, knowing "this is really happening." He let me hang onto him and supported me through each surge that coursed through my body. We finally made it to triage, where I was examined and told I was dilated at 6 cm and fully effaced.

My doula came, as well as my OB (to my great surprise!), and we all walked to my birth room. There, I chose a chair to kneel in front of, on top of a cushion, and worked through many contractions. Sitting on the toilet actually felt nice too, but I could tell I was making my nurse and OB nervous that I would deliver into the toilet, so I moved toward the bed. I felt extremely relieved to not be forced to have a hep-lock placed into my hand. Quickly, I realized the nurse attendant was extremely respectful of our crunchy wishes (no medication, no IV, ability to freely move, intermittent fetal monitoring, no vaccinations, eye goo, etc.), and she asked me before she did anything to me or in preparation of the baby's arrival. It was such a stark contrast from my previous experiences. It was so nice to be fully mentally present and feel fully integrated into my labor and delivery of our child, not just a vessel.

I began to be so uncomfortable that I sought different positions. The labor bed had the capability to transform into a sort of stepladder shape so that I could squat on it forward or backward, with different handles for me to use for support or to hang on to. The nurse and my doula attached a huge metal bar, encased with foam, as I decided to turn forward and rest semi-upright on my back in between contractions. (Not typical of a natural birthing mom, but it brought my tailbone some relief!) I began to feel some relief in pushing and cried out during the intense waves of insanity that went through my lower back and hips.

I was pushing, but our baby wasn't moving. With each push, the pain intensified instead of bringing the reported relief that each laboring mother is supposed to experience. As I had just finished a particularly shocking contraction, we heard a knock on the door and in walked a man with a table full of tools and medicines. "I hear someone called for an epidural?" he sang merrily. "NOOO!!!" shouted everyone synonymously. "No, thank you," I heard myself squeak. And everyone laughed at my little, polite refusal. Out backed the epidural man with his table of drugs. If I had a chance to back down and get an epidural, I'd lose it now, I thought to myself with a sense of finality and triumph over the temptation to escape the fear of the unknown.

The contractions were double-peaking and so closely on top of each other by now that I refused to let my OB (who'd remained in the room with us the entire time) check my cervix for progress. When he finally did check me, he informed me that he needed to aid in pulling the cervical lip back, that it was keeping our baby from being pushed to the point of crowning which explained the abnormal pain. So instead of my OB doing the typical perineum stretching that happens in the final pushing stage, he was aiding in cervical stretching. And it hurt like nothing I'd ever experienced before. At this moment, I closed my eyes and did not open them to anyone for the last half of my labor. It was me against myself, by myself.

I held a long, low note of a male tenor with each contraction and crazily thought I might be auditioning for the part of a pirate in a musical. I bellowed like a blind, old cow. I barked like a constipated, fat dog. I wailed like a banshee. I screamed like a girl riding down a roller coaster. When hollering proved insufficient, I punched my own thigh in disbelief of the reality of the pain. I slapped it as if I could not believe such sensations were gaining victory over me. I thrashed my head — shaking it, saying, "NO NO NO NO NOOOO!!!!!" absolutely forbidding the pain to triumph. And then, after each contraction, I raised one hand or the other into the air, eyes closed, like a passionate gospel singer, and slowly grasped at absolutely nothing.

At this point, soaked in sweat, I actually sobbed, saying, "I don't want to do this anymore!!! What else can I do! Please!!" I looked my husband full in the face for the first time, and I knew there was nothing. He firmly urged me on. My nurse urged me, and my doula reminded me that I was born to do this. Finally, my water broke — and I felt a new pain. A welcome pain. Our little boy was descending, finally descending. I gave two great pushes, and out came our little boy's head.

"Open your eyes and look down!" I was told. But I refused to open them until my husband placed our boy on my chest. Craig caught our little Collin John Paul. I opened my eyes as Collin was handed to me, and I was completely taken aback by the shock of jet-black hair covering his head, his beautifully colored, baby-pink skin (our other boys came out grayish/ purple because of the epidural, I believe), and the amount of vernix still coating his little body (indicating that he perhaps wasn't overdue, as we'd all believed).

And it was love at first sight. I was filled to the brim with a complete sense of peace and of love. (And then I barked, "NEVER AGAIN!" to the whole room. Fifteen minutes later, I caught myself saying, "Well, next time …")

This birth humbled me to my core. It fulfilled my identity as a woman. My life is full of incompletes, of goals never accomplished, of things started backward, or not carried out from A to Z. But this one. This I can humbly claim. I can know in my heart, "I really did it." It wasn't easy. It wasn't enjoyable. It wasn't. But it was amazing. It was better than winning a sporting event. Better than winning a gold medal. Better than getting a raise, a promotion, a new possession, being famous, walking the runway, jumping from an airplane … better than any achievement, award, reward, or drug I could ever possibly attain. And I got to experience it. I did. Just me. And I am humbled by that privilege.

....

The Birth of Elsa Rose
By Amelia B., mom to five

On the evening of Monday, September 10, I started to feel some cramping and noticed light pink spotting. I had never really had any spotting in pregnancy before, and I had a fear of placental abruption, so I called the midwife that night and asked her about it. She reassured me that a small amount was normal before labor started and to only worry if it gets to be actual bleeding instead of just spotting. The next day I had bloody show throughout the day and contractions/cramping periodically throughout the day, but I didn't really think anything of it.

Around 4:00 p.m. the contractions got a bit stronger, and at 5:00 p.m. I decided to start dinner, even though I had no appetite (which is a sure sign of labor for me: I hate eating while I am in labor and can barely stomach anything). I made chicken alfredo and swiss chard for everyone and managed to eat a little myself, even though I didn't really want to, all the time having contractions that were about six or seven minutes apart and strong enough that I needed to walk through them. Around 6:00 p.m. I told Ben that I was pretty sure this was it, and I called Dawn (my midwife) to give her a head's up but said that I didn't really think I needed her.

For the next hour and a half, contractions continued to be between five and ten minutes apart, but they kept getting stronger and more painful. I felt them mostly in my back as well, and I was worried about back labor. At 7:00 p.m. I decided to get into the shower, and the warm water helped, although the contractions started to slow down. They picked up again when I got out, and I told Ben to call the midwife and have her come over. She got here around 8:00 p.m. and, by this time, the contractions were still about eight to ten minutes apart, but when they came, they were very painful and hard to manage.

Around 8:40 p.m. or so, I had to go to the bathroom during a contraction, so I ran in there and went. Afterward, I started having really strong contractions right on top of each other that I just *had* to walk through. I had maybe five or six of those when I started feeling lots of pressure and like I was ready to push. Meanwhile, no one (not Ben nor the midwife) knew that I was suddenly having strong contractions super-close together, and Dawn had just texted her assistant and said that things were slow and she could take her time. It took a lot for me to walk out of the bathroom and call to the midwife for help (she was waiting in the living room), but I did NOT want to give birth in the bathroom by myself. So I walked out into the office, and called out for her. She came in and right at that very moment my water broke all over the carpet and she started throwing towels down. Ben brought me a chair to lean on since I was standing up. At that point, I could feel the head right there, and started grunting, and Dawn asked if I was pushing and started throwing chux pads down. I said yes and asked if the head is there. She said yes. I pushed two or three times and she was out … born a little before 9:00 p.m. The assistant never even made it over.

Elsa had a short cord (same as my older son), so Dawn cut it right away as there was no other way she could hand me the baby or anything. She was born very red/pink and crying … good Apgars! I sat down on the couch under all these chux pads and she latched on right away. After a few minutes, I started feeling more contractions, handed her off to Ben and delivered the placenta (with some help from Dawn). It was such a relief to get that out! Elsa spent the next hour or so nursing, before being weighed/measured/examined.

Giving birth at home was such a different experience than being in the hospital. I loved being mostly left to myself … no blood draws, no vaginal checks, no constant monitoring being strapped down, and no one taking the baby away after birth. Mostly, I loved being free to move around and have privacy if I wanted it and to give birth in whatever position I wanted to. I definitely think being at home is why this birth was so much quicker and shorter than my other ones. I'm still kind of shocked at how quickly things went, since I felt as if I went from contractions eight or so minutes apart to birth in less than twenty minutes! None of us were expecting birth to go that fast, but I'm so thankful it did!

The Birth of Sarah Mabel Elizabeth

By Ginny Foreman, mom to eight

WWW.GSHELLER.COM

I've birthed seven babies, my first an induced, medicated, hospital birth, and the five that followed were born at home. I never dreamed I would choose a cesarean birth for my seventh, but I did. Nearly a year later, I still don't regret my decision.

My obstetrician was surprised when I broached the subject of cesarean birth about six months into my pregnancy, though he knew I had come to his practice because I felt that home birth wasn't the right choice for me this time around. My babies were getting progressively larger, and my last one had been over ten pounds. He had severe shoulder dystocia at birth, and to say that the experience was terrifying would be an understatement. Between the fear of another dystocia birth and a few other troubling matters, I came to the conclusion on my own that a c-section birth might be the safest option for this baby. My doctor was sensitive to my concerns and considered the possibility of a c-section this time around to be a valid choice, despite his reputation for being a male midwife of sorts and an advocate for low-intervention birth. I spent another two weeks thinking things over, but ultimately chose to schedule my daughter's birth for the first day of summer, via c-section. I'll never forget sobbing tears of relief the entire way home.

The morning of the surgery the internal contradiction I felt was strong — afraid and confident at the same time. I put on comfortable clothes, including items made by two of my friends who had passed away in the previous couple of years: a clay bead bracelet made by my friend Sarah, and socks knitted by my friend Elizabeth. The daughter we would be welcoming in a few hours was to be named Sarah Mabel Elizabeth, after these friends, and my husband's grandmother, Mabel. I put on a brave face and hugged my children goodbye.

Once we were settled into our room and nurses began arriving to start prepping me for the surgery, things started to feel surreal for both me and my husband, Jonny. Honestly, he may have been more nervous about my impending surgery than I was. He told me later that it would have only taken one word and he would have gotten me out of there. But I knew I was making the right choice, and despite my fear of the experience ahead, I had peace.

My doctor stopped by to let me know that he was ready, and we were just waiting on me to finish getting prepped and for the surgical team to assemble. He glanced at my recent, uncharacteristically high blood pressure reading and said, "You're scared, aren't you?"

"Yeah, I guess so."

He reassured me and told me he'd see me soon.

Soon after, I met the nurse anesthetist who would be administering my spinal block. She was an elderly woman with a wicked sense of humor. She seemed trained in setting people at ease, and I loved her immediately.

The surgical dress code was a hospital gown and slip-resistant socks, no jewelry. I stated simply that I couldn't be parted from my bracelet, that I wore it every day, a birthday gift from a dear friend who died, for whom my baby would be named. The same went for the socks, my hand-knit Elizabeth socks. The nurses were concerned that I might slip, so I agreed to wear my Birkenstocks over my wool socks on the way down the hall to the operating room.

Looking back, I have no idea how I said goodbye to Jonny and turned to walk down the hall to the operating room. It was one of the bravest moments of my life. It felt a little like walking the plank. I must sound a little dramatic to those who have more experience with surgery, but this was my first, and I was truly afraid of the unknown that lay before me.

The operating room was stark and cold and busy. While the spinal was being placed, a surgical tech stood in front of me, instructing me to hug her neck and relax. Relaxing while hugging a stranger is outside my comfort zone, most especially when I am being told to essentially lay my face upon a stranger's breast while a needle is inserted in my back. But I did, I hugged her, and I relaxed, chanting Hail Marys over and over in my head. I never even felt a pinch as the spinal was placed. After that, things happened quickly. I felt a combination of sensations physically that were new and terrifying. Through some combination of heat and panic my anxiety level became so intense that I thought I was going to pass out. My worst fear was that I would not be mentally present when my daughter was born. I had spoken with my obstetrician extensively about that, the fact that I only wanted whatever drugs were necessary and nothing additional to "take the edge off." I fought for mental control. The nurses kept up an ongoing dialogue with me to reassure me that what I was feeling was normal. I would say, I'm feeling this, and they would say: "That's good. That's what you are supposed to be feeling. Everything is going exactly as it should."

The surgical tech asked me if I was religious, if I wanted to pray. I told her that I hadn't stopped praying since I entered the operating room. Hail Marys were replaced with my own desperate prayer of reassurance: "Jesus is with me. Jesus is with me." Those four words were all I could manage.

Looking back on my birth experience, I see now that the profound lesson I learned that day was one of trust. During my home births, with the exception of my shoulder dystocia birth, I relied on myself to bring my babies into the world. It was ultimately up to me to do the hard work of laboring, of pushing. Yes, I prayed for strength, but it's another matter entirely to give over control in its entirety. This time, I had to trust a team of medical professionals to do the work for me. Throughout the surgery I had a sensation of being held, carried by this team of near strangers, and by Jesus. For me, trusting the surgical team was directly linked to trusting Jesus.

When my doctor entered the room, I uncharacteristically thought to myself, "I really want to hold his hand for just a minute." As I struggled internally with how to voice my need, he came around to sit beside my head and reached under the sheet to grab my hand. I never had to ask. He simply said: "Don't be afraid. Just relax. I've got this. I'm going to take care of you now." I believed him.

Soon after, Jonny was brought into the room, and he replaced the nurse anesthetist who had been seated next to my head, constantly talking to me, letting me know that I was all right. With him now seated next to me, I was able to more fully relax. We kept up a steady conversation, which helped to distract me from the unexpected sensations of the surgery itself.

The surgical tech warned me that as the doctor pulled my daughter from my body it would feel like I had an elephant on my chest. I was glad she did, because I had no idea that so much external force would be used to help Mabel be born. I guess I expected that in a c-section the baby was just gently pulled out, quick and easy. Later, my doctor told me that Mabel was quite cozy where she was and wasn't very cooperative when it came to being born.

Prior to the surgery, my doctor and I had discussed at length the way I wanted things to happen immediately after Mabel's birth. Before I could even ask him, he told me that with his c-section births he delayed cord clamping and cutting. I knew that Mabel would have to be whisked over to the warmer to be looked over by the pediatrician, and I was okay with that, but I asked that he show me her face first, even for just a second.

I'll never forget him saying, "Here's your baby!" as he held her up over the sheet so I could see her. With that familiar sensation of knowing, all I could think was: "It's you! It was you all along." As she was taken from my sight, I asked Jonny to go to her while she was examined. I had stuffed a pair of knitted wool socks and a hat in his pocket earlier, and as I asked, he placed them on her little feet and her head. She was then wrapped in a blanket and brought to me. I knew it would be awkward to try to hold her while lying flat on my back, and it was. In the weeks leading up to the surgery, I wondered if I would grieve over the loss of holding her in my arms the second she was born, keeping her with me, and nursing her while midwives did what they needed to do while I was holding her. I didn't, and I haven't. I can honestly say that I haven't had any sadness over my first moments with Mabel, because those moments were so precious. How could I want them any way other than exactly as they occurred? She had her little face next to mine, and I kept thinking, as I always do, "She's here, she's really here!" And it was just me and her in that room. Never mind that I was in the process of being sewn back together. Nothing in the world mattered to me other than the fact that my daughter was here and she was safe.

Many years before that day, shortly after my first natural birth, I remember feeling an elation, a sense of pride in what I had done in bringing my child into the world without assistance. I felt brave and strong. As I was wheeled to recovery after my cesarean birth, I felt the same. Each pregnancy, each birth, each baby requires something different. Bravery is choosing what you believe to be best, and trusting Jesus with the rest.

....

The Birth of Michael Benedict and Raphael James
By Nicole Wright, mom to eight on Earth and one in eternity

I definitely was not pregnant. At that morning playdate, I took the test in an act of camaraderie with two of my friends who were hoping theirs were positive. Unfortunately, theirs were not. But guess whose was? To say I was incredulous would be a bit of an understatement. Surely these cheap, bulk Amazon tests were not accurate. I couldn't possibly be pregnant! Again. The night before I was drinking martinis. My youngest was only seven months old and I already had four kids five years and under. I had just gotten my cycles back the month prior. I hadn't even caught my breath from the last baby! I just wasn't ready!

A week or so later, a blood test confirmed it, and I was scheduled to go in for my first appointment at what would put me at a little past nine weeks. My husband was still in denial. I was a bit, too. Something felt different from my other four pregnancies — a little more tired than usual, but not an ounce of morning sickness to speak of. Weird. Although that had been getting progressively better with each pregnancy, I usually felt a little something. This time, though, nothing. I just didn't feel pregnant. I felt great. Maybe the tests were wrong?

When I got into the office that afternoon, my doctor did a quick, in-house sonogram to determine gestational age. I half jokingly, half seriously asked him, "Am I even pregnant?" Dr. P. chuckled and said: "Oh, you are pregnant all right. And not just with one baby, but two!" Didn't phase me in the least. My doctor and I always enjoyed some good-natured banter. I knew he was just teasing me.

"Good one, but really. Everything okay?"

I think it must have taken three more back-and-forths between the two of us until, finally, he turned the screen around to show me. I saw two little beans with matching beating hearts. After maniacally asking my doctor over and over if it were true, I called my husband. He had the same response as me. Completely and totally flabbergasted. We were having twins!

We literally were the last ones out of our friends who needed to speed up the frequency of our pregnancies with a two-for-one deal. I mean, how was I going to manage having six kids under six? How big would I get? I always went natural with labor and delivery, but how the heck was I going to push out two babies? How much more painful would this be? Would I be able to breastfeed them? For how long? But behind all the swirling doubt and questions racing through my head, I felt excited. Almost a bit euphoric. Twins! That was something different, something I never experienced before. I didn't even know anyone who had twins. And from the ultrasound, it looked as if they were encased in the same sac, so that meant identical twins, which is not based on heredity at all but just a random occurrence. How cool. How special … almost as if God just wanted me to have them.

I must say, when it comes to pregnancy, I am a bit of a worrywart. Everything has always been normal, with relatively fast, natural, and manageable labors, but, geez, they were still pretty darn painful. So, the moment I find out I am pregnant, I always start asking for prayers to temper the anxiety and stress. This pregnancy was no exception. I think I asked every person I knew to pray for me, on multiple occasions. I would even ask strangers at the playground, grocery store, or checkout line to pray for me and the twins. The godmother we chose for our twins was particularly hammered with prayer requests, which, of course, she graciously obliged.

A twin pregnancy is automatically labeled high risk in the medical world. The fact that they were identical did not make things any easier. The first fear was that they were sharing an amniotic sac, but an ultrasound confirmed that they indeed had separate amniotic sacs. Phew, crisis averted. However, they did appear to be sharing a placenta. The risk with that is something referred to as Twin to Twin Transfusion Syndrome, in which the twins' blood supply can become connected and flow disproportionately between the two. One twin gets too little and his or her growth and development is stunted, while the other twin gets too much, which can strain his or her heart and lead to heart failure. If this were the case, I would have to fly out of state for laser surgery to disrupt the connected blood vessels. More prayers please! Thankfully, this did not appear to be the case as my monthly and then bimonthly ultrasounds showed the twins healthy and growing at an even rate. The routine fetal monitoring was still in place though, and by the end of the pregnancy an ultrasound was a weekly occurrence.

In retrospect, while I knew a lot about singleton pregnancies and felt comfortable and competent advocating for myself and my babies when I felt unnecessary medical intervention was requested, I wasn't as comfortable with multiples. I was faced with a whole new gamut of risks that I never had to think about with my prior four pregnancies. I researched as much as I could, but I also did not know anyone who had been pregnant with twins before. So, I really wasn't aware of my options or if all this worry was warranted. I did have an excellent relationship with my doctor, and although he was a bit more medically conservative than me, he always let me exercise as much freedom as he could when it came to labor and delivery and adhering to my wishes. I trusted him and knew his intentions were in the right place. I do not regret how things were handled, and I am not sure if I had to do it again if I would proceed any differently, but I do think the testing and anxiety it caused could have been lessened. Never once were the results anything but normal. I was so incredibly thankful for that.

Time ticked on, and I got bigger and bigger. We found out we were having identical twin boys. Yay! The sweetest group of twenty-seven family and friends threw me a baby shower, even though these were not my first babies, but numbers five and six. I received everything from car seats to Pack 'n Plays to baby swings. I had friends help clean the house, tutor my oldest, whom I had just started to home-school, and my husband took up grocery shopping. The support, affirmation, and love I felt during that time was amazing. It was humbling and beautiful. I was still worried and anxious that I might go into labor at any moment, or that the babies wouldn't be okay, or what labor and delivery would be like, but the support I received helped immensely.

During the end of the pregnancy, especially late at night, when I felt the most anxious, I would read Saint Faustina's diary, *Divine Mercy in My Soul*, which gave me so much comfort. I also started to write down prayer intentions for which to offer up the pains of labor and delivery. This was something I always tried to do with each pregnancy. There weren't many times in my life that I was in real physical pain, and I always felt that I didn't want to waste it when it came. I had never gotten an epidural before, but went natural, even during a pregnancy in which I was induced. I wanted the same for this labor and delivery, and writing down my intentions prior helped me focus on the fact that this pain was worth something and I could use it. Added bonus, I also got an awesome little baby at the end, and this time two. However, since this pregnancy was different, I was open to doing whatever I needed to do to ensure they were delivered safely, whether that entailed an epidural or cesarean.

I was able to carry the twins all the way up until thirty-eight weeks, at which point my doctor advised induction. This is the one thing I wish I would have researched more, but I just wanted my babies to be healthy and safe. Both twins were head down, as they had been for the previous few weeks, and they were doing great. We scheduled an induction for the day after Thanksgiving.

I moseyed in a little after 9:00 a.m. with my husband, as I refused to come in at the crazy requested time of 6:00 a.m. Mama needs her rest if she is going to push out some babies! I was 4 cm walking in, pretty standard for me at that stage. By noon I was hooked up to the Pitocin (gah, I hate that stuff), in my comfy birthing skirt and tank, and prayed the Divine Mercy Chaplet with my husband to get me started. My doctor came in only for me that day and stuck around our room pretty much the whole time. As per my request, we ran the Pitocin slow, only upping it once every hour. I feel that this has helped me immensely with managing the pain, if Pitocin is administered slowly during an induction, by about half what they usually call for, and fully stopped once regular contractions are achieved. I got up to move a lot, as is my routine. I like to hang out in the bathroom, where the nurses don't bother me and where I can get some reprieve from the fetal-heart and contraction monitors, a nonnegotiable this time around with the twins. I sway with contractions, rock, hold on to towel bars or my husband and go up on my tippy toes. My favorite position is just standing upright. The babies were doing beautifully, and I was dilating about a centimeter an hour. That is on the slow side for me, but I wasn't feeling any pain with the contractions other than some pressure and mild cramping, so that was A-Okay. I knew that early on in labor my pain was pretty manageable, but that about 6 cms or so, things start to get intense. When I got to 6 cms, with still no real pain, I declined when my doctor asked if I wanted my water broken. He said it would speed things up, but I also knew it could change my pain level and the rhythm I had going on. In my last labor, my water was intact all the way up to the end and transition was so much more manageable. I hoped to achieve the same thing with this labor. Unless the pain started to feel unbearable and I needed things to move along, I did not want to have any more interventions.

By that time I was having regular contractions a minute apart, so I asked them to no longer increase the Pitocin. I mainly stayed standing in the bathroom, away from the monitors or anyone bothering me, just me and my husband. Still not much pain to speak of, but I knew it must be coming, and standing and moving around was always better than sitting in the hospital bed. I got checked often to gauge where I was in the labor. Before I knew it, I was 7 cms and then 8. Still no pain. Yes, some mild cramping and tightening, but this was not my first rodeo and I knew what real labor pain felt like. This was not it. This was amazing: 9 cms and a new nurse comes in and asks how my epidural is doing? I say, "What epidural? I don't have one." She says, "But you are 9 cms!" The doctor checks me one more time to see if they need to get me over to the operating room (another nonnegotiable at our hospital if you are delivering twins) and he fiddles around during a contraction to push me to 10 cm … and then comes the pain I know so well. All right, wheel me in. And thus we make our way to the OR.

We get to the OR, now with me in full-on labor pain and having to lie flat on my back (aka worst position ever) and then they ask the unthinkable. Can I move myself over to the teeny, tiny little operating table that looks to be about half the size of the bed that I am now in? Why that table is so small, the world may never know. I somehow manage to get my lumbering self over there. They start preparing the room, putting my legs into stirrups, and I notice there are about a dozen people in the room. A bit disconcerting. And then another contraction hits.

I go into this little cave when I am in pain. I close my eyes, I tense up, I don't talk, I don't want anyone talking to me or really touching me. But I hear him telling me to push. Okay, here comes the tough part. How long will this take? Will the other baby come out right after? Will everything be okay? I push once and Michael Benedict is born weighing 6 lbs., 7 oz. My husband and doctor are laughing and trying to joke with me. Hello, people?! You *do* know I have another baby to push out. And all of the sudden it is time. I give another push, and Raphael James is born two minutes after his brother weighing 5 lbs., 15 oz. Everyone is so excited and exclaiming, "He is en-caul! Baby is born en-caul!" What does that mean? My husband is telling me to look. Great idea if only my legs weren't in these darn stirrups. "Nick, the baby is under water. The baby is still in his amniotic sac!" And before I knew what was going on, the water broke. I miss all the good stuff.

There we are, in a room full of people with nothing to do because we just had two perfectly healthy little sons. Bye-bye, anesthesiologist; see ya later, NICU doc; clear out, all seventeen residents and twenty-eight nurses (I might be mildly exaggerating). And here they come, my two little bundles, one to rest in the crook of each arm. My husband and I just look at them and then each other, amazed that we really just did this. I pushed out two babies in what was undoubtedly my most pain-free labor and easiest delivery. Thank you, dear Lord. You have blessed me so much. How was this even possible?

Things are a little fuzzy after that. Recovery was uneventful. This was the first time I didn't need stitches. That made a big difference. But boy, did nursing two babies make up for it with the postpartum contractions. Apparently, if babies are born under or over a certain weight, they like to take their blood sugar soon after birth. Our second, slightly smaller twin, Raphael, had some wonky reads, and he wasn't keeping it up consistently. Again, it was hospital policy that they gave him formula. I was disappointed, but kept trying to nurse him as often as I could.

The night before we were supposed to be discharged, they decided to admit Raphael to the NICU for an IV, monitoring, and more bottle feeding. I was so upset. I was torn because now my two babies were on different floors and I had to keep alternating every few hours between nursing them both. I was so afraid the twin in the NICU would have trouble breastfeeding with all the supplementing they were giving him, and I knew the colostrum I was producing was best and still wanted to make sure he got all of it. The most upsetting time, though, was not with the NICU but when a nurse from the nursery decided to give the other breastfed-only twin formula "so I could get some rest." Only problem was, I didn't. I stayed up waiting for the nursery to bring him back. When I found out why they hadn't, I was so shaken and angry. They made a judgment call without my permission. With the stress of one baby in the NICU and then this, when my doctor came to check on me, I was shaky and on the verge of tears. This was the first time I ever saw my doctor get angry. He wanted to know the name of the nurse who did that and said it was totally unacceptable and he would deal with it to make sure it didn't happen again. I was so relieved I had his support. We ended up staying one extra night and were thankfully sent home with both of our babies, healthy and safe.

Even now, years later (since adding another two babies, bringing our family to eight kids ten years and under), I still marvel at the pregnancy and their births. God really held us in the palm of his hand and took us through it all in ways I could have never imagined possible. A practically pain-free labor? The stuff of fairy tales! Pushing out two babies in two minutes with one push each? Only in movies! A baby born in his intact amniotic sac? Oh, only 1 in every 80,000 births! Nursing two babies? I was able to do it for two years. It all worked out so well in the end. And it was none of my doing; it was all God's. His presence was made apparent to me in such a powerful way that day. And while I had been skeptical of the power of prayer, I undoubtedly believe it was those very prayers that saw me through it all. The prayers that reached the heart of God and moved him to extend his grace and his loving care down on an anxious-ridden, overwhelmed little family showed us that, despite all our worries and fears, he would take care of us. Despite all our doubts, he would teach us to trust. And we did, and we still try to. Thank you, Lord, for the blessing of the twins and all of our children.

....

The Birth of Mateo Benedicto
By April Jaure, mom to four on Earth and four in eternity
WWW.MYFEMININEMIND.COM

The births of my four children have all been quite different. I've birthed in the hospital with an obstetrician attending. I've had a home birth. I've birthed at the hospital with a midwife. Now my fourth child would be born in a birth center. Internally, I've been in different places, too, when it came time to give birth. My first was born after I had lost my job when I was eight months pregnant and I had no idea how we would provide for her. My second daughter started out in the wrong position, and so the labor was long and difficult. Not having the level of communication I needed from my care provider, I was fearful and tense. The feelings of fear and the level of pain I experienced made for a traumatic birth experience. With my third, almost four years later, I knew the importance of feeling safe and secure in order to help labor progress quickly. This time, I was also supremely confident in my body's ability to birth my third daughter without intervention. Although my forty-week due date came and went, I knew she would come at the day and time planned by God, and I was at peace. Finally, at forty-one weeks, I was in labor. Before her birth and during the labor I felt as if I was in "the zone." My meditation was "Let it be done to me according to your word." In labor, as each contraction came, I allowed it. I would completely relax my whole body, and, though painful, at no point did the contractions become more than I could handle. The labor progressed quickly, and before I knew it she was born.

This time, however, things were different. Mentally, I just didn't know how to get into that same calm confidence. Frankly, I was scared of the pain, and I didn't know how to psychologically be okay with it. Part of me wonders if perhaps my feelings were a lack of trust, a sort of pessimistic thinking that two perfect births would be too good to be true. But part of me thinks, maybe I just knew. Maybe I knew that this birth would be more challenging and that was God's grace preparing me. As it turned out, this child would be in a posterior position — face up rather than face down — which made for a longer and more painful labor. Funny thing is that now, if I were going to do it all over again — that is, go into labor at midnight and give birth about 2:40 tomorrow afternoon — I would have no fear about it. I would simply take each contraction as it came and be at peace. Even knowing that it would be difficult and painful, it would be fine, because now I know what to expect, and I know beforehand when would be the end. I guess it's the unknown that causes me so much vexation. But why? Knowing that it will be quite difficult is fine. Not knowing what to expect, however, but *fearing* it might be very difficult, is not fine. So why can't we just be at peace and know that, whether particular moments of our lives will be easy or difficult, God will give us the grace we need when the time comes?

When I went into labor on the date my child was born, despite my mental hang-ups, I was still able to fully relax my body during the contractions. I noticed that fully relaxing into the contractions increased the intensity of the pain a bit. In labor there is a choice. The woman can remain tense and disallow the fullness of the contractions, though doing so will prolong labor. But if she can "let it be done," labor will progress more quickly. Bearing life is not passive. We don't exactly have to "do," but we have to allow it. Women are the bearers of life, and if it is to be fully realized, it requires our yes. Perhaps this is the gift of femininity, our huge contribution to the world. We teach others to say yes to life. We teach others to let life unfold. My American culture likes to have everything planned, like a very neatly arranged museum, beautiful but essentially cold and lifeless. Life, however, is not that way. It rarely goes according to plan, literally and figuratively. Pregnancies happen when they weren't planned. Or maybe we planned for a pregnancy, but it doesn't come. Or maybe it comes but then ends too soon, and loss becomes part of our lives, and somehow in the struggle we have to learn to give our assent to that kind of pain instead.

As I labored, sometime in the middle of the night my in-laws arrived at my house to stay with our sleeping children, and my husband and I went to the birth center. Shortly after that, my doula, Jeannie, arrived to help me usher this child into the world, as she had done with the last. Along with some of her doula tools she arrived with her spiritual "tools" — her Bible; seven first-class relics of the Martyrs of Thailand; Oil of St. Joseph; holy water with Essence of St. Nicholas; gold, frankincense, and myrrh; and, most importantly, the Eucharist.

When she arrived, Jeannie placed the pyx holding the Eucharist on the nightstand next to the bed, along with a candle. The relics she placed in my hand while praying and rubbing the oils on my forehead and hands. Although I didn't have the assurance that labor would be swift, I knew that however it went, Jesus would be with me, not just in his omnipresence, but in the physicality of the Eucharist as well. I knew that when I chose to receive him, I could. It's likely that the first birth blessed with the presence of Jesus was John the Baptist's. Perhaps Mary, with Jesus in her womb, assisted her cousin in birth before she returned home again. What a gift it would be if the Eucharist could be brought to all Catholic women about to birth.

Toward morning, after I had been laboring all night, Jeannie prayed aloud the Litany for Laboring Women (see Appendix A), which contains the names of every saint I could find who had given birth. Once again, as at my last birth, I felt surrounded with the presence of the many women who have gone before me, praying for me in that moment before the face of God, women who also had the vocation of motherhood, who experienced childbirth, and who achieved great holiness. This time, I also added a petition to my four miscarried babies. It read, "Isabela, Solanus, Angel, and Rosario, please pray for your sibling who is now being born."

The last time I had been in labor, I had decided that I wanted to receive the Eucharist moments before I entered transition — that is, the most difficult part of labor, when contractions are their strongest, experienced just before the woman can begin pushing. This time I decided I needed the Eucharist even though I wasn't so close to the end yet. Sitting in a chair, with a blanket wrapped around my shoulders, Jeannie prayed, and I prayed with her when I could. After a few minutes, she placed the Eucharist in front of my eyes and said, "The Body of Christ." A contraction was beginning, and I could not even get "Amen" out, but I opened my mouth and Jeannie placed the Eucharist on my tongue. The contraction mounted. As the Eucharist sat on my tongue it felt as if my hips were going to break apart. This is my body broken for you.

I bowed my head in my hands and cried. During my pregnancy I had felt so distant from God. I couldn't pray when I tried to, and some days I hadn't even tried. But now, during this moment when I needed him the most, he came to me. He was here, being broken for me whether I felt warm and fuzzy or whether I felt distant. Because God is God, he does not change who he is based upon our whims, our successes, or even our failures.

The thing about back labor with a posterior baby is that it's too painful, more painful than we can handle. Although people say that God will never give us more than we can handle, I don't think I believe that. Sometimes things in life happen that ARE more than we can handle. People bear the pain of their spouses' infidelity. Parents have children who die. Couples face the unbearable pain of infertility. There are millions of children who are abused and trafficked. We can't handle it, and we break. Maybe that's the point, though. Maybe it's in that moment, in the breaking, that we come to understand the profundity of Christ's love for us: "This is my body broken for you." Broken. For YOU. Jesus, too, was given more than he could bear. That's why he fell three times. He was broken. In fact, his breaking literally killed him. But even though he could have stopped it, he allowed his own breaking. For you.

Finally, toward midafternoon, my body began to shiver. I wasn't cold, but my body shook just the same. Almost as soon as one double-peaking contraction ended another one began again. I knew I was in transition. I could no longer complete the breathing exercises designed to help me cope. Although the pain was nearly unbearable, exactly twice I was able to give a small yes. I couldn't completely and thoroughly relax my whole body through the contractions, as I had before. Two times, however, I decided that I could relax my body just a little bit. I couldn't give my full yes, but maybe I could give just a little more than I was. I didn't know it then, but it would be enough.

I had been on my side and then sat up. I wanted to bury my face in my husband's chest, and I wanted his arms surrounding me. He's always been my safe place, and I was done. I couldn't handle anymore. I whispered to my husband that I couldn't do this anymore. There was just no end in sight, and I didn't care if I got a cesarean or an epidural, just as long as the pain stopped. He looked at me. Even I, ever the optimist, had given up.

As I looked at him, waiting for his reaction, it happened. My body began to bear down — involuntarily and forcefully bear down. It's called the fetal ejection reflex, and I yelled through a half grunt, "Baby's coming!!!" I tried to scramble to the edge of the bed, and the others helped me. When that contraction ended, I moved to a kneeling position on the floor. When another contraction came, I pushed with all my strength. I decided I didn't like that position, and after that contraction ended I moved to the birthing tub.

In the tub I tried to refocus. I had just given up and had fully embraced the thought of a cesarean, even though I knew the recovery would be its own kind of challenge. But as long as it meant being pain-free in the present, I was okay with that. Now, suddenly baby was coming, and I needed to do a mental shift. I took a deep breath. "I can do this," I said aloud. It was nearly over for me. All I had to do was push my baby out. So I pushed, and my husband pushed with all his strength on my back. As I felt the baby getting lower, I knew his head was low in my pelvis. My water broke. I could feel that my baby was in the birth canal, then crowning. I pushed again and his head was out. One more push and I knew I'd be done.

From the moment on the bed when I yelled that the baby was coming to the moment he was born was about fifteen minutes. At the moment I had given up I didn't know that I had already had my last unbearable contraction. I didn't know that I wasn't hours from the end. I was just mere minutes.

My son was born very healthy and strong. And, oh, is there any relief greater than when your baby is out of your body? Once the umbilical cord was cut, Jeannie held the baby while I got out of the tub and walked to the bed. I was ready to lie down, get skin-to-skin, and nurse my little one. When everything was over, my husband and I took a nap together with our son. When we woke up at 5:30 that evening, we got our things together and went home to join the rest of our family and to introduce our newest addition to his three older sisters. Being born on the feast of Saint Benedict, we named him Mateo Benedicto.

....

Childbirth, Tupac, and "Offering It Up"
By Jennifer Fulwiler, mom to six
(ORIGINALLY POSTED AT WWW.JENNIFERFULWILER.COM.
REUSED HERE WITH PERMISSION.)

Not surprisingly, I find that labor is a great opportunity to think about the topic of suffering. With my first child, I was still basically an atheist, so my thoughts on suffering during the difficult eighteen-hour labor all basically fell in the category of "how to avoid it." But my second and third children were born after my conversion, leaving me thinking a lot about the topic from a religious perspective.

In the early stages of labor with this last baby, I thought a lot about the idea of "offering it up," uniting our own sufferings with Christ's for the good of someone else. For a while I considered what intention I might want to offer this labor for, but got sidetracked trying to figure out how this redemptive suffering thing works. It's something I'd puzzled about a lot in the past. I tend to get so overly analytical [that] I didn't understand how, specifically, you go from "just suffering" to "offering your suffering to God by uniting it with Christ's." I mean, is there some form we fill out where we describe the time and place of the suffering involved, check the "offer it up" box, and submit it to God with our signature? It didn't seem like simply saying the words that you're offering your suffering to God would really change anything.

In typical fashion, I always got so caught up in analyzing it that I'd never actually tried it. And in this case too, I just kind of forgot about the idea of offering up my labor because I couldn't get a full intellectual understanding of how exactly to do it. Instead, I put on my iPod headphones and began my pain-management technique of listening to rap. Yes, rap. It's always been one of my favorite genres of music, and for some reason I find that blasting a good rap song is far better than anything I ever learned in Bradley Method class in terms of labor pain management. I've found that Tupac's songs in particular — the infectious beats mixed with rhythmic laments about the human experience — somehow put me in the right state of mind for coping with great pain.

And, with baby number three, there was plenty of pain to cope with.

Ever since the diagnosis of a blood-clotting disorder, all my labors have to be induced, and I have to be hooked up to an IV, a few different monitors, and my legs placed in pneumatic boots to prevent blood clots. In other words, I can't move. Between the machines and wires and boots I can't even turn on my side. To manage the notoriously painful Pitocin-induced contractions while almost completely immobile is no easy thing, as I was reminded a few hours into my labor that day. Because I'm no fan of needles near my spinal cord, I waited until the pain was shatteringly unmanageable to ask for an epidural.

Unfortunately, there was a problem.

The anesthesiologist had reviewed my charts and wasn't sure whether or not my medical issues would cause bleeding in the spinal cord if he gave me the epidural, so he needed to make some calls and pull some other charts — after he helped a couple of other patients. In other words, the epidural was not coming anytime soon. I felt a tinge of panic so severe that I thought I might lose my mind if I gave in to it. I had mentally checked out of dealing with the pain since I thought it was only minutes until it all went away. In the midst of such profound, all-consuming suffering, I didn't know how to mentally check back in and get back to managing it. I felt myself begin to spiral out of control. I knew that the only way out of this mess was to go through the pain, but it seemed impossible that I could take one more second of it.

Flat on my back, devoured by the gnawing of seemingly unbearable suffering, I did the first thing that came to mind: I turned up the volume on my iPod and tried to lose myself as much as possible in the song that was playing, Tupac's posthumously released track "Changes." I instantly connected with the pain that informed so many of his lyrics, though his pain came from a life growing up amidst violence and gangs, never knowing another way, understanding that this lifestyle he felt so drawn to would mean that his time on this Earth would be short. I thought of the old pictures in the video where he grinned freely as a young child, and felt angry when I contrasted that innocent child's face to the face of the hardened notorious rapper who became involved in just about every bad thing a person could be involved in, wishing that I could somehow go back in time and shield that young boy from the tumultuous, sinful world he was born into. I thought of Tupac's painful death in a hospital bed after he'd been hunted down by enemies and shot multiple times, and the fact that he suffered the final ignominy of some of his equally misguided friends mixing his cremated remains with marijuana and smoking them in a joint. I thought of his life, his death, and the lives and deaths of others like him, and worried about their souls.

As a new surge of pain hit me, I decided that I would offer up my suffering for his soul, and for the souls of anyone else who was ever born into a life where the deck was stacked against them from day one.

And there in the midst of suffering so overwhelming that it left me with no mental resources for analysis, I finally got a glimpse of the power of "offering it up."

When I turned my mind to God in the midst of my agony to offer up my suffering for all the Tupacs of the world, a distinct, almost palpable shift occurred. I realized that instead of just doing everything in my power to get as far away from this pain as possible, I was now saying: "I accept it. If it helps these souls for whom I'm praying, I accept it." And what did that do? What's the big difference between trying to escape pain and accepting it for the benefit of someone else? The answer was something I could not have put into words but that I understood on a primal level: *it generates love.*

I'm no theologian and don't know how to defend that statement with high doctrinal analysis, but it's something I knew with complete certainty in my suffering there in the hospital. That feeling I sensed the moment I turned to Christ crucified and asked him to accept my suffering along with his own for those for whom I prayed was the feeling of an explosion of love. Through suffering, love had been generated where there were only impotent well wishes and kind words before. And though it's still not something I can put into words, I could feel how God could use such love for the benefit of us all. To put more of that real, meaty love into the world — that kind of love that can only spring from self-sacrifice on behalf of another — is to put more of God himself into the world.

I ended up getting the epidural (that didn't fully work) only ten minutes before the baby was born, and my suffering finally passed. But ever since that experience I've felt as if I finally understand the mystery of redemptive suffering a little better, even if I struggle to articulate it. I offer this story not as some thorough explanation of the subject, but more as food for thought in case anyone else finds it interesting. All I know is that, there on the hospital bed, pain and a desire to help a lost soul and the Cross the only things on my mind, I sensed some intimate — possibly inextricable?

— connection between love and willingness to suffer, and understood the power of this kind of love to save the world.

....

The Birth of Aliya Elizabeth

By Micaela Darr, mom to seven on Earth
and two in eternity, birth educator
WWW.MICAELADARR.COM

My first was just shy of nine months old when we found out we were pregnant again. I was still working full time and had a very high-needs baby. Added to that stress, I was very much hoping for a VBAC (vaginal birth after cesarean) with this baby, and I knew that doctors really prefer more space between pregnancies if you plan to do that. What's an information-ophile to do but begin her research, good and early.

So I read, and I researched, and I read and researched some more. Much to my delight, I came to discover that research shows that, in many cases, VBACs are safer than repeat cesareans. I found a doctor who supported my choice, and we were on our way. An important doctor note: my OB practice contained two OBs, one an older guy with a ton of experience and a laid-back attitude who was nonchalant about our choice for a VBAC. The other was young and significantly more uptight. She claimed to be supportive, but at every visit she made her caveats known. IF I didn't gain too much weight and IF the baby didn't go overdue and IF the stars and the moons were aligned with Jupiter, etc., I would be able to *attempt* a VBAC. In labor, you get whichever doctor is on call. Can you guess which one I was hoping for?

I also began a hard-sell campaign to get a doula for this birth. I knew that doulas were beneficial in most births, and especially in VBACs, but originally my husband and I had worried that a doula would somehow come between us in the delivery room. The more I talked to people, the more I understood this was not true. I happened to ask at a local mom group meeting, and lo and behold, the leader was a doula. After meeting her, Kevin got on board quickly.

I stopped work one week before my due date. The following Thursday afternoon I started having contractions but wasn't sure anything was "really" happening. While this was my second baby, it was my first labor. I was clueless. I called Kevin at work and told him he should swing by Target and pick up a new watch. He did, and when he got home he found my daughter and I in the front yard. I was giddy with anticipation, and she was covered in mud. Around 6:00 p.m. the contractions came regularly about six minutes apart and one minute long, but still weren't very intense. I called my parents at about 8:00 p.m., and they prepared to make the four-hour drive down to our house. My in-laws (who live just a few miles away) were put on notice.

I thought the contractions might subside at night, but no such luck! They didn't get closer together, but they got a LOT stronger around 2:00 a.m. (about the time my parents got to our house). We all tried to sleep, but I didn't have very much luck. I took a couple of showers to relieve the pain, but otherwise it was sleep–contraction–sleep. I'd have a contraction, wake up, and get on all fours, and then immediately lie down and fall asleep again when it went away. It really was the oddest thing, to go from asleep to wide awake to asleep again in just seconds.

At 6:00 a.m. my water broke. It took me a minute to figure out what that was, and in the interim I had a flash of panic that I was bleeding. After I realized what it was, and saw that the amniotic fluid was clear, the whole mood in the house shifted. My mom, who has given birth eleven times, was anxious for us to head to the hospital. Meanwhile, my contractions slowed down a bit and I was smiling nonstop. I knew we were well on our way to a VBAC, and that thrilled me to no end. My in-laws arrived a few minutes later and took over care of my daughter. The rest of us decided to make our way to the hospital. I called my doula, and she said she would meet us there. Enter hiccups one and two: (1) We found out on the way to the hospital that the uptight doctor was on call. Bummer. Big bummer. I had an inkling that she had an itchy c-section trigger and worried about what that would mean for the VBAC. (2) In the car, I had sat on a hospital pad. When I got out I noticed that the amniotic fluid was no longer clear, and I knew that meant meconium, which might mean more intervention or anxiety from the staff.

When I arrived at the L&D wing, the nurse directed me to a room to prep me for a cesarean (because they saw on my chart that I had a previous one). I was in the throes of a contraction and laid a death grip on my husband's arm. My knight in a shining sweatshirt calmly said: "Um, no thank you. We're planning a VBAC." In that moment we became "those" patients: the troublemakers. (I was kind of getting used to the title.) The nurses eyed us warily from behind the desk as we made our way down the hall to our room. I knew they were calculating the amount of fuss I would put up in the labor room. At that point, though (7:30 a.m.), I was deep in the birth forest of Don't Care What You Think. Fortunately, our nurse was an angel of sweetness and light. There weren't many babies being born on the floor, so she was in our room almost the whole time, yet gave us plenty of space to labor.

My husband called the doctor to let her know about the meconium, but she didn't seem worried! I ended up being monitored the whole time so they could watch the baby's heart rate, but I could get up and move around the room, so that was fine. My doula was such a pro that anytime the nurse got freaked out by the heart rate dropping, she just stepped in and adjusted the monitor, reminded me to breathe, etc. She constantly assured me that the baby was doing fine so I was able to focus on my contractions.

I want to take a moment to talk about my husband in the delivery room. At that point in our marriage, we had never been more intimately connected than those moments when his face was inches from mine, encouraging me, supporting me, loving me. He believed in me more than I believed in myself. I was a sweaty ball of whining and curses, and yet he never stopped telling me how beautiful I was. With the birth of my first, we missed out on that intimacy. I am blessed beyond measure to have had him there.

Back to the details. When I got there at 7:30ish a.m., I was dilated 5–6 cm; by 9:15 I was 8 cm. Twenty minutes later, my doula asked me between contractions if I had begun pushing. I don't remember my exact words, but I believe it was something along the lines of, "Ummmm, I don't really know?" She called a reluctant nurse over to check me again. Boy, was that nurse surprised when I measured at 10 cm. The nurse firmly ordered me not to push, though, because the doctor was finishing up surgery upstairs. I looked at my doula with what I'm sure was a panicked look. Not push? Is that even a thing? How, pray tell, does one override that primal instinct? I'll never forget the serene smile on her face as she said: "Micaela, someone will catch the baby. You go ahead and push if you feel like it." God bless her.

Did I mention that my mom and dad, my husband's mom and dad, my doula, my husband, plus my nurse and a NICU team (because of the meconium staining) were all in the room? The grandpas kept a respectful distance over my shoulders and everyone was really quiet. While I had planned to only have my husband, my doula, and my mom in the room, at that point, I didn't care. I started "officially" pushing at 10:12 (tried several different positions), and our baby was born at 10:32. Aliya Elizabeth weighed 9 lbs, 0.3 oz, and measured 21.5 inches long. I looked at my mom and croaked, "I did it."

Not that there weren't any complications, though. I sustained a tear and lost some blood from it, and my doctor (who did, after all, breeze in at the last minute and catch the baby) had to do some serious stitching. My blood pressure dropped, and I became dizzy and weak. They gave me a saline IV and made me drink, drink, drink. Meanwhile, they were suctioning Aliya's stomach and lungs to make sure the meconium didn't cause complications, which was a little nerve-racking. I didn't get up for two hours, and when I did get up, I almost passed out, so they had me lie down for another two hours. One of the sweetest memories of that foggy time was waking up to see my husband curled up on the delivery room couch, all 6 feet 2 inches of him lovingly cradling our newborn miracle.

While my recovery from Aliya's birth was better than my first, it was still painful due to the tearing and was worse than I expected. But because it didn't negatively affect my future births the way a repeat cesarean would have, I counted it all as joy. This little David conquered Goliath with a mighty stone of faith. Not without injury and not without fear, but with my army of loving protectors and a whole lot of grace, it happened. In most things, I wouldn't call myself a warrior. In birth, I do.

....

The Birth of Zeno Aquinas
By Melody Lyons, mom to eight on Earth and one in eternity
WWW.THEESSENTIALMOTHER.COM

My youngest child was born at home in the quiet and dark with a blessed candle to light his way into the world. It was our first home birth and, under the circumstances, the safest and healthiest option available to us. It was also one of the most profoundly beautiful experiences of my life.

I have always been committed to having unmedicated labors and have been mostly able to achieve that in the last twenty years and eight births (apart from one "necessary" nightmarish Pitocin experience). My reasons for wanting to go "natural" from the beginning were simple. As a young, first-time mother (twenty years old), I read about common labor medications and simply ruled them out. They all crossed the placenta and all reached the babies. They all brought a certain measure of risk to both mother and child in otherwise low-risk pregnancies. Maybe it was my youthful naiveté. Or stubbornness. Or fierce maternal instinct. But it made sense to me on a fundamental level to accept the pain in order to better protect my child. After getting through my first doozy of a birth naturally,

I simply never looked back. I credit youthful impetuousness, not any real courage of my own, and the subsequent knowledge that, yes, I can do this really hard thing. We went on to have seven hospital births without pain medication and also one miscarriage at home at thirteen weeks.

In spite of my commitment to natural birth, I didn't start dreaming of a home birth in earnest until my sixth child was born. He arrived after a forty-five-minute hurricane labor in which I barely made it into the delivery room. In theory, forty-five minutes sounds perfectly lovely. In reality, it was brutal. The stress level was extremely high, the pain difficult to manage, and the baby distressed. I didn't ever want to go through that again.

So the seed was planted, and the idea of peacefully, gently, quietly welcoming any additional babies into the world began to take root. We did our best to plan that kind of hospital birth for baby number seven, and it was much better, but still a far cry from the unfolding dream that I couldn't shake. I continued to research and imagine and learn about my body and God's design for birth. And then we found out that we were expecting our eighth child.

My pregnancies are difficult, and this one was no exception. The first few months were a complete blur of misery followed by remaining months of unconquerable fatigue and sickness. Every once in a while, I'd think about upcoming labor and tremble. I'm no fan of pain, especially labor pain. You might say it even terrifies me. I was tired, sick, and lacking courage. The thought of the hospital scene kept rising up before me, and one thing was absolutely clear to me: *I didn't want to step foot in a hospital to deliver this child if I didn't absolutely have to.* The thought of the noisy, crowded, intervening medical scene filled me with anxiety. The very image reminded me of PAIN, and my mind would take refuge again in the dream of just staying home. The dream always went something like this: Contractions would start or my water would break … and I would just … stay. In the quiet. In the dark. In my room. With my husband. And then our son would be born. That was all.

And in the end, that really is what happened.

I had been laboring for weeks, just like my previous pregnancies. The textbooks call it "prodromal labor," but I just call it the world's longest labor. There are many false starts to active labor and many nights filled with contractions too strong to sleep through. The one advantage to this is that once active labor starts, my babies are born within a couple of hours. I deal with the uncertainty of timing by sticking close to home for many weeks. Waiting … waiting … waiting. Knowing this time that I didn't have to leave to go to the hospital or arrange for complicated child care was significant. My anxiety level didn't rise with contractions. My heart, mind, and body stayed rooted in place ... rooted at home.

On the afternoon of the 26th, I noticed a slight increase in the regularity of my contractions. I paid attention, but not too much. After all, it was typical of my labors and might taper off. I did notice that I was crankier than usual, and that I felt an urgency to get something done. "Let's take the kids out for ice cream," I said. So we did.

Contractions were coming irregularly (typical for me), at about one every fifteen to forty minutes, but I noticed that they were getting a little sharper when they did come: *Duly noted, body. You've faked me out more times than I can count, but I'm paying attention for the moment.* At 10:00 p.m., we arrived home from ice cream.

At 11:30 p.m., after waiting for our oldest to get home from work, we said late family prayers. I was feeling a little serious at that point, but the rest of the family didn't seem to be on the same page. I felt very restless and irritable. This is probably it, I thought. I suddenly felt much more earnest about getting the kids into bed. Unfortunately, my desire and my toddler clashed, and she didn't fall asleep until night passed into morning. By that time, I knew we were going to have a baby. Soon.

At 12:30 a.m. came active labor. It was around that time that we called the midwives. The doula was the first to arrive, and my husband directed her downstairs to wait. I don't remember telling him that I wanted to be alone, but I suppose we must have talked about it enough. Whatever the case, he knew what to do, and I continued my labor in the quiet and dark of my room.

Quiet and dark and cool. It was the labor scenario of my dreams. There isn't a whole lot of room to wander in our tiny bedroom, but it was enough. I rested on the bed in front of the fan and then shuffled back and forth, the affirmations I had been looking at for at least a month running through my head and the music of my pre-labor playlist coming back to my mind in little bits and pieces. As labor intensified, most of those mental words fell away until I was left with only a few. I didn't choose them consciously ... they just seemed to be the ones I needed most.

> *Open.*
> *Come down, Baby.*
> *Sweet Jesus, carry me.*
> *Sing low.*

I began to sing to myself when the waves of the contractions crested. I never would have done that in the hospital and probably not in front of the midwives either; but alone, I sang. The words were from the chorus of a Chris Rice song:

And my soul wells up ...
And my soul wells up ...
And my soul wells up in an alleluia ...

As the wave would rise, I would imagine the pain rising up to Jesus — the one prayer I could give in the moment — and an effective way to surrender to the intensity and then give it away. The pain didn't disappear, but it was manageable. It was purposeful. And I never panicked.

I sang an octave lower than usual so that my jaw would stay loose, since a loose jaw means a relaxed pelvic floor. My plan had been to hum or sing low (sort of like a cow mooing, to be honest), but the actual singing was working beautifully. So I danced and sang in the quiet and the dark.

In the hospital, I have never been able to rise from a side lying position. I lie down, close my eyes, and wait for babies to be born. It is the way that I cope with the pain in what I find to be a highly stressful environment. The moment I open my eyes and see a nurse or a monitor is the moment I start to panic. At home it was different. I found relief in the standing. I saw our wedding picture faintly in the dark. I watched the fan. I danced and sang and there was no one to judge or to shush me. No intrusions.

Around 1:10 a.m. the midwives arrived and stayed downstairs with my daughter and husband, chatting at the kitchen table. I would need my husband soon, but not yet, and he intuitively knew that. A midwife entered my room to briefly check on the baby. I stayed standing while she listened to his heartbeat, which was strong even through a tough contraction. She left as quietly as she came.

My water broke gently during a contraction at 1:25 a.m., and I knew that I would need my husband with me. I felt the baby drop and recognized that feeling. It wouldn't be long now. A midwife asked my husband to make sure the fluid was clear. It was. My husband didn't leave my side after that point, and as I leaned into his arms and rocked I couldn't help but think that we were dancing our son into the world.

And he prayed. He prayed Hail Marys, and he prayed for protection. He prayed when I couldn't. And when I did call out to Jesus, he joined in with me, and it was, in many ways, like singing in one voice to God. The meaning of our marriage vows in those moments of suffering love was illuminated. I'm not sure I can put words to that kind of intimacy and joy.

In the meantime, the midwives waited downstairs. As the baby came closer to birth, my sounds began to change. I knew that, being good midwives, they would hear and know when to come. I laughed to myself a little at the time, thinking about my groanings as a birthy way of communicating with the women downstairs — like birdcalls or something. And they were listening and moving, first downstairs, then up to the kitchen, then to the base of the stairs leading to my room.

I felt those panicky feelings that come with transition. I wanted to squeal, but instead I focused on dropping my voice low and thinking only of the baby. There was no way around this moment. It is always a rather terrible moment when control slips away and is wholly replaced by a need to surrender to pain … but it was almost over. The difference between my earlier births and later births is that the pain took over every part of me, even my mind, like a white-hot blanket. In my more recent births, I have learned how to focus better and to work with my body instead of raging against it. Still gotta go through it, but that shift in mindset makes all the difference.

As we moved through transition, I got on my hands and knees on the bed, something I never would have attempted in the hospital. My husband stayed by my side supporting me, and I felt the baby descend. Prior to this delivery, I had only experienced pushing while on my back or on my side at the hospital. Lying down was how I coped in the hospital, but I didn't just want to cope: I wanted to thrive. The books all said that standing, squatting, or hands and knees were better and faster and less painful, so I decided that's what I would do. I wanted to spend as little time in transition as possible. The books were right. Everything opened quickly but gently.

"He's coming."

And suddenly, the midwives were there, quietly, steadily, as my baby crowned.

At 1:52 a.m., his head was delivered with one push and his body followed right after. And just as I had dreamed, he was born in the relative silence and darkness of the night, with only those there who belonged. They handed him to me immediately, and our family was changed again forever.

It was the quick labor and birth that I knew I would have. It was the gentle and joyful birth that I knew I could have. Thank God it was over. Thank God he was here. Thank God for the peace, for the quiet, for the joy, for the birthday.

After they gave the baby to me, I held him while we waited for the cord to stop pulsing and he received all the blood that rightfully belonged to him. I held him and nursed him while we waited for the placenta. No one pulled or tugged to make it go faster. There was no excess bleeding. No tearing. And we rested. I was helped to the bathroom to clean up a little while the bed was quickly changed. I returned to a fresh resting place and the baby was finally weighed and admired. He was quiet and calm through it all. The midwives retired downstairs to give us time to be alone and bond before they came in to check on the baby again.

After checking the different milestones of recovery, the midwives finally went home, and my husband and daughter continued with a little chatting, baby admiring, and a couple of minor points of clean up. My husband finally went downstairs to eat his "dinner" and my daughter went to bed. I prepared myself for what I knew would be a long night of afterpains, consoled by the presence of the sweetest baby on planet Earth. I nursed him and kissed him while the sun rose in the sky and the birds took over the songs of our night of joy.

Everyone slept in that morning, and the children straggled from their beds one at a time over a period of hours. I will never forget each awed face as it passed our door and realized that there was a tiny human being resting next to Mommy. All the children except for three had slept soundly through the miracle of the night. My oldest daughter wouldn't have missed it for the world, and my two oldest boys lay awake in the dark, hearing the sounds of our little community and of birth. If they minded, they didn't say, but one of them did pay attention and marked the time of his little brother's arrival by his clock. I can't help but think that such a memory (even though only through sound) will have significance in their lives. They will know ...

Birth is important.
Birth is natural and God-designed.
Birth is beautiful.
Birth is God's gift to the family.
Birth is a time to celebrate even while we carry the cross.
Birth looks a lot like real Christian love.

With some of my births, I have surrendered to a spirit of fear instead of surrendering to love; and I allowed that fear to increase pain and rob the moments of a fullness of joy. God allowed this home birth to be a source of tremendous healing for me, and I recognize it as his victory through my weakness. After the previous eight births, I felt as if I had nothing left to bring to the table. No courage. No emotional or physical strength. But in this moment, he allowed me to overcome anxiety, labor in hope, rest in peace, and drink in the joy. Thanks be to God.

APPENDICES

APPENDIX A

Prayers

Order for the Blessing of Parents before Childbirth
This blessing can be found from your priest or at www.usccb.org/prayer-and-worship/sacraments-and-sacramentals/sacramentals-blessings/persons/blessing-parents-before-childbirth.cfm.

The Rite for the Blessing of a Child in the Womb
This blessing can be obtained from your priest or found at www.usccb.org/about/pro-life-activities/prayers/upload/Rite-for-the-Blessing-of-a-Child-in-the-Womb.pdf.

A Prayer to Saint Gerard before Birth
O almighty and everlasting God who through the operation of the Holy Christ, didst prepare the body and soul of the glorious Virgin Mary to be a worthy dwelling place of thy divine Son; and, through the operation of the same Holy Ghost, didst sanctify Saint John the Baptist, while still in his mother's womb; hearken to the prayers of thy humble servant who implore thee, through the intercession of Saint Gerard, to protect me; that it may be cleansed by the saving water of baptism and, after a Christian life on Earth, it may with its mother, attain everlasting bliss in heaven. Amen.

Prayer of Saint Gianna
God our Father, we praise you and we bless you because in Saint Gianna Beretta Molla you have given us one who witnessed to the Gospel as a young woman, as a wife, as a mother, and as a doctor. We thank you because through the gift of her life we can learn to welcome and honor every human person.

You, Lord Jesus, were for Gianna a splendid example. She learned to recognize you in the beauty of nature. As she was questioning her choice of vocation she went in search of you and the best way to serve you. Through her married love she became a sign of your love for the Church and for humanity. Like you, the Good Samaritan, she cared for everyone who was sick, small, or weak. Following your example, out of love, she gave herself entirely, generating new life.

Holy Spirit, source of every perfection, give us wisdom, intelligence, and courage so that, following the example of Saint Gianna and through her intercession, we may know how to place ourselves at the service of each person we meet in our personal, family, and professional lives, and thus grow in love and holiness. Amen.

The Christmas Anticipation Prayer (also known as the Saint Andrew Novena Prayer)

(This prayer is traditionally said during Advent, calling upon the hour of Christ's birth, which makes it appropriate for our own births at any time of year.)

Hail and blessed be the hour and moment in which the Son of God was born of the most pure Virgin Mary at midnight in Bethlehem in piercing cold. In that hour, vouchsafe, O my God, to hear my prayers and grant my desires through the merits of our Savior Jesus Christ and his Blessed Mother. Amen.

The Litany to Mothers

A beautiful litany for labor, invoking hundreds of women saints who gave birth, can be found at www.myfemininemind.com/2012/11/birth-resources.html. This litany was written by April Jaure.

Prayer to Our Lady of La Leche

To you, lovely Lady of La Leche, and to your divine Son, do I now dedicate this little baby whom our Father in heaven has given me. Grateful for the trust he has placed in me, I beg you to obtain for me the physical and spiritual graces I need to fulfill my duties at every moment. Inspire me with the motherly sentiments you felt during your days with the Child Jesus. Make it possible for me, in imitation of you, O Lady of La Leche, to nurse my child to perfect health. In all things help me to follow the example which you, as the perfect model of all mothers, have given to me. Let my family mirror the virtues of your Holy Family of Nazareth. Finally, I commend to your loving care all the mothers of Earth, in whose hands he has entrusted the souls of his little children. Amen.

Novena Prayer to Our Lady of La Leche

Lovely Lady of La Leche, most loving mother of Jesus, and my mother, listen to my humble prayer. Your motherly heart knows my every wish, my every need. To you only, his spotless Virgin Mother, has your divine Son given to understand the sentiments which fill my soul. Yours was the sacred privilege of being the mother of the Savior. Intercede with him now, my loving mother, that in accordance with his will (mention your request). This I ask, O Lady of La Leche, in the name of your divine Son, my Lord and Savior. Amen.

V. O Mary, conceived without sin,
R. Pray for us who have recourse to you.

Our Lady of La Leche, pray for us.
Amen.[160]

....

In addition, *Mothers' Manual* by A. Francis Coomes, S.J., contains dozens of beautiful prayers for pregnancy, birth, postpartum, and motherhood, and are very specific in intention. It's a valuable spiritual resource highly recommended.

Prayers for Pregnancy and *Prayers for Birth* are two e-books written by Laura Kelly Fanucci that also contain appropriate prayers for pregnant mothers. They both can be found at www.motheringspirit.com.

APPENDIX B

Scriptures for Use in Labor and Birth

Some women choose one or a few Scriptures that resonate with them to bring to their labor. Others prefer simply to have any of them read at the discretion of the support person. The verses here have been divided up for use at different times during your labor, depending on your needs at particular moments. These (as well as many of the Scriptures opening each chapter) are just a few suggestions of the many that are appropriate for pregnancy, labor, and birth.

General Use

- "Yet you are he who took me from the womb; you kept me safe upon my mother's breasts." ~ Psalms 22:9

- "You formed my inward parts, you knitted me together in my mother's womb." ~ Psalms 139:13

- "They shall not labor in vain, or bear children for calamity; for they shall be the offspring of the blessed of the LORD, and their children with them." ~ Isaiah 65:23

- "Shall I bring to the birth and not cause to bring forth? says the LORD." ~ Isaiah 66:9

- "Come to me, all who labor and are heavy laden, and I will give you rest." ~ Matthew 11:28

- "And he took a child, and put him in the midst of them; and taking him in his arms, he said to them, 'Whoever receives one such child in my name, receives me; and whoever receives me, receives not me but him who sent me.'" ~ Mark 9:36–37

- "This is my body which is given for you. Do this in remembrance of me." ~ Luke 22:19

- "I appeal to you therefore, brethren, by the mercies of God, to present your bodies as a living sacrifice, holy and acceptable to God, which is your spiritual worship." ~ Romans 12:1

- "Do you not know that your body is a temple of the Holy Spirit within you, which you have from God? You are not your own; you were bought with a price. So glorify God in your body." ~ 1 Corinthians 6:19–20

- "Therefore, my beloved brethren, be steadfast, immovable, always abounding in the work of the Lord, knowing that in the Lord your labor is not in vain." ~ 1 Corinthians 15:58

- "And I am sure that he who began a good work in you will bring it to completion at the day of Jesus Christ." ~ Philippians 1:6

- "We give thanks to God always for you all, constantly mentioning you in our prayers, remembering before our God and Father your work of faith and labor of love and steadfastness of hope in our Lord Jesus Christ." ~ 1 Thessalonians 1:2–4

For Endurance

- "When a woman is in labor, she has pain, because her hour has come; but when she is delivered of the child, she no longer remembers the anguish, for joy that a child is born into the world." ~ John 16:21

- "Love bears all things, believes all things, hopes all things, endures all things." ~ 1 Corinthians 13:7

- "And after you have suffered a little while, the God of all grace, who has called you to his eternal glory in Christ, will himself restore, establish, and strengthen you." ~ 1 Peter 5:10

For Moments of Pain or Suffering

- "Be brave, my child; the Lord of heaven and earth grant you joy in place of this sorrow of yours. Be brave, my daughter." ~ Tobit 7:18

- "More than that, we rejoice in our sufferings, knowing that suffering produces endurance, and endurance produces character, and character produces hope, and hope does not disappoint us, because God's love has been poured into our hearts through the Holy Spirit who has been given to us." ~ Romans 5:3–5

- "I consider that the sufferings of this present time are not worth comparing with the glory that is to be revealed to us." ~ Romans 8:18

- "For as we share abundantly in Christ's sufferings, so through Christ we share abundantly in comfort too." ~ 2 Corinthians 1:5

- "Now I rejoice in my sufferings for your sake, and in my flesh I complete what is lacking in Christ's afflictions for the sake of his body, that is, the Church." ~ Colossians 1:24

- "That I may know him and the power of his resurrection, and may share his sufferings, becoming like him in his death." ~ Philippians 3:10

- "But rejoice in so far as you share Christ's sufferings, that you may also rejoice and be glad when his glory is revealed." ~ 1 Peter 4:13

For Moments of Fear or Anxiety

- "Be strong and of good courage, do not fear or be in dread of them: for it is the LORD your God who goes with you; he will not fail you or forsake you." ~ Deuteronomy 31:6

- "Be strong and of good courage, and do it. Fear not, be not dismayed; for the LORD God, even my God, is with you. He will not fail you or forsake you, until all the work for the service of the house of the LORD is finished."
  ~ 1 Chronicles 28:20

- "I sought the Lord, and he answered me, delivered me from all my fears." ~ Psalms 34:4

- "When I am afraid, I put my trust in you. In God, whose word I praise, in God I trust without a fear. What can flesh do to me?" ~ Psalms 56:3–5

- "With the Lord on my side I do not fear. What can man do to me?" ~ Psalms 118:6

- "Fear not, for I am with you; be not dismayed, for I am your God." ~ Isaiah 41:10

- "I can do all things in him who strengthens me."
  ~ Philippians 4:13

After Baby Is Born

- "My soul magnifies the Lord, and my spirit rejoices in God my Savior, for he has regarded the low estate of his handmaiden. For behold, henceforth all generations will call me blessed; for he who is mighty has done great things for me, and holy is his name. And his mercy is on those who fear him from generation to generation. He has shown strength with his arm, he has scattered the proud in the imagination of their hearts, he has put down the mighty from their thrones, and exalted those of low degree; he has filled the hungry with good things, and the rich he has sent empty away." ~ Luke 1:46–55

- "For this child I prayed; and the LORD has granted me my petition which I made to him. Therefore I have lent him to the LORD; as long as he lives, he is lent to the LORD."
  ~ 1 Samuel 1:27–28

- "Praise the LORD! O give thanks to the LORD, for he is good; for his mercy endures forever!" ~ Psalms 106:1

- "Behold, sons are a heritage from the LORD, the fruit of the womb a reward." ~ Psalms 127:3

- "Praise the LORD! Praise the LORD, O my soul! I will praise the LORD as long as I live; I will sing praises to my God while I have being." ~ Psalms 146:1–2

- "For what thanksgiving can we render to God for you, for all the joy which we feel for your sake before our God?"
  ~ 1 Thessalonians 3:9

- "Amen! Blessing and glory and wisdom and thanksgiving and honor and power and might be to our God for ever and ever! Amen." ~ Revelation 7:12

APPENDIX C

Saint Quotes for Pregnancy, Labor, and Birth

- "I am not afraid; I was born to do this." ~ *Saint Joan of Arc*

- "Teach us to give and not count the cost." ~ *Saint Ignatius of Loyola*

- "One cannot love without suffering or suffer without loving." ~ *Saint Gianna Beretta Molla*

- "There is no cross to bear that Christ has not already born for us, and does not now bear with us." ~ *Saint John Paul II*

- "I plead with you — never, ever give up on hope, never doubt, never tire, and never become discouraged. Be not afraid." ~ *Saint John Paul II*

- "Let nothing trouble you, let nothing make you afraid. All things pass away. God never changes. Patience obtains everything. God alone is enough." ~ *Saint Teresa of Ávila*

- "Apart from the cross, there is no other ladder by which we may get to heaven." ~ *Saint Rose of Lima*

- "We can do no great things, only small things with great love." ~ *Saint Teresa of Calcutta*

- "I know well that the greater and more beautiful the work is, the more terrible will be the storms that rage against it." ~ *Saint Faustina*

- "He who can preserve gentleness amid pains, and peace amid worry multitude of affairs, is almost perfect." ~ *Saint Francis de Sales*

- "Faith means battles; if there are no contests, it is because there are none who desire to contend." ~ *Saint Ambrose*

- "Christians must lean on the Cross of Christ just as travelers lean on a staff when they begin a long journey. They must have the Passion of Christ deeply embedded in their minds and hearts, because only from it can they derive peace, grace, and truth." ~ *Saint Anthony of Padua*

- "For me prayer is a surge of the heart, it is a simple look towards heaven, it is a cry of recognition and of love, embracing both trial and joy." ~ *Saint Thérèse of Lisieux*

- "If you are what you should be, you will set the whole world ablaze!" ~ *Saint Catherine of Siena*

- "Let us go forward in peace, our eyes upon heaven, the only one goal of our labors." ~ *Saint Thérèse of Lisieux*

- "I can't do big things. But I want all I do, even the smallest thing, to be for the greater glory of God." ~ *Saint Dominic Savio*

- "Suffering is a great grace; through suffering the soul becomes like the Savior; in suffering love becomes crystallized; the greater the suffering, the purer the love." ~ *Saint Faustina*

- "I fixed my gaze upon His sacred wounds and felt happy to suffer with Him. I suffered, and yet I did not suffer, because I felt happy to know the depth of His love, and the hour passed like a minute." ~ *Saint Faustina*

- "The past does not belong to me; the future is not mine; with all my soul I try to make use of the present moment." ~ *Saint Faustina*

- "In difficult moments I will fix my gaze upon the silent heart of Jesus, stretched upon the cross, and from the exploding flames of His merciful heart, will flow down upon me power and strength to keep fighting." ~ *Saint Faustina*

- "The loveliest masterpiece of the heart of God is the heart of a mother." ~ *Saint Thérèse of Lisieux*

- "May you trust God that you are exactly where you are meant to be." ~ *Saint Thérèse of Lisieux*

- "Do not look forward in fear to the changes in life; rather, look to them with full hope that as they arise, God, whose very own you are, will lead you safely through all things; and when you cannot stand it, God will carry you in His arms. Do not fear what may happen tomorrow; the same understanding Father who cares for you today will take care of you then and every day. He will either shield you from suffering or will give you unfailing strength to bear it. Be at peace and put aside all anxious thoughts and imaginations." ~ *Saint Francis de Sales*

APPENDIX D

Recommended Informational Resources

It should be noted that while these resources are helpful, not everything included in them may align with Catholic teaching. The recommendation of the work should not imply an endorsement of anything that is contrary to natural law or Catholic doctrine.

Websites

Ask Dr. Sears: Advice and information on pregnancy and childbirth, parenting and behavior, feeding and eating. www.askdrsears.com

Evidence-Based Birth: An online childbirth resource for expecting parents and birth-care practitioners to understand the latest, proven, evidence-based care practices. www.evidencebasedbirth.com

Lamaze International: Pregnancy, birth, and early parenting education. www.lamazeinternational.com

The Bradley Method (Husband Coached Natural Childbirth): Pregnancy and natural birth education. www.bradleybirth.com

Birth Boot Camp: Online or in-person classes in natural childbirth and breastfeeding. www.birthbootcamp.com

Spinning Babies: Techniques and recommendations for helping encourage baby into the optimal position for birth. www.spinningbabies.com

International Cesarean Awareness Network: Support for women before and after cesarean section. www.ican-online.org

VBAC Facts: Unbiased and evidence-based information on VBAC. www.vbacfacts.com

Mothering: Information and resources for pregnancy, childbirth, breastfeeding, and parenting. www.mothering.com

La Leche League International: A worldwide organization that provides support, encouragement, information, and education for breastfeeding. www.llli.org

Kelly Mom: Breastfeeding information and support. www.kellymom. com

The Guiding Star Project: A growing network of centers that provide support for natural means of family planning, fertility care, childbirth, breastfeeding, and family life. www.theguidingstarproject.com

Elizabeth Ministry International: An international ministry designed to offer hope and healing for women and their families on issues related to childbearing, sexuality, and relationships. Especially known for support and resources following miscarriage or loss. www.elizabethministry.com

Flourish in Hope: Catholic postpartum solidarity and support. www. flourishinhope.com

Books

The Healthy Pregnancy Book by William Sears and Martha Sears

The Birth Book by William Sears and Martha Sears

Pregnancy, Childbirth, and the Newborn by Penny Simkin, Janet Whalley, Ann Keppler, Janelle Durham, and April Bolding

Natural Childbirth the Bradley Way by Susan McCutcheon

Ina May's Guide to Childbirth by Ina May Gaskin

Gentle Birth, Gentle Mothering: A Doctor's Guide to Natural Childbirth and Gentle Early Parenting Choices by Sarah Buckley

HypnoBirthing: The Mongan Method by Marie Mongan

The Womanly Art of Breastfeeding by Diane Wiessinger and Diana West through La Leche League International

Breastfeeding and Catholic Motherhood by Sheila M. Kippley

Ina May's Guide to Breastfeeding by Ina May Gaskin

Breastfeeding Made Simple: Seven Natural Laws for Nursing Mothers by Nancy Mohrbacher and Kathleen Kendall-Tackett

The Baby Book by William Sears and Martha Sears

Mulieris Dignitatem (On the Dignity and Vocation of Women) by Pope Saint John Paul II

Gratissimam Sane (Letter to Families) by Pope Saint John Paul II

Letter to Women by Pope Saint John Paul II

Familiaris Consortio (On the Christian Family in the Modern World) by Pope Saint John Paul II

NOTES

1. Mt 10:30 and Ps 139:2.

2. Second Vatican Council, *Lumen Gentium* (Dogmatic Constitution on the Church) (Vatican City: Libreria Editrice Vaticana, 1964), 36, http://www.vatican.va/archive/hist_councils/ii_vatican_council/documents/vat-ii_const_19641121_lumen-gentium_en.html; also cited in the *Catechism of the Catholic*, 912 (emphasis added).

3. Penny Simkin, *Birth Trauma Definitions and Statistics*, PATTCh (Prevention and Treatment of Traumatic Childbirth) 2017, http://pattch.org/resource-guide/traumatic-births-and-ptsd-definition-and-statistics/.

4. WHO, UNICEF, UNFPA, The World Bank, and the United Nations Population Division, *Trends in Maternal Mortality: 1990 to 2013* (Geneva: World Health Organization, 2014), http://apps.who.int/iris/bitstream/10665/112682/2/9789241507226_eng.pdf?ua=1.

5. U.S. Central Intelligence Agency, *The World Factbook*, "Country Comparison: Infant Mortality Rate," https://www.cia.gov/library/publications/the-world-factbook/rankorder/2091rank.html (accessed October 3, 2017).

6. Department of Reproductive Health and Research, World Health Organization, *WHO Statement of Cesarean Section Rates* (Geneva: World Health Organization, 2015), http://apps.who.int/iris/bitstream/10665/161442/1/WHO_RHR_15.02_eng.pdf.; and BE Hamilton, JA Martin, MJK Osterman, et al., "Births: Final Data for 2014," *National Vital Statistics Reports*, vol. 64, no. 12 (2015): 2, https://www.cdc.gov/nchs/data/nvsr/nvsr64/nvsr64_12.pdf.

7. T. J. Matthews et al., U.S. Department of Health and Human Services, "Infant Mortality Statistics from the 2013 Period Linked Birth/Infant Death Data Set," *National Vital Statistics Reports,* vol. 64, no. 9 (2015), https://www.cdc.gov/nchs/data/nvsr/nvsr64/nvsr64_09.pdf.

8. John Paul II, *Familiaris Consortio* (Boston: Pauline Books and Media, 1993), 26.

9. See *Catechism of the Catholic Church*, 1753.

10. John Paul II, *Letter to Families* (Boston: Pauline Books and Media, 1994), 9.

11. *Catechism of the Catholic Church*, 2203, 2222.

12. John Paul II, *Familiaris Consortio*, 64.

13. *Catechism of the Catholic Church*, 2444; Mt 25:34–40 and Lk 14:12–14.

14. John Paul II. *Mulieris Dignitatem*, 19.

15. John Paul II, *Theology of the Body: Human Love in the Divine Plan* (Boston: Pauline Books and Media, 1997), 81. (Also referenced as TOB 20:3 in General Audience of March 12, 1980): "The constitution of the woman is different, as

compared with the man. We know today that it is different even in the deepest bio-physiological determinants. It is manifested externally only to a certain extent, in the construction and form of her body. Maternity manifests this constitution internally, as the particular potentiality of the female organism. With creative peculiarity it serves for the conception and begetting of the human being, with the help of man. Knowledge conditions begetting."

16. See *Catechism of the Catholic Church*, 239.

17. Freda Mary Oben, trans., *Essays on Women: The Collected Works of Edith Stein*, vol. 2 (Washington, D.C.: ICS Publications, 1996), 70–75.

18. *Letter to Families*, 7 (emphasis in original).

19. W. F. Chan et al., "Male Microchimerism in the Human Female Brain," *PLOS One — Public Library of Science Journal*, vol. 7, no. 9 (2012), https://www.ncbi.nlm. nih.gov/pubmed/23049819.

20. John Paul II, *Mulieris Dignitatem, 12 (emphasis in original)*.

21. Ibid., 13.

22. Ibid., 15.

23. Ibid., 7.

24. Second Vatican Council, *Gaudium et Spes* (Pastoral Constitution on the Church in the Modern World) (Vatican City: Libreria Editrice Vaticana, 1964), 24.

25. John Paul II, *Mulieris Dignitatem*, 18.

26. Gn 1:31.

27. Benedict XVI, *Deus Caritas Est* (2005), 5 http://w2.vatican.va/content/benedict-xvi/en/encyclicals/documents/hf_ben-xvi_enc_20051225_deus-caritas-est.html.

28. *Catechism of the Catholic Church*, 364 (originally in *Gaudium et Spes*, 14).

29. Ibid., 1004.

30. John Paul II, General Audience, February 11, 1981.

31. 1 Cor 6:13–20.

32. See Mt 19.

33. The Pontifical Council on the Family, *The Truth and Meaning of Human Sexuality* (Boston: Pauline Books and Media, 1996.), 30.

34. "Man and woman, created as a 'unity of the two' in their common humanity, are called to live in a communion of love, and in this way to mirror in the world the communion of love that is in God, through which the Three Persons love each other in the intimate mystery of the one divine life." John Paul II, *Mulieris Dignitatem*, 7.

35. *Catechism of the Catholic Church,* 1604.

36. Pius XI, *Casti Connubi*, encyclical letter, 11.

37. John Paul II, *Letter to Families*, 11.

38. Ibid., 7.

39. Ibid., 9 (emphasis added).

40. "This grace proper to the sacrament of Matrimony is intended to perfect the couple's love and to strengthen their indissoluble unity. By this grace they 'help one another to attain holiness in their married life and in welcoming and educating their children.'" *Catechism of the Catholic Church*, 1641.

41. *Catechism of the Catholic Church*, 1974.

42. John Paul II, *Theology of the Body*, 82.

43. "The Creed," Article III, *The Catechism of the Council of Trent* (Rockford: Tan Books and Publishers, 1982), 46.

44. Gn 3:17, English Hebrew Interlinear Translation, Bible Hub, http://biblehub.com/interlinear/genesis/3-17.htm.

45. Gn 3:16, English Hebrew Interlinear Translation, Bible Hub, http://biblehub.com/interlinear/genesis/3-16.htm.

46. Bible Hub, Hebrew Concordance Compilation, *Itstsabon*, 6093, http://biblehub.com/hebrew/6093.htm.

47. Bible Hub, Hebrew Concordance Compilation, *Atsab*, 6087, http://biblehub.com/hebrew/6087.htm.

48. John Paul II, *Mulieris Dignitatem*, 11.

49. Fulton Sheen, *Way to Happiness* (Garden City: Garden City, 1954).

50. John Paul II, *Mulieris Dignitatem*, 11.

51. *Catechism of the Catholic Church*, 968; see also *Lumen Gentium*, 61.

52. Alonso-Zaldívar, Ricardo, "Labeling Birth Control Preventive Medicine Could Make Contraception Free for U.S. Women," *Chicago Tribune*, October 31, 2010, http://www.chicagotribune.com/lifestyles/health/sns-ap-us-birth-control-story.html.

53. U.S. Department of Health and Human Services, Office on Women's Health, *Birth Control Methods Fact Sheet*, (Washington D.C., 2011), https://www.womenshealth.gov/publications/our-publications/fact-sheet/birth-control-methods.html.

54. P. Goodman, M. C. Mackey, and A. S. Tavakoli, "Factors Related to Childbirth Satisfaction," *Journal of Advanced Nursing*, (Blackwell Publishing, vol. 46, no. 2 (April 2004): 212–219, https://www.ncbi.nlm.nih.gov/pubmed/15056335.

55. John Paul II, *Mulieris Dignitatem, 18*.

56. Thomas F. Baskett and Fritz Naegele, "Naegele's Rule: A Reappraisal," *British Journal of Obstetrics and Gynaecology*, vol. 107 (2000), 1433–1435, http://onlinelibrary.wiley.com/doi/10.1111/j.1471-0528.2000.tb11661.x/epdf.

57. J. P. Newman et al., "Effects of Frequent Ultrasound During Pregnancy: A

Randomised Controlled Trial," *Lancet*, vol. 342, no. 8876 (1993): 887–891, http://www.thelancet.com/journals/lancet/article/PII0140-6736(93)91944-H/abstract.

58. ACOG, "Ultrasound Exams," FAQ025, June 2017, http://www.acog.org/Patients/FAQs/Ultrasound-Exams.

59. R. Mittendorf et al., "The Length of Uncomplicated Human Gestation," *Obstet Gynecol*, 75(6) (1990): 929–932, https://www.ncbi.nlm.nih.gov/pubmed/2342739.

60. Rebecca Dekker, "Evidence on Inducing Labor for Going Past Your Due Date," *Evidence Based Birth*, http://evidencebasedbirth.com/evidence-on-inducing-labor-for-going-past-your-due-date/.

61. J. M. Nicholson et al., "New Definition of Term Pregnancy," *Journal of the American Medical Association,* vol. 310, no. 18 (2013): 1985–1986, http://jama.jamanetwork.com/article.aspx?articleid=1769878.

62. Lu Sao et al., "Steroid Receptors Coactivators 1 and 2 Mediate Fetal-to-Maternal Signaling that Initiates Parturition," The *Journal of Clinical Investigation*, vol. 125, no. 7 (2015): 2808–2824, http://www.jci.org/articles/view/78544.

63. John Paul II, *Letter to Families*, 16 (emphasis added).

64. See Eph 5:25–28.

65. Pius XII, *Allocution to Midwives*, October 29, 1951.

66. Marian F. MacDorman et al., "Trends in Out-of-Hospital Births in the United States 1990–2012," NCHS Data Brief, no. 144 (2014), https://www.cdc.gov/nchs/data/databriefs/db144.pdf.

67. Ellen D. Hodnett et al., "Continuous Support for Women During Childbirth," *Cochrane Database of Systematic Reviews*, issue 7, no. CD003766 (2013), http://onlinelibrary.wiley.com/doi/10.1002/14651858.CD003766.pub5/full.

68. ACOG, "Safe Prevention of the Primary Cesarean Delivery," *Obstet Gynecol*, no. 1 (2014, reaffirmed in 2016): 693–711. Published concurrently in the *American Journal of Obstetrics and Gynecology*, March 2014 issue, http://www.acog.org/Resources-And-Publications/Obstetric-Care-Consensus-Series/Safe-Prevention-of-the-Primary-Cesarean-Delivery.

69. John Paul II, *Letter to Women*, 12, emphasis in original.

70. John Paul II, *Letter to Families*, 16.

71. N. O. Enaruna et al., "Clinical Significance of Low Serum Magnesium in Pregnant Women," *Nigerian Journal of Clinical Practice*, vol. 16, no. 4 (2013): 448–453, https://www.ncbi.nlm.nih.gov/pubmed/23974737.

72. Lisa M. Bodnar et al., "Early-Pregnancy Vitamin D Deficiency and Risk of Preterm Birth Subtypes," *Obstetrics and Gynecology,* vol. 125, no. 2 (2015): 439–447, https://www.ncbi.nlm.nih.gov/pmc/articles/PMC4304969/.

73. American Society of Anesthesiologists, "Moms-to-Be with Low Vitamin D Levels Could Have More Painful Labors," *Science Daily* (2014), https://www.sciencedaily.com/releases/2014/10/141014170634.htm.

74. O. Al-Kuran et al., "The Effect of Late Pregnancy Consumption of Date Fruit on Labour and Delivery," The *Journal of Obstetrics and Gynecology*, vol. 31, no. 1 (2011): 29–31, https://www.ncbi.nlm.nih.gov/pubmed/21280989.

75. Carla Wintersgill, "C-Section Not Best Option for Breech Birth," *The Globe and Mail*, August 23, 2012, http://www.theglobeandmail.com/life/parenting/c-section-not-best-option-for-breech-birth/article597103/.

76. W. F. McCool and S. A. Simeone, "Birth in the United States: An Overview of Trends Past and Present," The *Nursing Clinics of North America*, vol. 37, no. 4 (2002): 735–746, https://www.ncbi.nlm.nih.gov/pubmed/12587371.

77. Adrian Feldhusen, "The History of Midwifery and Childbirth in America: A Timeline," *Midwifery Today*, 2000, https://www.midwiferytoday.com/articles/timeline.asp.

78. Emily Stevens et al., "A History of Infant Feeding," The *Journal of Perinatal Education*, vol. 18, no. 2 (2009): 32–39, https://www.ncbi.nlm.nih.gov/pmc/articles/PMC2684040/.

79. J. Riordan and B. A. Countryman, "Basics of Breastfeeding. Part 1: Infant Feeding Patterns Past and Present," *Journal of Obstetric, Gynecologic, and Neonatal Nursing*, vol. 9, no. 4 (1980): 207–210, https://www.ncbi.nlm.nih.gov/pubmed/7001126; and Rima D. Apple, *Mothers and Medicine: A Social History of Infant Feeding 1890–1950* (Madison: University of Wisconsin Press, 1987).

80. *Lex orandi, lex credenda* (loosely translated, "The law of prayer is the law of belief").

81. *Catechism of the Catholic Church,* 1670.

82. Pius XII, *Allocution to Midwives.*

83. James T. Sharkey et al., "Melatonin Synergizes with Oxytocin to Enhance Contractility of Human Myometrial Smooth Muscle Cells," The *Journal of Clinical Endocrinology and Metabolism,* vol. 94, no. 2 (2009): 421–427, https://www.ncbi.nlm.nih.gov/pmc/articles/PMC2730229/.

84. See *Catechism of the Catholic Church*, 1883–1885.

85. American College of Obstetricians and Gynecologists, "Don't Perform Prenatal Ultrasounds for Non-Medical Purposes," *Choosing Wisely, An Initiative by the ABIM Foundation*, 2016, http://www.choosingwisely.org/clinician-lists/american-college-obstetricians-gynecologists-prenatal-ultrasounds-for-non-medical-purposes/.

86. Mark Bradford, "New Study: Abortion After Prenatal Diagnosis of Down Syndrome Reduces Down Syndrome Community by 30 Percent," Charlotte Lozi-

er Institute, April 21, 2015, https://www.ncbi.nlm.nih.gov/pubmed/22418958.

87. A. K. Johri et al., "Group B Streptococcus: Global Incidence and Vaccine Development," *Nature Reviews Microbiology*, vol. 4, no. 12 (2006): 932–942, http://www.ncbi.nlm.nih.gov/pubmed/17088932.

88. Jennifer R. Verani et al., "Prevention of Perinatal Group B Streptococcal Disease," Centers for Disease Control and Prevention, MMWR, 59 (2010): 1–32, https://www.cdc.gov/mmwr/preview/mmwrhtml/rr5910a1.htm?s_cid=rr5910a1_w.

89. P. T. Heath et al., "Group B Streptococcal Disease in Infants: A Case Control Study," *Archives of Disease in Childhood — BMJ Journal*, vol. 94, no. 9 (2009): 674–680, http://www.ncbi.nlm.nih.gov/pubmed/19457879; and C. E. Adair et al., "Risk Factors for Early Onset Group B Streptococcal Disease in Neonates: A Population-Based Case Control Study," *Canadian Medical Association Journal*, vol. 169, no. 3 (2003): 198–203, http://www.ncbi.nlm.nih.gov/pubmed/12900477.

90. Rebecca Dekker, "Evidence on: Group B Strep in Pregnancy," July 17, 2017, https://evidencebasedbirth.com/groupbstrep/.

91. ACOG, "Safe Prevention of the Primary Cesarean Delivery," *Obstet Gynecol*, no. 1 (2014, reaffirmed in 2016): 693–711; published concurrently in the American Journal of Obstetrics and Gynecology, March 2014 issue, http://www.acog.org/Resources-And-Publications/Obstetric-Care-Consensus-Series/Safe-Prevention-of-the-Primary-Cesarean-Delivery.

92. R. Gone et al., "Prediction of Successful Induction of Labor: Comparison of Transvaginal Ultrasonography and the Bishop Score," *European Journal of Ultrasound*, vol. 7, no. 3 (1998): 183–187, http://cat.inist.fr/?aModele=afficheN&cpsidt=2381313.

93. L. Jansen et al., "First Do No Harm: Interventions During Childbirth," *Journal of Perinatal Education*, vol. 22, no. 2 (2013), https://www.ncbi.nlm.nih.gov/pmc/articles/PMC3647734/.

94. ACOG, "Approaches to Limit Intervention During Labor and Birth — Committee Opinion No. 687," Obstet Gynecol (February 2017): 129:e20–8, http://www.acog.org/Resources-And-Publications/Committee-Opinions/Committee-on-Obstetric-Practice/Approaches-to-Limit-Intervention-During-Labor-and-Birth?IsMobileSet=false.

95. Ibid.

96. R. M. D. Smyth, C. Markham, C., and T. Dowswell, "Amniotomy for Shortening Spontaneous Labour," *Cochrane*, June 18, 2013, http://www.cochrane.org/CD006167/PREG_amniotomy-for-shortening-spontaneous-labour.

97. Rebecca Dekker, "Evidence-Based Fetal Monitoring," Evidence Based Birth, July 17, 2012, http://evidencebasedbirth.com/evidence-based-fetal-moni-toring/.

98. American College of Obstetricians and Gynecologists, "ACOG Practice Bulletin Number 106: Intrapartum Fetal Heart Rate Monitoring; Nomenclature, Interpretation, and General Management Principles," *Obstet Gynecol*, vol. 114, no. 1 (2009): 192–202. http://journals.lww.com/greenjournal/Citation/2009/07000/ACOG_Practice_Bulletin_No__106__Intrapartum_Fetal.51.aspx.

99. "Approaches to Limit Intervention During Labor and Birth — Committee Opinion No. 687."

100. Z. Alfirevic et al., "Continuous Cardiotocography (CTG) as a Form of Electronic Fetal Monitoring (EFM) for Fetal Assessment During Labor," *Cochrane Database of Systematic Reviews*, 5 (2013), https://www.ncbi.nlm.nih.gov/pubmed/23728657.

101. M. Singata et al., "Restricting Oral Fluid and Food Intake During Labor," The *Cochrane Database of Systematic Reviews*, Iss. 8, No. CD003930 (2013). https://www.ncbi.nlm.nih.gov/pubmed/20091553.

102. "Most Healthy Women Would Benefit from a Light Meal During Labor," American Society of Anesthesiologists, November 6, 2015, http://www.asahq.org/about-asa/newsroom/news-releases/2015/10/eating-a-light-meal-during-labor.

103. "Approaches to Limit Intervention During Labor and Birth — Committee Opinion No. 687."

104. Ibid.

105. Justin R. Happen and Dana R. Gusset, "Changes in Episiotomy Practice: Evidence-Based Medicine in Action," *Medscape, Expert Review of Obstet Gynecol*, vol. 5, no. 3 (2010): 301–309, http://www.medscape.com/viewarticle/721538.

106. ACOG, "Delayed Umbilical Cord Clamping After Birth," ACOG Committee Opinion No. 684 (2017), http://www.acog.org/Resources-And-Publications/Committee-Opinions/Committee-on-Obstetric-Practice/Delayed-Umbilical-Cord-Clamping-After-Birth.

107. World Health Organization, "Optimal Timing of Cord Clamping for the Prevention of Iron Deficiency Anaemia in Infants," E-Library of Evidence for Nutritious Actions (2015), http://www.who.int/elena/titles/cord_clamping/en/.

108. Gina Eichenbaum-Pikser et al., "Delayed Clamping of the Umbilical Cord: A Review with Implications for Practice," *Journal of Midwifery and Women's Health*, vol. 5, no. 4 (2009): 321–326, http://www.medscape.com/viewarticle/708616_3.

109. Margaret R. Thomas et al., "Providing Newborn Resuscitation at the Mother's Bedside: Assessing the Safety, Usability and Acceptability of a Mobile Trolley," *BMC Pediatrics*, vol. 14 (2014), https://www.ncbi.nlm.nih.gov/pmc/articles/PMC4055396/.

110. Elizabeth Moore et al., "Early Skin-to-Skin Contact for Mothers and Their Healthy Newborn Infants," *Cochrane Database Systemic Review*, May 16, 2012, https://www.ncbi.nlm.nih.gov/pmc/articles/PMC3979156/; and Charpak, Nathalie, et al., "Twenty-Year Follow-Up of Kangaroo Mother Care Versus Traditional Care," *Pediatrics*, December 2016. http://pediatrics.aappublications.org/content/early/2016/12/08/peds.2016-2063.

111. Catholic Physicians' Guild, "Disposal of Amputated Members," *The Linacre Quarterly*, vol. 15, no. 3, art. 13 (1948), http://epublications.marquette.edu/lnq/vol15/iss3/13/.

112. "Epidural Anesthesia," AmericanPregnancy.org, updated August, 2016. http://americanpregnancy.org/labor-and-birth/epidural/.

113. American College of Obstetricians and Gynecologists, "Medications for Pain Relief During Labor and Delivery," ACOG FAQ086, (March 2014), http://www.acog.org/Patients/FAQs/Medications-for-Pain-Relief-During-Labor-and-Delivery.

114. See Col 1:24.

115. Thérèse of Lisieux, *The Story of a Soul*, trans. John Beevers (New York: Doubleday, 1957), 139–140.

116. Ashwin Ramachandrappa and Lucky Jain, "Elective Cesarean Section: Its Impact on Neonatal Respiratory Outcome," *Clinics in Perinatology*, 35(2) (2008): 373-vii, http://www.ncbi.nlm.nih.gov/pmc/articles/PMC2453515/.

117. World Health Organization, "WHO Statement on Cesarean Section Rates" (Geneva: World Health Organization, 2010), http://apps.who.int/iris/bitstream/10665/161442/1/WHO_RHR_15.02_eng.pdf?ua=1.

118. B. E. Hamilton, J. A. Martin, M. J. K. Osterman et al., "Births: Final Data for 2014," *National Vital Statistics Reports*, vol. 64, no. 12 (2015): 2, https://www.cdc.gov/nchs/data/nvsr/nvsr64/nvsr64_12.pdf; and "Childbirth Indicators by Place of Residence," Canadian Institute for Health Information (2016).

119. American College of Obstetricians and Gynecologists, "Safe Prevention of the Primary Cesarean Delivery." http://www.acog.org/Resources-And-Publications/Obstetric-Care-Consensus-Series/Safe-Prevention-of-the-Primary-Cesarean-Delivery.

120. Ibid.

121. Mayo Clinic, *Labor Induction* (2014), http://www.mayoclinic.org/tests-procedures/labor-induction/basics/risks/prc-20019032.

122. ACOG, "Safe Prevention of the Primary Cesarean Delivery," http://www.acog.org/Resources-And-Publications/Obstetric-Care-Consensus-Series/Safe-Prevention-of-the-Primary--Delivery.

123. Rebecca Dekker, "What Is the Evidence for Induction or C-Section for a Big Baby?," Evidence Based Birth, 2013 and updated June 8, 2016, http://evidencebasedbirth.com/evidence-for-induction-or-c-section-for-big-baby/.

124. Ellen D. Hodnett et al., "Continuous Support for Women During Childbirth," http://onlinelibrary.wiley.com/doi/10.1002/14651858.CD003766.pub5/full.

125 . ACOG, "ACOG Practice Bulletin No. 115: Vaginal Birth After Previous Cesarean Delivery," *Obstet Gynecol*, 2 (pt. 1) (2010): 450–463, https://www.ncbi.nlm.nih.gov/pubmed/20664418.

126. Ibid.

127. Nicole Churchin, "Evidence on: The Vitamin K Shot in Newborns," Evidence Based Birth, March 18, 2014, https://evidencebasedbirth.com/evidence-for-the-vitamin-k-shot-in-newborns/.

128. Rebecca Dekker, "Evidence on: Erythromycin Eye Ointment for Newborns," Evidence Based Birth, August 3, 2017, https://evidencebasedbirth.com/is-erythromycin-eye-ointment-always-necessary-for-newborns/.

129. Gloria Casas, "Sherman Nurse's 'Wait to Bathe' Newborns Policy Adopted by Hospitals," *Chicago Tribune*, June 11, 2017, http://www.chicagotribune.com/suburbs/elgin-courier-news/news/ct-ecn-elgin-sherman-nurse-baby-policy-st-0612-20170611-story.html.

130. "Checking Blood Glucose in Newborn Babies," *Paediatrics & Child Health*, vol 9., no. 10 (2004): 731–732, https://www.ncbi.nlm.nih.gov/pmc/articles/PMC2724151/.

131. Gal 5:2–6.

132. The Council of Florence, *Bull of Union with the Copts* (February 4, 1442), session 11, EWTN Library, https://www.ewtn.com/library/COUNCILS/FLORENCE.HTM.

133. Centers for Disease Control, "Trends in In-Hospital Newborn Male Circumcision — United States 1999–2010," *Morbidity and Mortality Weekly Report (MMWR)*, 60(34) (2011): 1167–1168, https://www.cdc.gov/mmwr/preview/mmwrhtml/mm6034a4.htm?s_cid=mm6034a4_w.

134. World Health Organization, *Neonatal and Child Male Circumcision: A Global Review, Joint United Nations Programme on HIV/AIDS (UNAIDS)* (2010): 7, http://www.who.int/hiv/pub/malecircumcision/neonatal_child_MC_UNAIDS.pdf?ua=1.

135. Aaron J. Krill et al., "Complications of Circumcision," *Scientific World Journal*, vol. 11, 2011, https://www.ncbi.nlm.nih.gov/pmc/articles/PMC3253617/;

and Dan Bollinger, "Lost Boys: An Estimate of U.S. Circumcision-Related Infant Deaths," *Thymos: Journal of Boyhood Studies*, vol. 4, no. 1, spring (2010): 78–90. http://www.academia.edu/6394940/Lost_Boys_An_Estimate_of_U.S._Circumcision-Related_Infant_Deaths.

136. "Except when performed for strictly therapeutic medical reasons, directly intended *amputations, mutilations, and sterilizations performed on innocent persons are against the moral law." Catechism of the Catholic Church, 2297 (emphasis added).*

137. National Institutes of Health, "Postpartum Depression Facts," U.S. Department of Health and Human Services, Publication No. 13-8000, https://www.nimh.nih.gov/health/publications/postpartum-depression-facts/index.shtml.

138. Ibid.

139. Aimee R. Kroll-Desrosiers et al., "Association of Peripartum Synthetic Oxytocin Administration and Depressive and Anxiety Disorders Within the First Year," *Depression and Anxiety: The Official Journal of the AADD*, Vol. 34, Iss. 2, February 2017: 137–146, http://onlinelibrary.wiley.com/wol1/doi/10.1002/da.22599/abstract.

140. Elvin Ystrom, "Breastfeeding Cessation and Symptoms of Anxiety and Depression: A Longitudinal Cohort Study," *BioMed Central Pregnancy and Childbirth*, 2012, http://bmcpregnancychildbirth.biomedcentral.com/articles/10.1186/1471-2393-12-36.

141. G. Stern and L. Kruckman, "Multi-Disciplinary Perspectives on Post-Partum Depression: An Anthropological Critique," *Social Science and Medicine,* vol. 17, no. 15 (1983): 1027–1041, https://www.ncbi.nlm.nih.gov/pubmed/6623110.

142. Mayo Clinic, "Dilation and Curettage (D&C)" (2016), http://www.mayoclinic.org/tests-procedures/dilation-and-curettage/basics/risks/prc-20013836.

143. Whitney C. Harris, "How Risky Is Having a D&C After a Miscarriage?" *Fit Pregnancy and Baby,* http://www.fitpregnancy.com/pregnancy/getting-pregnant/how-risky-having-dc-after-.

144. "Cervical Scar Tissue — A Cause of Unnecessary C-Sections," *Improving Birth*, July 25, 2012, https://improvingbirth.org/2012/07/cervical-scar-tissue-a-cause-of-unnecessary-c-sections/.

145. Jacqueline Levine, "Pelvic Exams Near Term: Benefit or Risk? Talking to Mothers About Informed Consent and Refusal," *Science and Sensibility,* November 1, 2012 and updated March 9, 2016, https://www.scienceandsensibility.org/p/bl/et/blogid=2&blogaid=522.

146. Your priest should have a copy of the *Book of Blessings,* but it can also be found at http://www.catholicculture.org/culture/liturgicalyear/prayers/view. cfm?id=711.

147. *Catechism of the Catholic Church,* 1261.

148. International Theological Commission, *The Hope of Salvation for Infants Who Die Without Being Baptized,* (Vatican City: 2007), 102, http://www. vatican.va/roman_curia/congregations/cfaith/cti_documents/rc_con_cfaith_ doc_20070419_un-baptised-infants_en.html.

149. John Paul II, "Address on Breastfeeding," May 12, 1995, 2-3.

150. American Academy of Pediatrics, "Breastfeeding and the Use of Human Milk," *Pediatrics,* vol. 129, no. 3 (2012): 827–841, http://pediatrics. aappublications.org/content/129/3/e827.

151. Isabel Woodman, "Breastfeeding Reduces Risk of Breast Cancer, Says Study," *British Medical Journal,* vol. 325, no. 7357 (2002): 184, https://www.ncbi. nlm.nih.gov/pmc/articles/PMC1143616/.

152. Gwen Dewar, "The Best Infant Feeding Schedule: Why Babies Are Better Off Feeding on Cue," *Parenting Science,* last updated March 2014, http://www. parentingscience.com/infant-feeding-schedule.html.

153. Elizabeth Moore et al., "Early Skin-to-Skin Contact for Mothers and Their Healthy Newborn Infants," *Cochrane Database Systemic Review,* May 16, 2012, https://www.ncbi.nlm.nih.gov/pmc/articles/PMC3979156/.

154. Benedict XVI, "The Prayer of Jacob," General Audience, May 25, 2011, http://www.ewtn.com/library/PAPALDOC/b16chrstpryr4.htm.

155. *Catechism of the Catholic Church,* 1213.

156. *Catechism of the Catholic Church,* 1250–1251.

157. *Code of Canon Law,* see Canon 867.

158. Ibid, see Canons 872-874; see also *Catechism of the Catholic Church,* 1255.

159. "Churching of Women," New Advent, http://www.newadvent.org/ cathen/03761a.htm.

160. http://missionandshrine.org/.